RUSSIA

KAZAKHSTAN

MONGOLIA

TURKEY
GEORGIA ARM. AZER. UZBEK KIRGIZ
CYPRUS TURKEY TURKMEN TAJIK
SYRIA
LEB. IRAQ IRAN AFGH.
ISR.JOR. KUWAIT
EGYPT BAH. PAKISTAN NEPAL BHU.
QATAR
SAUDI UAE B'DESH
ARABIA OMAN INDIA MYANMAR LAOS
SUDAN ERITREA YEMEN THAILAND VIETNAM
DJIB. CAMBODIA
ETHIOPIA SOMALIA SRI
UGAN. KENYA LANKA
ZAIRE TANZANIA

CHINA

N. KOREA
S. KOREA JAPAN

HONG
KONG TAIWAN
MACAO

PHILIPPINES

BRUNEI
MALAYSIA
SING.
INDONESIA

PAPUA
NEW GUINEA

ZAMBIA MALAWI
ZIMB. MOZ. MADAGASCAR MAURITIUS
BOT. SWAZI
OUTH LESOTHO
RICA

FIJI

AUSTRALIA

NEW ZEALAND

# POCKET WORLD IN FIGURES

# The Economist

===== POCKET =====

# WORLD IN FIGURES

THE ECONOMIST IN ASSOCIATION WITH
HAMISH HAMILTON LTD

Published by the Penguin Group
Penguin Books Ltd, 27 Wrights Lane, London W8 5TZ, England
Penguin Books USA Inc., 375 Hudson Street, New York,
New York 10014, USA
Penguin Books Australia Ltd, Ringwood, Victoria, Australia
Penguin Books Canada Ltd, 10 Alcorn Avenue, Toronto,
Ontario, Canada M4V 3B2
Penguin Books (NZ) Ltd, 182–190 Wairau Road, Auckland 10,
New Zealand

Penguin Books Ltd, Registered Offices: Harmondsworth,
Middlesex, England

First published by The Economist Books Ltd 1991
Second edition published by The Economist Books Ltd 1992
Third edition published by Hamish Hamilton Ltd in association
with The Economist 1993
This edition published by Hamish Hamilton Ltd in association
with The Economist 1994

1 3 5 7 9 10 8 6 4 2

Copyright © The Economist Books Ltd, 1991, 1992, 1993, 1994

**Material researched and compiled by** Michael Coulman,
Fiona Haynes, Peter Holden, Carol Howard, Stella Jones,
Liz Mann, David McKelvey, Justene McNeice, Keith Potter,
Sara Pritchard, Nick Wiseman, Anna Wolek

Design and makeup Jonathan Harley, Peter Sonderskov,
Liz Conway, Ruth Taylor

The greatest care has been taken in compiling this book. However,
no responsibility can be accepted by the publishers or compilers
for the accuracy of the information presented.

Printed in Great Britain by William Clowes Limited,
Beccles and London

A CIP catalogue record for this book is available
from the British Library

ISBN 0-241-00261-3

# Contents

# Notes

The country profiles cover some 60 major countries, including Russia and Ukraine, and a selection of statistics for the other ex-Soviet republics. The world rankings consider 163: all those with a population of at least 1m or a GDP of at least $1bn. The extent and quality of the statistics available varies from country to country. Every care has been taken to specify the broad definitions on which the data are based and to indicate cases where data quality or technical difficulties are such that interpretation of the figures is likely to be seriously affected. Nevertheless, figures from individual countries will often differ from standard international statistical definitions.

Statistics do not yet fully reflect the changes that have taken place in Germany, Yemen, the Czech Republic and Slovakia, ex-Yugoslavia and the former Soviet Union. Where possible, 1992 or later data have been combined to show Eastern and Western Germany as one and North and South Yemen as one. Data for Cyprus normally refer to Greek Cyprus only. For other countries such as Morocco and Indonesia they exclude disputed areas.

## Statistical basis

The all-important factor in a book of this kind is to be able to make reliable comparisons between countries. Although this is never quite possible for the reasons stated above, the best route, which this book takes, is to compare data for the same year or period and to use actual, not estimated, figures wherever possible. The research for this edition of *The Economist Pocket World in Figures* was carried out in 1994 using the latest available sources that present data on an internationally comparable basis. Data, therefore, unless otherwise indicated, refers to the year ending December 31 1992.

In the country profiles, population density, population under 15 and over 65, and number of men per 100 women refer to forecasts for 1995; life expectancy, crude birth, death and fertility rates are based on 1990–95 averages; human development indices and GDP per head in purchasing power parity to 1990; energy data refer to 1991; structure of manufacturing data to 1990; household data and marriage and divorce data refer to the latest year with available figures, 1985–92. In a number of cases, data are shown for the latest year within a range.

## Other definitions

Data shown on country profiles may not always be consistent with those shown on the world rankings because the definitions or years covered can differ. Data may also differ between two different rankings.

Most countries' national accounts are now compiled on a GDP basis so, for simplicity, the term GDP has been used interchangeably with GNP. GDP figures in this book come from the World Bank. It bases its rouble conversions on purchasing power parities.

Statistics for principal exports and principal imports are normally based on customs statistics. These are generally compiled on different definitions to the visible exports and imports figures shown in the balance of payments section.

Definitions of the statistics shown are given in the glossary at the end of the book. Figures may not add exactly to totals, or percentages to 100, because of rounding or, in the case of GDP, statistical adjustment. Sums of money have generally been converted to US dollars at the official exchange rate ruling at the time to which the figures refer.

Energy consumption data are not always reliable, particularly for the major oil producing countries. Consumption per head data may therefore be higher than in reality. Energy exports can exceed production and imports can exceed consumption if transit operations distort trade data or oil is imported for refining and re-exported.

## Abbreviations

| | | | |
|---|---|---|---|
| bn | billion (one thousand million) | m | million |
| kg | kilogram | NDP | Net domestic product |
| km | kilometre | NMP | Net material product |
| GDP | Gross domestic product | PPP | Purchasing power parity |
| GNP | Gross national product | ... | not available |
| GRT | Gross tonnage | | |

# ═══ Part I ═══
# WORLD RANKINGS

# Countries: *natural facts*

## Countries: *the largest*
*'000 sq km*

| | | | | | |
|---|---|---|---|---|---|
| 1 | Russia | 17,075 | 31 | Nigeria | 924 |
| 2 | Canada | 9,976 | 32 | Venezuela | 912 |
| 3 | China | 9,561 | 33 | Namibia | 824 |
| 4 | United States | 9,373 | 34 | Mozambique | 802 |
| 5 | Brazil | 8,512 | 35 | Pakistan | 796 |
| 6 | Australia | 7,687 | 36 | Turkey | 779 |
| 7 | India | 3,288 | 37 | Chile | 757 |
| 8 | Argentina | 2,767 | 38 | Zambia | 753 |
| 9 | Kazakhstan | 2,717 | 39 | Myanmar | 677 |
| 10 | Sudan | 2,506 | 40 | Afghanistan | 652 |
| 11 | Algeria | 2,382 | 41 | Somalia | 638 |
| 12 | Zaire | 2,344 | 42 | CAR | 623 |
| 13 | Saudi Arabia | 2,150 | 43 | Ukraine | 604 |
| 14 | Mexico | 1,958 | 44 | Madagascar | 587 |
| 15 | Indonesia | 1,905 | 45 | Botswana | 582 |
| 16 | Libya | 1,760 | 46 | Kenya | 580 |
| 17 | Iran | 1,648 | 47 | France | 552 |
| 18 | Mongolia | 1,565 | 48 | Yemen | 528 |
| 19 | Peru | 1,285 | 49 | Thailand | 513 |
| 20 | Chad | 1,284 | 50 | Spain | 505 |
| 21 | Niger | 1,267 | 51 | Turkmenistan | 488 |
| 22 | Angola | 1,247 | 52 | Cameroon | 475 |
| 23 | Mali | 1,240 | 53 | Papua New Guinea | 463 |
| 24 | Ethiopia | 1,223 | 54 | Sweden | 450 |
| 25 | South Africa | 1,221 | 55 | Morocco | 447 |
| 26 | Colombia | 1,139 | | Uzbekistan | 447 |
| 27 | Bolivia | 1,099 | 57 | Iraq | 438 |
| 28 | Mauritania | 1,026 | 58 | Paraguay | 407 |
| 29 | Egypt | 1,001 | 59 | Zimbabwe | 391 |
| 30 | Tanzania | 945 | 60 | Japan | 378 |

## Mountains: *the highest*[a]

| | Name | Location | Height (m) |
|---|---|---|---|
| 1 | Everest | Nepal-China | 8,848 |
| 2 | K2 (Godwin Austen) | Pakistan | 8,611 |
| 3 | Kangchenjunga | Nepal-Sikkim | 8,586 |
| 4 | Lhotse | Nepal-China | 8,516 |
| 5 | Makalu | Nepal-China | 8,463 |
| 6 | Cho Oyu | Nepal-China | 8,201 |
| 7 | Dhaulagiri | Nepal | 8,167 |
| 8 | Manaslu | Nepal | 8,163 |
| 9 | Nanga Parbat | Pakistan | 8,125 |
| 10 | Annapurna I | Nepal | 8,091 |
| 11 | Gasherbrum I | Pakistan-China | 8,068 |
| 12 | Broad Peak | Pakistan-China | 8,047 |
| 13 | Xixabangma (Gosainthan) | China | 8,046 |
| 14 | Gasherbrum II | Pakistan-China | 8,035 |

a  Includes separate peaks which are part of the same massif.

## Rivers: *the longest*

| | Name | Location | Length (km) |
|---|---|---|---|
| 1 | Nile | Africa | 6,695 |
| 2 | Amazon | South America | 6,516 |
| 3 | Yangtze | Asia | 6,380 |
| 4 | Mississippi-Missouri | North America | 6,019 |
| 5 | Ob'-Irtysh | Asia | 5,570 |
| 6 | Yenisey-Angara | Asia | 5,550 |
| 7 | Hwang He (Yellow) | Asia | 5,464 |
| 8 | Congo | Africa | 4,667 |
| 9 | Parana | South America | 4,500 |
| 10 | Mekong | Asia | 4,425 |
| 11 | Amur | Asia | 4,416 |
| 12 | Lena | Asia | 4,400 |
| 13 | Mackenzie | North America | 4,250 |
| 14 | Niger | Africa | 4,030 |
| 15 | Missouri | North America | 3,969 |
| 16 | Mississippi | North America | 3,779 |
| 17 | Murray-Darling | Australia | 3,750 |
| 18 | Volga | Europe | 3,688 |
| 19 | Kolyma | Asia | 3,513 |
| 20 | Madeira | South America | 3,200 |
| 21 | Yukon | North America | 3,185 |
| 22 | Indus | Asia | 3,180 |
| 23 | Syrdar'ya | Asia | 3,078 |
| 24 | Salween | Asia | 3,060 |
| 25 | Sao Francisco | South America | 2,900 |
| 26 | Rio Grande | North America | 2,870 |
| 27 | Danube | Europe | 2,850 |
| 28 | Brahmaputra | Asia | 2,840 |
| 29 | Euphrates | Asia | 2,815 |
| 30 | Para-Tocantis | South America | 2,750 |

## Waterfalls: *the highest*

| | Name | Location | Height (m) |
|---|---|---|---|
| 1 | Angel | Venezuela | 979 |
| 2 | Tugela | South Africa | 948 |
| 3 | Utigard | Norway | 800 |
| 4 | Mongefossen | Norway | 774 |
| 5 | Yosemite | California, USA | 739 |
| 6 | Mardalsfossen | Norway | 656 |
| 7 | Tyssestrengane | Norway | 646 |
| 8 | Cuquenan | Venezuela | 609 |
| 9 | Ribbon | California, USA | 491 |
| 10 | Della | Canada | 440 |

**Notes:** Estimates of the lengths of different rivers vary widely according to the rules adopted concerning the selection of tributaries to be followed, the path to take through a delta, where different hydrological systems begin and end etc. The Nile is normally taken as the world's longest river but some estimates put the Amazon as longer if a southerly path through its delta leading to the River Para is followed. Likewise, difficulties in waterfall measurements exist depending on which breaks in the fall are counted. The more famous waterfalls, Niagara and Victoria, are surprisingly small, 50m and 108m respectively; their notoriety evolving from their width and accessibility.

# Population: *explosions revealed*

## Largest populations, 1992
*Millions*

| | | | | | |
|---|---|---|---|---|---|
| 1 | China | 1,166.14 | 31 | Argentina | 33.10 |
| 2 | India | 883.47 | 32 | Canada | 27.84 |
| 3 | United States | 255.41 | 33 | Sudan | 26.59 |
| 4 | Indonesia | 184.27 | 34 | Algeria | 26.38 |
| 5 | Brazil | 153.85 | 35 | Morocco | 26.26 |
| 6 | Russia | 148.92 | 36 | Tanzania | 25.97 |
| 7 | Japan | 124.32 | 37 | Kenya | 25.84 |
| 8 | Pakistan | 119.35 | 38 | Romania | 22.87 |
| 9 | Bangladesh | 112.83 | 39 | North Korea | 22.61 |
| 10 | Nigeria | 101.88 | 40 | Peru | 22.37 |
| 11 | Mexico | 84.97 | 41 | Afghanistan | 21.56 |
| 12 | Germany | 80.55 | 42 | Uzbekistan | 21.29 |
| 13 | Vietnam | 69.23 | 43 | Taiwan | 20.75 |
| 14 | Philippines | 64.19 | 44 | Venezuela | 20.31 |
| 15 | Iran | 59.79 | 45 | Nepal | 19.89 |
| 16 | Turkey | 58.47 | 46 | Iraq | 19.18 |
| 17 | Thailand | 57.99 | 47 | Malaysia | 18.61 |
| 18 | Italy | 57.84 | 48 | Australia | 17.54 |
| 19 | United Kingdom | 57.70 | 49 | Uganda | 17.48 |
| 20 | France | 57.34 | 50 | Sri Lanka | 17.40 |
| 21 | Egypt | 54.81 | 51 | Kazakhstan | 16.95 |
| 22 | Ethiopia | 54.79 | 52 | Mozambique | 16.57 |
| 23 | Ukraine | 52.12 | 53 | Saudi Arabia | 15.91 |
| 24 | Myanmar | 43.72 | 54 | Ghana | 15.82 |
| 25 | South Korea | 43.66 | 55 | Netherlands | 15.17 |
| 26 | Zaire | 39.79 | 56 | Chile | 13.60 |
| 27 | South Africa | 39.76 | 57 | Yemen | 13.13 |
| 28 | Spain | 39.08 | 58 | Syria | 12.95 |
| 29 | Poland | 38.37 | 59 | Côte d'Ivoire | 12.84 |
| 30 | Colombia | 33.41 | 60 | Madagascar | 12.38 |

## Largest populations, 2010
*Millions*

| | | | | | |
|---|---|---|---|---|---|
| 1 | China | 1,409.95 | 14 | Philippines | 89.34 |
| 2 | India | 1,189.40 | 15 | Ethiopia | 89.04 |
| 3 | United States | 296.09 | 16 | Germany | 84.11 |
| 4 | Indonesia | 245.29 | 17 | Turkey | 78.95 |
| 5 | Pakistan | 197.67 | 18 | Egypt | 77.68 |
| 6 | Nigeria | 197.37 | 19 | Zaire | 68.59 |
| 7 | Brazil | 194.00 | 20 | Thailand | 66.74 |
| 8 | Bangladesh | 177.49 | 21 | Myanmar | 61.63 |
| 9 | Russia | 162.21 | 22 | France | 60.03 |
| 10 | Japan | 130.58 | 23 | United Kingdom | 59.72 |
| 11 | Mexico | 118.46 | 24 | South Africa | 58.45 |
| 12 | Iran | 104.12 | 25 | Italy | 58.30 |
| 13 | Vietnam | 97.10 | 26 | Ukraine | 55.30 |

## Fastest growing populations, 1985-92
*Average annual growth, %*

| | | | | | |
|---|---|---|---|---|---|
| 1 | Qatar | 6.0 | 12 | Botswana | 3.4 |
| 2 | Jordan | 5.8 | | Ethiopia | 3.4 |
| 3 | Yemen | 4.4 | | Malawi | 3.4 |
| 4 | Côte d'Ivoire | 4.0 | 15 | Congo | 3.3 |
| 5 | Oman | 3.8 | | Ghana | 3.3 |
| 6 | Iran | 3.7 | | Iraq | 3.3 |
| | Togo | 3.7 | | Syria | 3.3 |
| 8 | Libya | 3.6 | | Zaire | 3.3 |
| 9 | Kenya | 3.5 | 20 | Bahrain | 3.2 |
| | Saudi Arabia | 3.5 | | Benin | 3.2 |
| | Zambia | 3.5 | | Brunei | 3.2 |

## Slowest growing populations, 1985-92
*Average annual growth, %*

| | | | | | |
|---|---|---|---|---|---|
| 1 | Kuwait | -2.3 | | Italy | 0.2 |
| 2 | Portugal | -0.7 | | Spain | 0.2 |
| 3 | Hungary | -0.6 | 14 | Barbados | 0.3 |
| 4 | Ireland | -0.1 | | Belgium | 0.3 |
| 5 | Bulgaria | 0.0 | | Ukraine | 0.3 |
| | Latvia | 0.0 | | United Kingdom | 0.3 |
| 7 | Czech Republic | 0.1 | 18 | Croatia | 0.4 |
| | Denmark | 0.1 | | Japan | 0.4 |
| | Romania | 0.1 | | Norway | 0.4 |
| 10 | Bosnia & Hercegovina | 0.2 | | Poland | 0.4 |
| | Estonia | 0.2 | | Slovakia | 0.4 |

## Fastest growing populations, 1995-2010
*Average annual growth, %*

| | | | | | |
|---|---|---|---|---|---|
| 1 | Oman | 3.5 | | Rwanda | 3.2 |
| 2 | Côte d'Ivoire | 3.4 | 9 | Kenya | 3.1 |
| 3 | Syria | 3.3 | | Liberia | 3.1 |
| | Yemen | 3.3 | | Madagascar | 3.1 |
| 5 | Angola | 3.2 | | Niger | 3.1 |
| | Jordan | 3.2 | | Saudi Arabia | 3.1 |
| | Libya | 3.2 | | Tanzania | 3.1 |

## Slowest growing populations, 1995-2010
*Average annual growth, %*

| | | | | | |
|---|---|---|---|---|---|
| 1 | Belgium | 0.0 | | Portugal | 0.1 |
| | Bulgaria | 0.0 | 10 | Austria | 0.2 |
| | Italy | 0.0 | | Estonia | 0.2 |
| 4 | Denmark | 0.1 | | Finland | 0.2 |
| | Greece | 0.1 | | Germany | 0.2 |
| | Hungary | 0.1 | | Japan | 0.2 |
| | Ireland | 0.1 | | Spain | 0.2 |
| | Latvia | 0.1 | | United Kingdom | 0.2 |

# Population: *city living*

## Biggest cities
*Population millions, latest year*

| | | | |
|---|---|---|---|
| 1 | Sao Paolo | Brazil | 11.13 |
| 2 | Bombay | India | 9.93 |
| 3 | Seoul | South Korea | 9.64 |
| 4 | Mexico City | Mexico | 8.83 |
| 5 | Moscow | Russia | 8.80 |
| 6 | Tokyo | Japan | 8.28 |
| 7 | Jakarta | Indonesia | 7.89 |
| 8 | New York | United States | 7.32 |
| 9 | Delhi | India | 7.21 |
| 10 | London | United Kingdom | 6.79 |
| 11 | Cairo | Egypt | 6.66 |
| 12 | Lima[a] | Peru | 6.41 |
| 13 | Istanbul | Turkey | 6.29 |
| | Shanghai | China | 6.29 |
| 15 | Rio de Janeiro | Brazil | 6.04 |
| | Tehran | Iran | 6.04 |
| 17 | Bangkok | Thailand | 5.88 |
| 18 | Beijing | China | 5.53 |
| 19 | Karachi[a] | Pakistan | 5.18 |
| 20 | Tianjin | China | 5.15 |
| 21 | St Petersburg | Russia | 4.47 |
| 22 | Calcutta | India | 4.40 |
| 23 | Santiago | Chile | 4.39 |
| 24 | Bogota[a] | Colombia | 4.18 |
| 25 | Shenyang | China | 3.94 |
| 26 | Madras | India | 3.84 |
| 27 | Sydney | Australia | 3.66 |
| 28 | Pusan | South Korea | 3.51 |
| 29 | Los Angeles | United States | 3.49 |
| 30 | Berlin | Germany | 3.43 |

## Highest urban pop.
*% pop. living in urban areas, 1995*

| | | |
|---|---|---|
| 1 | Bermuda | 100 |
| | Singapore | 100 |
| 3 | Macao | 99 |
| 4 | Belgium | 97 |
| | Kuwait | 97 |
| 6 | Hong Kong | 95 |
| 7 | Israel | 93 |
| | Venezuela | 93 |
| 9 | Iceland | 92 |
| 10 | Qatar | 91 |

## Lowest urban pop.
*% pop. living in urban areas, 1995*

| | | |
|---|---|---|
| 1 | Bhutan | 6 |
| | Burundi | 6 |
| | Rwanda | 6 |
| 4 | Cambodia | 13 |
| | Ethiopia | 13 |
| | Oman | 13 |
| | Uganda | 13 |
| 8 | Malawi | 14 |
| | Nepal | 14 |
| 10 | Papua New Guinea | 18 |

a  Urban agglomeration.
**Note:** Estimates of cities' populations vary according to where geographical boundaries are defined. As far as possible the data refer to the city proper; urban agglomeration includes adjacent suburbs, eg, the population of the extended agglomeration of Paris (which includes 309 communes) is 8.51m; the population of Paris excluding these communes is 2.19m.

## Highest population density
*Population per sq km, 1995*

| | | | | | |
|---|---|---|---|---|---|
| 1 | Macao | 31,063 | 22 | Haiti | 259 |
| 2 | Hong Kong | 5,677 | 23 | Trinidad & Tobago | 254 |
| 3 | Singapore | 4,617 | 24 | United Kingdom | 238 |
| 4 | Bermuda | 1,155 | 25 | Netherlands Antilles | 236 |
| 5 | Malta | 1,139 | 26 | Jamaica | 232 |
| 6 | Bangladesh | 891 | 27 | Philippines | 231 |
| 7 | Bahrain | 852 | 28 | Burundi | 228 |
| 8 | Barbados | 608 | | Germany | 228 |
| 9 | Taiwan[a] | 576 | 30 | Vietnam | 223 |
| 10 | Mauritius | 554 | 31 | North Korea | 198 |
| 11 | South Korea | 456 | 32 | Italy | 192 |
| 12 | Puerto Rico | 415 | 33 | Pakistan | 170 |
| 13 | Netherlands | 379 | 34 | Switzerland | 168 |
| 14 | Japan | 333 | 35 | Dominican Republic | 162 |
| 15 | Belgium | 329 | 36 | Nepal | 157 |
| 16 | Rwanda | 316 | 37 | Luxembourg | 149 |
| 17 | Lebanon | 291 | 38 | Nigeria | 137 |
| 18 | India | 283 | 39 | Czech Republic[a] | 131 |
| 19 | Sri Lanka | 280 | 40 | China | 129 |
| 20 | Israel | 279 | | Moldova | 129 |
| 21 | El Salvador | 274 | | | |

## Lowest population density
*Population per sq km, 1995*

| | | | | | |
|---|---|---|---|---|---|
| 1 | Australia | 2 | | Oman | 9 |
| | Botswana | 2 | | Papua New Guinea | 9 |
| | Mauritania | 2 | | Russia[a] | 9 |
| | Mongolia | 2 | 24 | Algeria | 12 |
| | Namibia | 2 | | Argentina | 12 |
| 6 | Canada | 3 | | Paraguay | 12 |
| | Iceland | 3 | | Sudan | 12 |
| | Libya | 3 | | Zambia | 12 |
| | Suriname | 3 | 29 | New Zealand | 13 |
| 10 | Chad | 5 | | Norway | 13 |
| | Gabon | 5 | 31 | Finland | 15 |
| 12 | CAR | 6 | 32 | Somalia | 16 |
| | Kazakhstan[a] | 6 | 33 | Uruguay | 18 |
| 14 | Bolivia | 7 | 34 | Brazil | 19 |
| | Niger | 7 | | Chile | 19 |
| 16 | Congo | 8 | | Peru | 19 |
| | Saudi Arabia | 8 | | Sweden | 19 |
| | Turkmenistan[a] | 8 | | Zaire | 19 |
| 19 | Angola | 9 | 39 | Bahamas | 20 |
| | Mali | 9 | | Mozambique | 20 |

a 1992.

**Note:** Estimates of population density refer to the total land area of a country. In countries such as Japan and Canada, where much of the land area is virtually uninhabitable, the effective population densities of the habitable areas are much greater than the figures suggest.

# Population: *age and sex*

## Youngest populations
*% aged under 15, 1995*

| | | | | | | |
|---|---|---|---|---|---|---|
| 1 | Rwanda | 49.9 | 21 | Liberia | 46.0 |
| 2 | Yemen | 49.3 | 22 | Iran | 45.9 |
| 3 | Malawi | 49.2 | | Nicaragua | 45.9 |
| 4 | Côte d'Ivoire | 49.0 | 24 | Togo | 45.8 |
| 5 | Uganda | 48.7 | 25 | Madagascar | 45.7 |
| 6 | Zambia | 48.5 | 26 | Congo | 45.6 |
| 7 | Niger | 48.1 | 27 | Ghana | 45.3 |
| | Zaire | 48.1 | | Libya | 45.3 |
| 9 | Tanzania | 47.9 | 29 | CAR | 45.1 |
| 10 | Syria | 47.6 | 30 | Mauritania | 45.0 |
| 11 | Somalia | 47.5 | | Namibia | 45.0 |
| 12 | Kenya | 47.4 | | Sierra Leone | 45.0 |
| | Mali | 47.4 | 33 | Botswana | 44.9 |
| 14 | Benin | 47.2 | | Burkina Faso | 44.9 |
| 15 | Angola | 47.1 | | Mozambique | 44.9 |
| | Guinea | 47.1 | 36 | Laos | 44.8 |
| 17 | Nigeria | 46.9 | 37 | Zimbabwe | 44.6 |
| 18 | Oman | 46.6 | 38 | Senegal | 44.5 |
| 19 | Ethiopia | 46.5 | 39 | Sudan | 44.4 |
| 20 | Burundi | 46.3 | 40 | Guatemala | 44.3 |

## Oldest populations
*% aged over 65, 1995*

| | | | | | | |
|---|---|---|---|---|---|---|
| 1 | Sweden | 17.4 | 21 | Estonia | 12.7 |
| 2 | Norway | 15.9 | 22 | United States | 12.6 |
| 3 | Belgium | 15.7 | 23 | Uruguay | 12.3 |
| 4 | Italy | 15.6 | 24 | Lithuania | 12.2 |
| | United Kingdom | 15.6 | 25 | Ex-Czechoslovakia | 12.1 |
| 6 | Austria | 15.4 | 26 | Canada | 12.0 |
| | Denmark | 15.4 | | Ukraine | 12.0 |
| | Greece | 15.4 | 28 | Barbados | 11.8 |
| 9 | Switzerland | 15.1 | 29 | Australia | 11.6 |
| 10 | France | 14.9 | | Ireland | 11.6 |
| 11 | Germany | 14.8 | 31 | Romania | 11.3 |
| 12 | Spain | 14.7 | 32 | New Zealand | 11.2 |
| 13 | Bulgaria | 14.4 | 33 | Iceland | 11.1 |
| 14 | Portugal | 14.2 | 34 | Belorussia | 11.0 |
| 15 | Finland | 14.1 | 35 | Malta | 10.9 |
| 16 | Luxembourg | 14.0 | | Poland | 10.9 |
| 17 | Hungary | 13.9 | 37 | Ex-Yugoslavia | 10.6 |
| | Japan | 13.9 | 38 | Cyprus | 10.2 |
| 19 | Latvia | 13.1 | 39 | Hong Kong | 10.1 |
| 20 | Netherlands | 13.0 | 40 | Russia | 10.0 |

## Most male populations
*Number of men per 100 women[a], 1995*

| | | | | | | |
|---|---|---|---|---|---|---|
| 1 | UAE | 194.0 | 21 | Fiji | 103.5 |
| 2 | Qatar | 183.3 | | Iran | 103.5 |
| 3 | Bahrain | 133.8 | | Kuwait | 103.5 |
| 4 | Saudi Arabia | 123.8 | 24 | Dominican Republic | 103.4 |
| 5 | Oman | 110.7 | | Egypt | 103.4 |
| 6 | Libya | 108.7 | 26 | Singapore | 103.2 |
| 7 | Pakistan | 108.3 | 27 | Côte d'Ivoire | 103.1 |
| 8 | Papua New Guinea | 107.2 | | Panama | 103.1 |
| 9 | Hong Kong | 106.7 | 29 | Philippines | 102.8 |
| | India | 106.7 | 30 | Bhutan | 102.6 |
| 11 | Taiwan[c] | 106.6 | 31 | Paraguay | 102.5 |
| 12 | Bangladesh | 106.0 | 32 | Costa Rica | 102.3 |
| 13 | China | 105.7 | 33 | Tunisia | 102.2 |
| | Nepal | 105.7 | 34 | Liberia | 102.1 |
| 15 | Albania | 105.6 | 35 | Guatemala | 102.0 |
| 16 | Brunei | 105.2 | 36 | Malaysia | 101.8 |
| 17 | Jordan | 105.0 | | Mongolia | 101.8 |
| 18 | Afghanistan | 104.7 | | Syria | 101.8 |
| 19 | Turkey | 104.1 | 39 | Honduras | 101.7 |
| 20 | Iraq | 103.7 | 40 | North Korea | 101.6 |

## Most female populations
*Number of men per 100 women, 1995*

| | | | | | | |
|---|---|---|---|---|---|---|
| 1 | Ukraine[b] | 86.1 | | Uruguay | 95.0 |
| 2 | Latvia | 88.1 | 24 | Ex-Czechoslovakia | 95.1 |
| | Russia[b] | 88.1 | | Lebanon | 95.1 |
| 4 | Belorussia[b] | 88.2 | | Poland | 95.1 |
| 5 | Estonia | 89.5 | 27 | France | 95.2 |
| 6 | Lithuania | 90.5 | 28 | Azerbaijan[b] | 95.4 |
| 7 | Georgia[b] | 90.6 | | United States | 95.4 |
| 8 | Moldova[b] | 91.1 | 30 | Netherlands Antilles[d] | 95.5 |
| 9 | Cambodia | 92.2 | | Nicaragua | 95.5 |
| 10 | Botswana | 92.4 | 32 | Congo | 95.7 |
| 11 | Hungary | 92.5 | | Kirgizstan[b] | 95.7 |
| 12 | Barbados | 92.7 | 34 | El Salvador | 95.8 |
| 13 | Austria | 93.1 | 35 | Burundi | 95.9 |
| 14 | Portugal | 93.4 | 36 | Belgium | 96.1 |
| 15 | CAR | 94.1 | | United Kingdom | 96.1 |
| 16 | Kazakhstan[b] | 94.2 | 38 | Bulgaria | 96.3 |
| 17 | Macao[c] | 94.4 | 39 | Haiti | 96.4 |
| 18 | Italy | 94.6 | | Switzerland | 96.4 |
| 19 | Germany | 94.7 | 41 | Armenia[b] | 96.5 |
| 20 | Finland | 94.8 | 42 | Luxembourg | 96.7 |
| 21 | Puerto Rico | 94.9 | 43 | Sierra Leone | 96.8 |
| 22 | Lesotho | 95.0 | | | |

a Large numbers of immigrant workers, mostly men, result in the high male ratios of several Middle East countries.
b mid 1990.
c 1992.
d 1989.

# Population: *matters of breeding*

## Highest crude birth rates
*No. of live births per 1,000 population, 1990-95*

| | | | | | |
|---|---|---|---|---|---|
| 1 | Malawi | 54.5 | 26 | Congo | 44.7 |
| 2 | Afghanistan | 52.8 | 27 | CAR | 44.5 |
| 3 | Rwanda | 52.1 | | Togo | 44.5 |
| 4 | Angola | 51.3 | 29 | Chad | 43.7 |
| | Niger | 51.3 | | Kenya | 43.7 |
| 6 | Uganda | 51.0 | 31 | Senegal | 43.0 |
| 7 | Mali | 50.7 | 32 | Gabon | 42.6 |
| 8 | Guinea | 50.6 | 33 | Namibia | 42.5 |
| 9 | Somalia | 50.2 | 34 | Syria | 42.4 |
| 10 | Côte d'Ivoire | 49.9 | 35 | Sudan | 42.0 |
| 11 | Ethiopia | 49.1 | 36 | Libya | 41.9 |
| 12 | Benin | 48.9 | 37 | Ghana | 41.7 |
| 13 | Yemen | 48.3 | 38 | Cameroon | 40.7 |
| 14 | Sierra Leone | 48.2 | 39 | Pakistan | 40.6 |
| 15 | Tanzania | 48.1 | | Zimbabwe | 40.6 |
| 16 | Zaire | 47.5 | 41 | Nicaragua | 40.5 |
| 17 | Liberia | 47.3 | | Oman | 40.5 |
| 18 | Burkina Faso | 46.7 | 43 | Bhutan | 40.0 |
| 19 | Zambia | 46.4 | 44 | Iran | 39.9 |
| 20 | Burundi | 46.0 | 45 | Jordan | 39.5 |
| | Mauritania | 46.0 | 46 | Cambodia | 39.2 |
| 22 | Madagascar | 45.5 | 47 | Iraq | 38.8 |
| 23 | Laos | 45.2 | 48 | Guatemala | 38.7 |
| | Nigeria | 45.2 | 49 | Bangladesh | 38.5 |
| 25 | Mozambique | 45.1 | 50 | Botswana | 38.4 |

## Highest fertility rates
*Average no. of children per woman, 1990-95*

| | | | | | |
|---|---|---|---|---|---|
| 1 | Rwanda | 8.49 | 21 | Togo | 6.58 |
| 2 | Malawi | 7.60 | 22 | Burkina Faso | 6.50 |
| 3 | Côte d'Ivoire | 7.41 | | Mauritania | 6.50 |
| 4 | Uganda | 7.30 | | Mozambique | 6.50 |
| 5 | Angola | 7.20 | | Sierra Leone | 6.50 |
| 6 | Yemen | 7.18 | 26 | Nigeria | 6.42 |
| 7 | Benin | 7.10 | 27 | Libya | 6.39 |
| | Mali | 7.10 | 28 | Saudi Arabia | 6.37 |
| | Niger | 7.10 | 29 | Zambia | 6.33 |
| 10 | Ethiopia | 7.00 | 30 | Congo | 6.29 |
| | Guinea | 7.00 | 31 | Kenya | 6.28 |
| | Somalia | 7.00 | 32 | CAR | 6.20 |
| 13 | Afghanistan | 6.90 | 33 | Pakistan | 6.17 |
| 14 | Burundi | 6.80 | 34 | Syria | 6.15 |
| | Liberia | 6.80 | 35 | Senegal | 6.06 |
| | Tanzania | 6.80 | 36 | Sudan | 6.05 |
| 17 | Oman | 6.71 | 37 | Namibia | 6.00 |
| 18 | Zaire | 6.70 | 38 | Ghana | 5.96 |
| 19 | Laos | 6.69 | 39 | Iran | 5.95 |
| 20 | Madagascar | 6.60 | 40 | Bhutan | 5.89 |

## Lowest crude birth rates
*Number of live births per 1,000 population, 1990-95*

| | | | | | |
|---|---|---|---|---|---|
| 1 | Italy | 10.0 | 21 | Estonia | 14.0 |
| 2 | Greece | 10.4 | | Sweden | 14.0 |
| 3 | Spain | 10.8 | 23 | Ex-Yugoslavia | 14.1 |
| 4 | Japan | 11.2 | 24 | Canada | 14.2 |
| 5 | Germany | 11.3 | | Ukraine | 14.2 |
| 6 | Austria | 11.6 | 26 | Poland | 14.3 |
| | Portugal | 11.6 | 27 | Ireland | 14.4 |
| 8 | Belgium | 12.1 | 28 | Bermuda[b] | 14.6 |
| 9 | Hungary | 12.3 | 29 | Belorussia | 14.7 |
| | Luxembourg | 12.3 | | Norway | 14.7 |
| 11 | Bulgaria | 12.5 | 31 | Lithuania | 14.8 |
| | Denmark | 12.5 | | Russia | 14.8 |
| 13 | Hong Kong | 12.7 | 33 | Slovakia[c] | 14.9 |
| | Switzerland | 12.7 | 34 | Taiwan | 15.0 |
| 15 | Finland | 12.8 | 35 | Australia | 15.1 |
| 16 | Czech Republic[a] | 13.3 | 36 | Malta | 15.2 |
| 17 | France | 13.5 | 37 | Georgia | 15.6 |
| 18 | Netherlands | 13.7 | 38 | Romania | 15.7 |
| 19 | Latvia | 13.9 | 39 | Barbados | 15.8 |
| | United Kingdom | 13.9 | 40 | United States | 15.9 |

## Lowest fertility rates
*Average number of children per woman, 1990-95*

| | | | | | |
|---|---|---|---|---|---|
| 1 | Italy | 1.31 | 21 | Bulgaria | 1.83 |
| 2 | Spain | 1.38 | | Hungary | 1.83 |
| 3 | Hong Kong | 1.44 | 23 | Cuba | 1.87 |
| 4 | Greece | 1.47 | 24 | United Kingdom | 1.88 |
| 5 | Portugal | 1.48 | 25 | Ex-Yugoslavia | 1.90 |
| 6 | Austria | 1.50 | 26 | Australia | 1.91 |
| | Germany | 1.50 | 27 | Ex-Czechoslovakia | 1.97 |
| 8 | Luxembourg | 1.60 | 28 | Latvia | 2.00 |
| 9 | Belgium | 1.65 | | Lithuania | 2.00 |
| | Japan | 1.65 | | Mauritius | 2.00 |
| | Switzerland | 1.65 | | Norway | 2.00 |
| 12 | Denmark | 1.70 | 32 | Bahamas | 2.01 |
| | Netherlands | 1.70 | 33 | Estonia | 2.05 |
| 14 | South Korea | 1.75 | | Poland | 2.05 |
| | Singapore | 1.75 | 35 | Malta | 2.07 |
| | Taiwan | 1.75 | | Sweden | 2.07 |
| 17 | Canada | 1.78 | | United States | 2.07 |
| 18 | Barbados | 1.80 | 38 | Belorussia | 2.09 |
| | Finland | 1.80 | | Macao | 2.09 |
| 20 | France | 1.82 | | Netherlands Antilles | 2.09 |

**Notes:** The crude birth rate is the number of live births in one year per 1,000 population. In addition to the fertility rate (see below) it depends on the population's age structure and will tend to be higher if there is a large proportion of women of childbearing age.

The fertility rate is the average number of children born to a woman who completes her childbearing years.

a  Provisional 1991.
b  1989.
c  1991.

# Economic strength

## Biggest economies
*GDP, $bn*

| | | | | | | |
|---|---|---|---|---|---|---|
| 1 | United States | 5,905 | | UAE | 37 |
| 2 | Japan | 3,508 | 50 | Egypt | 35 |
| 3 | Germany | 1,846 | 51 | Nigeria | 33 |
| 4 | France | 1,279 | 52 | Hungary | 31 |
| 5 | Italy | 1,187 | 53 | Belorussia | 30 |
| 6 | United Kingdom | 1,025 | 54 | Kazakhstan | 29 |
| 7 | Canada | 566 | 55 | Morocco | 27 |
| 8 | Spain | 548 | 56 | Bangladesh | 25 |
| 9 | China | 442 | | Czech Republic | 25 |
| 10 | Brazil | 424 | | Libya | 25 |
| 11 | Russia | 398 | | Romania | 25 |
| 12 | Netherlands | 312 | 60 | Puerto Rico | 24 |
| 13 | Australia | 299 | 61 | North Korea | 23 |
| 14 | South Korea | 296 | 62 | Iraq[a] | 22 |
| 15 | Mexico | 295 | | Kuwait | 22 |
| 16 | India | 272 | 64 | Peru | 21 |
| 17 | Switzerland | 249 | 65 | Uzbekistan | 18 |
| 18 | Sweden | 233 | 66 | Syria | 15 |
| 19 | Belgium | 210 | | Tunisia | 15 |
| 20 | Taiwan | 207 | 68 | Luxembourg | 14 |
| 21 | Argentina | 200 | 69 | Bulgaria | 12 |
| 22 | Austria | 175 | | Ecuador | 12 |
| 23 | Denmark | 134 | | Slovenia | 12 |
| 24 | Iran | 131 | 72 | Oman | 11 |
| 25 | Saudi Arabia | 126 | 73 | Cameroon | 10 |
| 26 | Indonesia | 123 | | Guatemala | 10 |
| 27 | Finland | 116 | | Slovakia | 10 |
| 28 | Turkey | 114 | | Uruguay | 10 |
| 29 | Norway | 110 | 77 | Côte d'Ivoire | 9 |
| 30 | Thailand | 107 | | Qatar | 9 |
| 31 | South Africa | 106 | | Sri Lanka | 9 |
| 32 | Hong Kong | 89 | | Vietnam | 9 |
| 33 | Ukraine | 87 | | Zaire | 9 |
| 34 | Greece | 75 | 82 | Angola[a] | 8 |
| | Poland | 75 | | Croatia[a] | 8 |
| 36 | Portugal | 73 | | Dominican Republic | 8 |
| 37 | Israel | 68 | | Kenya | 8 |
| 38 | Venezuela | 59 | 86 | Cyprus | 7 |
| 39 | Malaysia | 52 | | Ghana | 7 |
| 40 | Pakistan | 49 | | Yemen | 7 |
| | Philippines | 49 | 89 | Azerbaijan | 6 |
| 42 | Algeria | 48 | | Costa Rica | 6 |
| 43 | Colombia | 45 | | El Salvador | 6 |
| 44 | Myanmar | 44 | | Ethiopia | 6 |
| | Singapore | 44 | | Iceland | 6 |
| 46 | Ireland | 43 | | Panama | 6 |
| 47 | New Zealand | 41 | | Paraguay | 6 |
| 48 | Chile | 37 | | Senegal | 6 |

a  Estimate.

## Human development index

| | | | | | |
|---|---|---|---|---|---|
| 1 | Japan | 98.3 | 41 | Portugal | 85.3 |
| 2 | Canada | 98.2 | 42 | Costa Rica | 85.2 |
| 3 | Norway | 97.9 | 43 | Singapore | 84.9 |
| 4 | Switzerland | 97.8 | 44 | Brunei | 84.7 |
| 5 | Sweden | 97.7 | 45 | Ukraine | 84.4 |
| 6 | United States | 97.6 | 46 | Argentina | 83.2 |
| 7 | Australia | 97.2 | 47 | Armenia | 83.1 |
| 8 | France | 97.1 | | Poland | 83.1 |
| 9 | Holland | 97.0 | 49 | Georgia | 82.9 |
| 10 | United Kingdom | 96.4 | 50 | Venezuela | 82.4 |
| 11 | Iceland | 96.0 | 51 | Kuwait | 81.5 |
| 12 | Germany | 95.7 | 52 | Mexico | 80.5 |
| 13 | Denmark | 95.5 | 53 | Kazakhstan | 80.2 |
| 14 | Finland | 95.4 | | Qatar | 80.2 |
| 15 | Austria | 95.2 | 55 | Mauritius | 79.4 |
| | Belgium | 95.2 | 56 | Bahrain | 79.0 |
| 17 | New Zealand | 94.7 | | Malaysia | 79.0 |
| 18 | Luxembourg | 94.3 | 58 | Colombia | 77.0 |
| 19 | Israel | 93.8 | | Azerbaijan | 77.0 |
| 20 | Barbados | 92.8 | 60 | Moldova | 75.8 |
| 21 | Ireland | 92.5 | 61 | Suriname | 75.1 |
| 22 | Italy | 92.4 | 62 | Turkmenistan | 74.6 |
| 23 | Spain | 92.3 | 63 | Panama | 73.8 |
| 24 | Greece | 90.2 | | United Arab Emirates | 73.8 |
| | Hong Kong | 90.2 | 65 | Jamaica | 73.6 |
| 26 | Ex-Czechoslovakia | 89.2 | 66 | Brazil | 73.0 |
| 27 | Cyprus | 89.0 | | Fiji | 73.0 |
| 28 | Hungary | 88.7 | 68 | Turkey | 71.7 |
| 29 | Lithuania | 88.1 | 69 | Thailand | 71.5 |
| | Uruguay | 88.1 | 70 | Cuba | 71.1 |
| 31 | Trinidad and Tobago | 87.7 | 71 | Romania | 70.9 |
| 32 | Bahamas | 87.5 | 72 | Albania | 69.9 |
| 33 | Estonia | 87.2 | 73 | Uzbekistan | 69.5 |
| | South Korea | 87.2 | 74 | Syria | 69.4 |
| 35 | Latvia | 86.8 | 75 | Kirgizstan | 68.9 |
| 36 | Chile | 86.4 | 76 | Saudi Arabia | 68.8 |
| 37 | Russia | 86.2 | 77 | South Africa | 67.3 |
| 38 | Belorussia | 86.1 | 78 | Sri Lanka | 66.3 |
| 39 | Malta | 85.5 | 79 | Libya | 65.8 |
| 40 | Bulgaria | 85.4 | 80 | Tajikistan | 65.7 |

**Notes:** GDP or GDP per head is often taken as a measure of how developed a country is but its usefuless is limited as it refers only to economic welfare. In 1990 the UN Development Programme published its first estimate of a Human Development Index, which combined statistics on two other indicators – adult literacy and life expectancy – with income levels to give a better, though still far from perfect, indicator of human development. In 1991 average years of schooling was combined with adult literacy to give a knowledge variable. The index is shown here scaled from 0 to 100; countries scoring over 80 are considered to have high human development, those scoring from 50 to 79 have medium human development and those under 50 have low human development.

# World economies: *rich and poor*

## Highest GDP per head
$

| | | | | | | |
|---|---|---|---|---|---|---|
| 1 | Switzerland | 36,231 | 36 | Greece | 7,184 |
| 2 | Luxembourg | 35,260 | 37 | Bahrain | 6,936 |
| 3 | Japan | 28,217 | 38 | Netherlands Antilles | 6,912 |
| 4 | Sweden | 26,784 | 39 | South Korea | 6,787 |
| 5 | Bermuda[a] | 26,600 | 40 | Puerto Rico | 6,606 |
| 6 | Denmark | 25,927 | 41 | Barbados | 6,537 |
| 7 | Norway | 25,804 | 42 | Oman | 6,486 |
| 8 | Iceland | 23,667 | 43 | Macao | 6,366 |
| 9 | United States | 23,119 | 44 | Slovenia | 6,330 |
| 10 | Finland | 22,977 | 45 | Argentina | 6,051 |
| 11 | Germany | 22,917 | 46 | Libya | 5,141 |
| 12 | France | 22,300 | 47 | Gabon | 4,447 |
| 13 | UAE | 22,223 | 48 | Trinidad & Tobago | 3,939 |
| 14 | Austria | 22,106 | 49 | Suriname | 3,700 |
| 15 | Belgium | 20,878 | 50 | Mexico | 3,470 |
| 16 | Netherlands | 20,593 | 51 | Uruguay | 3,336 |
| 17 | Italy | 20,513 | 52 | Hungary | 3,006 |
| 18 | Canada | 20,320 | 53 | Belorussia | 2,912 |
| 19 | United Kingdom | 17,760 | 54 | Venezuela | 2,900 |
| 20 | Australia | 17,065 | 55 | Botswana | 2,792 |
| 21 | Qatar | 16,242 | 56 | Malaysia | 2,790 |
| 22 | Singapore | 15,748 | 57 | Estonia | 2,765 |
| 23 | Hong Kong | 15,379 | 58 | Brazil | 2,759 |
| 24 | Spain | 14,022 | 59 | Chile | 2,725 |
| 25 | Israel | 13,233 | 60 | Mauritius | 2,698 |
| 26 | Brunei | 12,821 | 61 | Russia | 2,671 |
| 27 | Ireland | 12,104 | 62 | South Africa | 2,666 |
| 28 | New Zealand | 12,060 | 63 | Panama | 2,440 |
| 29 | Bahamas | 12,019 | 64 | Czech Republic | 2,438 |
| 30 | Kuwait | 11,066 | 65 | Iran | 2,189 |
| 31 | Taiwan | 9,981 | 66 | Fiji | 2,013 |
| 32 | Cyprus | 9,888 | 67 | Costa Rica | 1,997 |
| 33 | Saudi Arabia | 7,942 | 68 | Poland | 1,962 |
| 34 | Portugal | 7,451 | 69 | Turkey | 1,954 |
| 35 | Malta | 7,239 | 70 | Latvia | 1,941 |

## Lowest GDP per head
$

| | | | | | | |
|---|---|---|---|---|---|---|
| 1 | Sudan[b] | 55 | 11 | Bhutan | 176 |
| 2 | Mozambique | 62 | 12 | Mongolia | 194 |
| 3 | Tanzania | 99 | 13 | Burundi | 205 |
| 4 | Somalia[b] | 100 | 14 | Malawi | 209 |
| 5 | Cambodia | 103 | 15 | Chad | 211 |
| 6 | Ethiopia | 113 | 16 | Zaire | 214 |
| 7 | Vietnam | 130 | 17 | Bangladesh | 219 |
| 8 | Nepal | 165 | 18 | Madagascar | 227 |
| 9 | Sierra Leone | 167 | 19 | Rwanda | 248 |
| 10 | Uganda | 169 | 20 | Laos | 252 |

a 1991
b Estimate.

## Highest purchasing power[a]

*GDP per head in PPP (USA = 100), 1990*

| | | | | | |
|---|---|---|---|---|---|
| 1 | United States | 100.0 | 36 | Barbados | 38.7 |
| 2 | Switzerland | 97.3 | 37 | Russia | 37.1 |
| 3 | Canada | 89.7 | 38 | Greece | 34.3 |
| | Luxembourg | 89.7 | 39 | Ex-Czechoslovakia[b] | 34.0 |
| 5 | Germany | 84.9 | 40 | Libya[b] | 32.6 |
| 6 | Japan | 82.1 | 41 | South Korea | 31.4 |
| 7 | France | 81.1 | 42 | Trinidad & Tobago | 30.8 |
| 8 | Sweden | 79.3 | 43 | Latvia | 30.1 |
| 9 | Denmark | 78.2 | 44 | Estonia | 30.0 |
| 10 | UAE | 78.1 | 45 | Venezuela | 28.8 |
| 11 | Austria | 76.9 | 46 | Malaysia | 28.6 |
| | Iceland | 76.9 | 47 | Hungary | 28.5 |
| 13 | Finland | 76.7 | 48 | Mexico | 27.6 |
| 14 | Belgium | 76.4 | | Uruguay | 27.6 |
| 15 | Australia | 74.8 | 50 | Mauritius | 26.8 |
| 16 | Norway | 74.7 | 51 | Belorussia | 26.7 |
| 17 | Italy | 74.1 | 52 | Ukraine | 25.3 |
| 18 | Singapore | 74.0 | 53 | Chile | 23.8 |
| 19 | United Kingdom | 73.7 | 54 | Lithuania | 22.9 |
| 20 | Holland | 73.2 | 55 | South Africa | 22.7 |
| 21 | Hong Kong | 72.7 | 56 | Syria | 22.2 |
| 22 | Kuwait | 70.8 | 57 | Armenia | 22.1 |
| 23 | Brunei[b] | 65.3 | 58 | Brazil | 22.0 |
| 24 | New Zealand | 62.9 | | Kazakhstan | 22.0 |
| 25 | Spain | 54.7 | 60 | Bulgaria | 21.9 |
| 26 | Qatar[b] | 53.1 | 61 | Turkey | 21.7 |
| 27 | Bahamas | 52.4 | 62 | Georgia | 21.3 |
| 28 | Saudi Arabia | 51.2 | 63 | Costa Rica | 21.2 |
| 29 | Israel | 50.5 | 64 | Fiji | 20.6 |
| 30 | Bahrain | 49.9 | 65 | Argentina | 20.0 |
| 31 | Ireland | 49.4 | 66 | Colombia | 19.8 |
| 32 | Oman | 46.5 | | Poland | 19.8 |
| 33 | Cyprus | 46.4 | 68 | Turkmenistan | 19.7 |
| 34 | Portugal | 40.9 | 69 | Gabon | 19.3 |
| 35 | Malta | 40.7 | 70 | Thailand | 18.6 |

## Lowest purchasing power[a]

*GDP per head in PPP (USA=100), 1990*

| | | | | | |
|---|---|---|---|---|---|
| 1 | Ethiopia | 1.7 | | Niger | 3.0 |
| | Zaire | 1.7 | 12 | Myanmar | 3.1 |
| 3 | Guinea | 2.3 | | Rwanda | 3.1 |
| 4 | Uganda | 2.4 | 14 | Afghanistan | 3.3 |
| 5 | Chad | 2.6 | | Madagascar | 3.3 |
| 6 | Mali | 2.7 | 16 | Togo | 3.4 |
| | Tanzania | 2.7 | 17 | Zambia | 3.5 |
| 8 | Burkina Faso | 2.9 | 18 | CAR | 3.6 |
| | Burundi | 2.9 | 19 | Bhutan[b] | 3.7 |
| 10 | Malawi | 3.0 | 20 | Somalia | 3.9 |

a See glossary for explanation of purchasing power parity.
b Estimate.

# Economic growth

## Fastest economic growth, 1985-92
*Average annual % increase in real GDP*

| | | | | | |
|---|---|---|---|---|---|
| 1 | China | 9.2 | | Oman | 5.5 |
| 2 | South Korea | 8.9 | 22 | India | 5.2 |
| 3 | Thailand | 8.6 | 23 | Nepal | 5.0 |
| 4 | Botswana | 7.5 | | Turkey | 5.0 |
| 5 | Mauritius | 6.9 | 25 | Ireland | 4.8 |
| 6 | Taiwan | 6.5 | | Vietnam | 4.8 |
| 7 | Singapore | 6.3 | 27 | Burundi | 4.7 |
| 8 | Chile | 6.2 | | Ghana | 4.7 |
| | Malaysia | 6.2 | 29 | Israel | 4.6 |
| 10 | Cyprus | 6.1 | 30 | Luxembourg | 4.5 |
| | Hong Kong | 6.1 | 31 | Kenya | 4.3 |
| 12 | Bhutan | 5.9 | 32 | Burkina Faso | 4.2 |
| 13 | Cambodia[a] | 5.8 | | Tunisia | 4.2 |
| | Indonesia | 5.8 | | Uganda | 4.2 |
| | Laos[a] | 5.8 | 35 | Costa Rica | 4.1 |
| 16 | Nigeria | 5.7 | | Japan | 4.1 |
| 17 | Pakistan | 5.6 | | Tanzania | 4.1 |
| 18 | Chad | 5.5 | 38 | Bangladesh | 4.0 |
| | Lesotho | 5.5 | | Colombia | 4.0 |
| | Malta | 5.5 | 40 | Sri-Lanka | 3.9 |

## Slowest economic growth, 1985-92
*Average annual % increase in real GDP*

| | | | | | |
|---|---|---|---|---|---|
| 1 | Georgia[be] | -14.5 | 21 | Suriname | -1.5 |
| 2 | Iraq[b] | -14.3 | | Trinidad & Tobago | -1.5 |
| 3 | Armenia[be] | -9.8 | 23 | Ex-Czechoslovakia | -1.4 |
| 4 | Lithuania[c] | -6.0 | 24 | Belorussia[ae] | -1.2 |
| 5 | Moldova[be] | -5.5 | | Somalia[d] | -1.2 |
| | Romania | -5.5 | 26 | Peru | -0.9 |
| 7 | Azerbaijan[be] | -5.4 | 27 | Bulgaria | -0.8 |
| 8 | Estonia[c] | -5.1 | 28 | Liberia | -0.6 |
| | Slovenia[a] | -5.1 | 29 | Poland | -0.5 |
| 10 | Latvia[c] | -4.8 | 30 | Myanmar | -0.4 |
| 11 | Albania | -4.5 | | Zaire | -0.4 |
| 12 | Russia[b] | -4.1 | 32 | Côte d'Ivoire | 0.1 |
| 13 | Afghanistan[d] | -3.8 | 33 | Congo | 0.2 |
| 14 | Cameroon | -3.2 | | New Zealand | 0.2 |
| 15 | Libya | -2.8 | 35 | Ethiopia | 0.4 |
| | Ukraine[ce] | -2.8 | | Turkmenistan[ce] | 0.4 |
| 17 | Nicaragua | -2.6 | 37 | South Africa | 0.5 |
| 18 | Haiti | -2.5 | | Zambia | 0.5 |
| 19 | Hungary | -1.7 | 39 | Mongolia | 0.8 |
| | Kirgizstan[c] | -1.7 | 40 | Barbados | 0.9 |

a  1988-92.
b  1987-92.
c  1986-92.
d  1985-92.
e  Net material product.

## Fastest economic growth, 1975-84
*Average annual % increase in real GDP*

| | | | | | |
|---|---|---|---|---|---|
| 1 | Botswana | 12.4 | | Malta | 7.2 |
| 2 | Oman | 10.3 | 12 | Egypt | 7.1 |
| 3 | Jordan | 9.0 | 13 | Malaysia | 7.0 |
| 4 | Hong Kong | 8.9 | | Thailand | 7.0 |
| 5 | Taiwan | 8.6 | 15 | Cameroon | 6.8 |
| 6 | Singapore | 8.0 | 16 | Paraguay | 6.6 |
| | South Korea | 8.0 | 17 | Mongolia | 6.5 |
| 8 | Congo | 7.6 | 18 | Bahrain | 6.2 |
| 9 | Niger | 7.4 | 19 | Vietnam | 6.1 |
| 10 | China | 7.2 | 20 | Bhutan | 6.0 |

## Slowest economic growth, 1975-84
*Average annual % increase in real GDP*

| | | | | | |
|---|---|---|---|---|---|
| 1 | Kuwait | -1.7 | 11 | Madagascar | -0.2 |
| 2 | Ghana | -1.5 | 12 | El Salvador | -0.1 |
| 3 | Nicaragua | -1.4 | | Zambia | -0.1 |
| | Nigeria | -1.4 | 14 | Switzerland | 0.0 |
| 5 | Chad | -1.3 | 15 | Argentina | 0.1 |
| 6 | Gabon | -0.9 | | Mozambique | 0.1 |
| 7 | Zaire | -0.8 | 17 | Uganda | 0.2 |
| 8 | Afghanistan | -0.6 | 18 | Papua New Guinea | 0.6 |
| 9 | Lesotho | -0.5 | 19 | Jamaica | 0.7 |
| 10 | Liberia | -0.4 | 20 | Sierra Leone | 0.8 |

## Highest industrial growth, 1980-91
*Average annual % increase in real terms*

| | | | | | |
|---|---|---|---|---|---|
| 1 | Bhutan | 14.8 | 6 | Oman | 9.6 |
| 2 | South Korea | 12.1 | | Thailand | 9.6 |
| 3 | China | 11.0 | 8 | Lesotho | 8.2 |
| 4 | Botswana | 10.7 | 9 | Malaysia | 7.7 |
| 5 | Mauritius | 10.1 | 10 | Pakistan | 7.5 |

## Highest services growth, 1980-91
*Average annual % increase in real terms*

| | | | | | |
|---|---|---|---|---|---|
| 1 | China | 11.2 | 6 | Bhutan | 7.3 |
| 2 | Botswana | 10.3 | | Chad | 7.3 |
| 3 | South Korea | 9.3 | | Singapore | 7.3 |
| 4 | Taiwan | 9.1 | 9 | Indonesia | 6.8 |
| 5 | Thailand | 8.0 | 10 | India | 6.7 |

## Highest agricultural growth, 1980-91
*Average annual % increase in real terms*

| | | | | | |
|---|---|---|---|---|---|
| 1 | Saudi Arabia | 14.0 | 6 | Togo | 5.3 |
| 2 | Jordan | 8.1 | 7 | Algeria | 5.0 |
| 3 | Oman | 7.1 | 8 | Benin | 4.9 |
| 4 | Morocco | 6.8 | | Nepal | 4.9 |
| 5 | China | 5.7 | 10 | Bhutan | 4.8 |

# Trading places

## Biggest traders
*% of total world exports (visible & invisible)*

| | | | | | |
|---|---|---|---|---|---|
| 1 | United States | 13.09 | 26 | Brazil | 0.74 |
| 2 | Germany | 10.09 | 27 | Russia | 0.66 |
| 3 | Japan | 9.40 | 28 | Indonesia | 0.65 |
| 4 | France | 7.28 | 29 | Ireland | 0.62 |
| 5 | United Kingdom | 6.51 | 30 | Finland | 0.54 |
| 6 | Italy | 4.80 | 31 | South Africa | 0.51 |
| 7 | Belgium/Luxembourg | 4.36 | 32 | Portugal | 0.46 |
| 8 | Netherlands | 3.44 | 33 | India | 0.45 |
| 9 | Canada | 2.83 | | Turkey | 0.45 |
| 10 | Switzerland | 2.25 | 35 | UAE | 0.39 |
| 11 | Spain | 1.96 | 36 | Israel | 0.37 |
| 12 | Taiwan | 1.78 | 37 | Poland | 0.35 |
| 13 | South Korea | 1.63 | 38 | Philippines | 0.31 |
| 14 | Austria | 1.51 | 39 | Iran | 0.30 |
| 15 | China | 1.47 | | Venezuela | 0.30 |
| 16 | Sweden | 1.45 | | Ex-Yugoslavia | 0.30 |
| 17 | Denmark | 1.27 | 42 | Ex-Czechoslovakia | 0.29 |
| 18 | Singapore | 1.20 | 43 | Argentina | 0.27 |
| 19 | Australia | 1.00 | | Greece | 0.27 |
| 20 | Saudi Arabia | 0.97 | 45 | Netherlands Antilles | 0.26 |
| 21 | Norway | 0.94 | 46 | Hungary | 0.25 |
| 22 | Hong Kong | 0.85 | 47 | Algeria[a] | 0.23 |
| 23 | Malaysia | 0.84 | | Chile | 0.23 |
| 24 | Mexico | 0.80 | | Nigeria | 0.23 |
| 25 | Thailand | 0.76 | | | |

## Most trade dependent
*Trade as % of GDP [b]*

| | | |
|---|---|---|
| 1 | Singapore | 101.9 |
| 2 | Bahrain | 96.8 |
| 3 | Panama | 88.9 |
| 4 | Malaysia | 73.8 |
| 5 | Malta[c] | 62.1 |
| 6 | Ireland | 57.2 |
| 7 | Belgium/Luxembourg | 55.6 |
| 8 | UAE | 51.5 |
| 9 | Netherlands Antilles | 50.0 |
| 10 | Mozambique | 49.3 |
| | Namibia | 49.3 |
| | Slovenia | 49.3 |
| 13 | Jordan | 47.9 |
| 14 | Lesotho | 47.8 |
| 15 | Mauritius | 46.7 |

## Least trade dependent
*Trade as % of GDP [b]*

| | | |
|---|---|---|
| 1 | Afghanistan[d] | 4.0 |
| 2 | Ethiopia[a] | 5.2 |
| 3 | Argentina | 6.5 |
| 4 | Brazil | 6.7 |
| 5 | Japan | 7.5 |
| 6 | India | 8.0 |
| | United States | 8.3 |
| 8 | Russia | 8.5 |
| | Rwanda | 8.5 |
| 10 | Haiti[a] | 9.3 |
| 11 | Uganda | 9.7 |
| 12 | Albania | 9.9 |
| 13 | Cameroon[a] | 10.0 |
| 14 | Bangladesh | 11.0 |
| | Burundi | 11.0 |

**Notes:** The figures are drawn from balance of payment statistics and, therefore, have differing technical definitions from trade statistics taken from customs or similar sources. The invisible trade figures do not show some countries, notably Eastern European, due to unavailable data. For Hong Kong and Singapore, domestic exports and retained imports only are used.

## Biggest visible traders
*% of world visible exports*

| | | | | | |
|---|---|---|---|---|---|
| 1 | United States | 12.02 | 21 | Malaysia | 1.09 |
| 2 | Germany | 11.11 | 22 | Russia | 1.01 |
| 3 | Japan | 9.03 | 23 | Brazil | 0.99 |
| 4 | France | 6.15 | 24 | Norway | 0.96 |
| 5 | United Kingdom | 5.12 | 25 | Indonesia | 0.89 |
| 6 | Italy | 4.85 | 26 | Thailand | 0.88 |
| 7 | Canada | 3.64 | 27 | Hong Kong | 0.82 |
| 8 | Netherlands | 3.51 | 28 | Ireland | 0.76 |
| 9 | Belgium/Luxembourg | 3.18 | 29 | Mexico | 0.75 |
| 10 | Taiwan | 2.23 | 30 | South Africa | 0.65 |
| 11 | Switzerland | 2.15 | 31 | Finland | 0.64 |
| 12 | South Korea | 2.05 | 32 | UAE | 0.59 |
| 13 | China | 1.90 | 33 | India | 0.54 |
| 14 | Spain | 1.75 | 34 | Portugal | 0.50 |
| 15 | Sweden | 1.51 | 35 | Iran | 0.44 |
| 16 | Austria | 1.18 | 36 | Turkey | 0.41 |
| 17 | Saudi Arabia | 1.17 | 37 | Poland | 0.38 |
| 18 | Australia | 1.16 | | Venezuela | 0.38 |
| 19 | Denmark | 1.11 | | Ex-Yugoslavia[a] | 0.38 |
| | Singapore | 1.11 | 40 | Israel | 0.36 |

## Biggest invisible traders
*% of world invisible exports*

| | | | | | |
|---|---|---|---|---|---|
| 1 | United States | 15.13 | 22 | Netherlands Antilles | 0.74 |
| 2 | Japan | 10.11 | 23 | Australia | 0.70 |
| 3 | France | 9.45 | 24 | Saudi Arabia | 0.61 |
| 4 | United Kingdom | 9.16 | 25 | Turkey | 0.54 |
| 5 | Germany | 8.13 | 26 | Thailand | 0.53 |
| 6 | Belgium/Luxembourg | 6.60 | 27 | Greece | 0.49 |
| 7 | Italy | 4.69 | 28 | Egypt | 0.46 |
| 8 | Netherlands | 3.31 | 29 | Portugal | 0.40 |
| 9 | Switzerland | 2.44 | 30 | Israel | 0.39 |
| 10 | Spain | 2.38 | | Philippines | 0.39 |
| 11 | Austria | 2.01 | 32 | Malaysia | 0.37 |
| 12 | Denmark | 1.58 | 33 | Ireland | 0.34 |
| 13 | Singapore | 1.37 | 34 | Finland | 0.33 |
| 14 | Sweden | 1.32 | 35 | India | 0.29 |
| 15 | Canada | 1.28 | | Poland | 0.29 |
| 16 | Taiwan | 0.94 | 37 | Brazil | 0.26 |
| 17 | Hong Kong | 0.89 | 38 | Ex-Czechoslovakia | 0.25 |
| | Mexico | 0.89 | 39 | South Africa | 0.24 |
| | Norway | 0.89 | 40 | Hungary | 0.20 |
| 20 | South Korea | 0.83 | | Indonesia | 0.20 |
| 21 | China | 0.77 | | | |

a   1991.
b   Average of imports and exports of goods as % of GDP.
c   1990.
d   1989.

# Current account

## Largest surpluses

*$bn*

| | | | | | | |
|---|---|---:|---|---|---|---:|
| 1 | Japan | 117.6 | | 17 | Hong Kong | 1.7 |
| 2 | Switzerland | 13.4 | | 18 | South Africa | 1.4 |
| 3 | Taiwan | 8.2 | | 19 | Colombia | 0.9 |
| 4 | Netherlands | 6.8 | | | Slovenia | 0.9 |
| 5 | China | 6.4 | | 21 | Bulgaria | 0.5 |
| 6 | Brazil | 6.3 | | 22 | Hungary | 0.4 |
| 7 | Belgium/Luxembourg | 5.4 | | 23 | Bangladesh | 0.2 |
| 8 | Denmark | 4.7 | | | Ethiopia | 0.2 |
| 9 | France | 4.1 | | 25 | Barbados | 0.1 |
| 10 | Norway | 2.9 | | | Botswana[b] | 0.1 |
| | Singapore | 2.9 | | | Israel | 0.1 |
| 12 | Egypt | 2.8 | | | Jamaica | 0.1 |
| 13 | Ireland | 2.6 | | | Lithuania | 0.1 |
| 14 | Algeria[a] | 2.4 | | | Namibia | 0.1 |
| 15 | Nigeria | 2.3 | | | Syria | 0.1 |
| 16 | Libya[b] | 2.2 | | | Trinidad & Tobago | 0.1 |

## Largest deficits

*$bn*

| | | | | | | |
|---|---|---:|---|---|---|---:|
| 1 | United States | -66.3 | | 28 | Bahrain | -1.0 |
| 2 | Germany | -25.6 | | 29 | Kuwait | -0.9 |
| 3 | Italy | -25.4 | | | Philippines | -0.9 |
| 4 | Canada | -23.0 | | | Tunisia | -0.9 |
| 5 | Mexico | -22.8 | | | Turkey | -0.9 |
| 6 | United Kingdom | -20.7 | | 33 | Jordan | -0.8 |
| 7 | Saudi Arabia | -19.4 | | | New Zealand | -0.8 |
| 8 | Spain | -18.5 | | 35 | Austria | -0.7 |
| 9 | Australia | -10.7 | | | Guatemala | -0.7 |
| 10 | Argentina | -8.4 | | | Nicaragua | -0.7 |
| 11 | Iran | -7.9 | | 38 | Chile | -0.6 |
| 12 | Thailand | -6.7 | | | Zaire[b] | -0.6 |
| 13 | Finland | -5.1 | | 40 | Angola | -0.5 |
| 14 | India | -5.0 | | | Bolivia | -0.5 |
| 15 | Sweden | -4.9 | | | Ecuador | -0.5 |
| 16 | South Korea | -4.5 | | | Paraguay | -0.5 |
| 17 | Indonesia | -3.7 | | | Sri Lanka | -0.5 |
| 18 | Venezuela | -3.4 | | | Sudan | -0.5 |
| 19 | Pakistan | -3.1 | | | Zimbabwe | -0.5 |
| | Poland | -3.1 | | 47 | Costa Rica | -0.4 |
| 21 | Russia | -2.7 | | | Dominican Republic | -0.4 |
| 22 | Greece | -2.1 | | | Ghana | -0.4 |
| | Peru | -2.1 | | | Morocco | -0.4 |
| 24 | Malaysia | -1.7 | | | Mozambique | -0.4 |
| 25 | Romania | -1.5 | | | Oman | -0.4 |
| 26 | Côte d'Ivoire | -1.3 | | | Papua New Guinea[a] | -0.4 |
| 27 | Ex-Yugoslavia[a] | -1.2 | | | Tanzania[b] | -0.4 |

## Largest surpluses as % of GDP
%

| | | | | | | |
|---|---|---|---|---|---|---|
| 1 | Libya[b] | 8.8 | 14 | Jamaica | 3.6 |
| 2 | Barbados | 8.1 | 15 | Denmark | 3.5 |
| | Egypt | 8.1 | | Lesotho | 3.5 |
| 4 | Slovenia | 7.3 | 17 | Japan | 3.4 |
| 5 | Nigeria | 6.9 | 18 | Ethiopia | 2.8 |
| 6 | Singapore | 6.6 | 19 | Netherlands Antilles | 2.7 |
| 7 | Ireland | 6.1 | 20 | Belgium | 2.6 |
| 8 | Namibia | 5.7 | | Norway | 2.6 |
| 9 | Switzerland | 5.4 | 22 | Trinidad & Tobago | 2.4 |
| 10 | Botswana[b] | 5.3 | 23 | Netherlands | 2.2 |
| 11 | Algeria[a] | 4.5 | 24 | Colombia | 2.0 |
| 12 | Taiwan | 4.0 | 25 | Hong Kong | 1.9 |
| 13 | Bulgaria | 3.8 | | | |

## Largest deficits as % of GDP
%

| | | | | | | |
|---|---|---|---|---|---|---|
| 1 | Nicaragua | -52.5 | 31 | Nepal | -5.5 |
| 2 | Mozambique | -36.8 | 32 | Ghana | -5.3 |
| 3 | Sudan | -34.9 | 33 | Dominican Republic | -5.2 |
| 4 | Bahrain | -26.9 | 34 | Madagascar | -4.8 |
| 5 | Jordan | -17.4 | | Sri Lanka | -4.8 |
| 6 | Somalia[c] | -15.6 | 36 | Rwanda | -4.7 |
| 7 | Saudi Arabia | -15.4 | 37 | Burundi | -4.5 |
| 8 | Tanzania[b] | -15.3 | 38 | CAR | -4.4 |
| 9 | Côte d'Ivoire | -15.1 | | Finland | -4.4 |
| 10 | Congo | -12.3 | 40 | Argentina | -4.2 |
| 11 | Zambia | -11.9 | 41 | Malawi[d] | -4.1 |
| 12 | Papua New Guinea[a] | -10.7 | | Canada | -4.1 |
| 13 | Bolivia | -10.5 | | Poland | -4.1 |
| 14 | Peru | -9.8 | 44 | Kuwait | -4.0 |
| 15 | Honduras | -8.4 | 45 | Ecuador | -3.9 |
| 16 | Zimbabwe | -8.3 | | Senegal | -3.9 |
| 17 | Mexico | -7.7 | 47 | Laos | -3.7 |
| | Paraguay | -7.7 | 48 | Australia | -3.6 |
| 19 | Zaire[b] | -7.6 | | Bahamas | -3.6 |
| 20 | Guatemala | -7.4 | 50 | Cyprus | -3.4 |
| 21 | Angola | -6.7 | | El Salvador | -3.4 |
| | Togo | -6.7 | | Iceland | -3.4 |
| 23 | Tunisia | -6.5 | | Oman | -3.4 |
| 24 | Chad | -6.3 | | Spain | -3.4 |
| | Thailand | -6.3 | | Uganda | -3.4 |
| 26 | Pakistan | -6.2 | 56 | Burkina Faso | -3.3 |
| 27 | Romania | -6.1 | | Malaysia | -3.3 |
| 28 | Iran | -6.0 | | Mali | -3.3 |
| 29 | Costa Rica | -5.9 | 59 | Cameroon | -3.2 |
| 30 | Venezuela | -5.7 | 60 | Indonesia | -3.0 |

a   1991.
b   1990.
c   1989.
d   1988.

# Inflation

## Highest inflation, 1992-93
*% consumer price inflation*

| | | | | | |
|---|---|---|---|---|---|
| 1 | Serbia[a] | 8,926.0 | 31 | Uganda[a] | 52.4 |
| 2 | Zaire[a] | 4,129.2 | 32 | Peru | 48.6 |
| 3 | Kazakhstan[a] | 2,567.8 | 33 | Kenya | 45.7 |
| 4 | Brazil | 2,110.0 | 34 | Ecuador | 45.0 |
| 5 | Ukraine[a] | 1,450.1 | 35 | Suriname[a] | 43.7 |
| 6 | Moldova[a] | 1,277.0 | 36 | Venezuela | 38.1 |
| 7 | Belorussia[a] | 1,074.5 | 37 | Poland | 35.3 |
| 8 | Estonia[a] | 1,069.0 | 38 | Iran | 35.0 |
| 9 | Lithuania[a] | 1,020.0 | 39 | Jamaica[a] | 30.6 |
| 10 | Turkmenistan[a] | 980.2 | 40 | Mozambique | 30.0 |
| 11 | Latvia[a] | 951.2 | 41 | Zimbabwe | 28.0 |
| 12 | Russia | 940.0 | 42 | Haiti[a] | 25.2 |
| 13 | Georgia[a] | 913.0 | 43 | Algeria | 25.0 |
| 14 | Kirgizstan[a] | 854.6 | | Lebanon | 25.0 |
| 15 | Armenia[a] | 790.0 | | Slovakia | 25.0 |
| 16 | Croatia[a] | 665.0 | | Vietnam[a] | 25.0 |
| 17 | Azerbaijan[a] | 607.2 | 47 | Malawi | 23.5 |
| 18 | Uzbekistan[a] | 515.0 | 48 | Hungary | 22.5 |
| 19 | Romania | 245.6 | 49 | Colombia | 22.4 |
| 20 | Slovenia[a] | 201.3 | 50 | Tanzania | 22.0 |
| 21 | Cambodia[a] | 176.8 | 51 | Myanmar[a] | 21.9 |
| 22 | Iraq[b] | 175.0 | 52 | Costa Rica[a] | 21.8 |
| 23 | Zambia | 130.0 | 53 | Czech Republic | 20.8 |
| 24 | Sudan[a] | 117.6 | 54 | China | 20.0 |
| 25 | Liberia[a] | 80.0 | 55 | Nicaragua | 19.5 |
| | Nigeria[a] | 80.0 | 56 | Paraguay | 18.5 |
| 27 | Bulgaria | 72.8 | 57 | Sierra Leone | 18.0 |
| 28 | Turkey | 66.0 | 58 | Lesotho[a] | 17.2 |
| 29 | Yemen | 55.0 | | Nepal[a] | 17.2 |
| 30 | Uruguay | 54.3 | 60 | Syria | 17.0 |

## Highest inflation, 1988-93
*% average annual consumer price inflation*

| | | | | | |
|---|---|---|---|---|---|
| 1 | Nicaragua | 1,479.9 | 16 | Cambodia[e] | 123.6 |
| 2 | Brazil | 1,178.7 | 17 | Belorussia[e] | 121.9 |
| 3 | Serbia[e] | 1,009.0 | 18 | Estonia[c] | 116.2 |
| 4 | Peru | 702.4 | 19 | Zambia | 116.0 |
| 5 | Zaire[c] | 478.1 | 20 | Lithuania[c] | 110.4 |
| 6 | Croatia[c] | 443.0 | 21 | Latvia[c] | 95.1 |
| 7 | Argentina | 383.3 | 22 | Vietnam[c] | 87.6 |
| 8 | Slovenia[c] | 351.0 | 23 | Turkmenistan[c] | 85.5 |
| 9 | Kazakhstan[d] | 309.2 | 24 | Georgia[c] | 80.3 |
| 10 | Moldova[d] | 235.0 | 25 | Kirgizstan[c] | 79.1 |
| 11 | Russia | 162.3 | 26 | Uruguay | 78.7 |
| 12 | Azerbaijan[d] | 148.9 | 27 | Romania | 76.6 |
| 13 | Iraq[b] | 146.6 | 28 | Liberia | 76.4 |
| 14 | Ukraine[e] | 137.0 | 29 | Sudan[c] | 68.0 |
| 15 | Poland | 124.2 | 30 | Turkey | 66.5 |

## Lowest inflation, 1992-93
*% consumer price inflation*

| | | | | | | |
|---|---|---|---|---|---|---|
| 1 | Togo[b] | -25.0 | | | France | 2.1 |
| 2 | Gabon[a] | -9.6 | | | Netherlands | 2.1 |
| 3 | Chad[a] | -4.0 | | 28 | Norway | 2.2 |
| 4 | Burkina Faso[a] | -1.9 | | 29 | Singapore | 2.4 |
| 5 | CAR[a] | -0.9 | | | Bahamas | 2.8 |
| 6 | Mali[a] | -0.8 | | | Belgium | 2.8 |
| 7 | Senegal[a] | -0.1 | | 32 | Taiwan | 2.9 |
| 8 | Bangladesh | 1.0 | | 33 | Benin[a] | 3.0 |
| 9 | Japan | 1.2 | | | Puerto Rico | 3.0 |
| 10 | Denmark | 1.3 | | | Qatar | 3.0 |
| | New Zealand | 1.3 | | | United States | 3.0 |
| 12 | Ireland | 1.4 | | 37 | Switzerland | 3.3 |
| | Netherlands Antilles[a] | 1.4 | | 38 | UAE | 3.5 |
| 14 | Malta[a] | 1.6 | | 39 | Austria | 3.6 |
| | Panama | 1.6 | | | Luxembourg | 3.6 |
| | United Kingdom | 1.6 | | | Malaysia | 3.6 |
| 17 | Canada | 1.8 | | | Thailand | 3.6 |
| | Saudi Arabia | 1.8 | | 43 | Côte d'Ivoire | 4.0 |
| 19 | Australia | 2.0 | | 44 | Iceland | 4.1 |
| | Bahrain | 2.0 | | | Western Germany | 4.1 |
| | Cameroon[a] | 2.0 | | 46 | Italy | 4.3 |
| | Congo | 2.0 | | 47 | Papua New Guinea[a] | 4.4 |
| | Oman | 2.0 | | 48 | Dominican Republic | 4.5 |
| 24 | Brunei | 2.1 | | 49 | Spain | 4.6 |
| | Finland | 2.1 | | 50 | Sweden | 4.7 |

## Lowest inflation, 1988-93
*% average annual consumer price inflation*

| | | | | | | |
|---|---|---|---|---|---|---|
| 1 | Niger[c] | -3.5 | | 16 | Netherlands | 2.3 |
| 2 | Togo[b] | -2.4 | | 17 | Singapore | 2.6 |
| 3 | CAR[c] | -1.4 | | 18 | Belgium | 2.7 |
| 4 | Gabon[c] | -1.0 | | | Côte d'Ivoire | 2.7 |
| 5 | Senegal[c] | -0.6 | | 20 | Congo | 2.8 |
| 6 | Bahrain | 0.9 | | 21 | Denmark | 2.9 |
| 7 | Panama | 1.0 | | | France | 2.9 |
| 8 | Cameroon[c] | 1.2 | | | Ireland | 2.9 |
| 9 | Burkina Faso[c] | 1.4 | | 24 | Benin[c] | 3.0 |
| 10 | Brunei[e] | 1.8 | | 25 | Austria | 3.1 |
| | Malta[c] | 1.8 | | | Luxembourg | 3.1 |
| | Saudi Arabia | 1.8 | | | Netherlands Antilles[c] | 3.1 |
| 13 | Chad[c] | 2.0 | | | Western Germany | 3.1 |
| | Japan | 2.0 | | 29 | Malaysia | 3.5 |
| 15 | Mali[c] | 2.2 | | | Taiwan | 3.5 |

| | | | | |
|---|---|---|---|---|
| a | 1991-92. | | d | 1990-92. |
| b | Estimate. | | e | 1989-92. |
| c | 1988-92. | | | |

**Notes:** Inflation is measured as the % increase in the consumer price index between two dates. The figures shown are based on the average level of the index during the relevant years.

# Debt

## Highest foreign debt[a]
$m

| | | | | | |
|---|---|---|---|---|---|
| 1 | Brazil | 121,110 | 21 | Peru | 20,297 |
| 2 | Mexico | 113,378 | 22 | Malaysia | 19,837 |
| 3 | Indonesia | 84,385 | 23 | Chile | 19,360 |
| 4 | Russia | 78,658 | 24 | Côte d'Ivoire | 17,997 |
| 5 | India | 76,893 | 25 | Colombia | 17,204 |
| 6 | China | 69,321 | 26 | Syria | 16,513 |
| 7 | Argentina | 67,569 | 27 | Ex-Yugoslavia | 16,294 |
| 8 | Turkey | 54,772 | 28 | Sudan | 16,085 |
| 9 | Poland | 48,521 | 29 | Iran | 14,166 |
| 10 | South Korea | 42,999 | 30 | Bangladesh | 13,189 |
| 11 | Egypt | 40,431 | 31 | Ecuador | 12,280 |
| 12 | Thailand | 39,424 | 32 | Bulgaria | 12,146 |
| 13 | Venezuela | 37,193 | 33 | Nicaragua | 11,126 |
| 14 | Philippines | 32,589 | 34 | Zaire | 10,912 |
| 15 | Portugal | 32,046 | 35 | Angola | 9,645 |
| 16 | Nigeria | 30,998 | 36 | Ex-Czechoslovakia | 9,328 |
| 17 | Algeria | 26,349 | 37 | Tunisia | 8,476 |
| 18 | Pakistan | 24,072 | 38 | Jordan | 7,977 |
| 19 | Hungary | 21,900 | 39 | Zambia | 7,041 |
| 20 | Morocco | 21,418 | 40 | Tanzania | 6,715 |

## Highest debt service[b]
$m

| | | | | | |
|---|---|---|---|---|---|
| 1 | Mexico | 20,701 | 21 | Ex-Yugoslavia | 2,080 |
| 2 | Indonesia | 11,709 | 22 | Morocco | 2,072 |
| 3 | Brazil | 9,518 | 23 | Ex-Czechoslovakia | 2,029 |
| 4 | Algeria | 9,277 | 24 | Russia | 1,600 |
| 5 | Turkey | 9,053 | 25 | Poland | 1,530 |
| 6 | China | 8,724 | 26 | Tunisia | 1,377 |
| 7 | South Korea | 6,770 | 27 | Côte d'Ivoire | 1,117 |
| 8 | India | 6,637 | 28 | Peru | 1,033 |
| 9 | Thailand | 5,956 | 29 | Ecuador | 981 |
| 10 | Portugal | 5,579 | 30 | Panama | 912 |
| 11 | Argentina | 5,204 | 31 | Syria | 908 |
| 12 | Hungary | 4,962 | 32 | Iran | 810 |
| 13 | Philippines | 4,888 | 33 | Jordan | 717 |
| 14 | Nigeria | 3,777 | 34 | Jamaica | 692 |
| 15 | Colombia | 3,756 | 35 | Papua New Guinea | 660 |
| 16 | Venezuela | 3,309 | 36 | Paraguay | 628 |
| 17 | Malaysia | 3,072 | 37 | Uruguay | 595 |
| 18 | Chile | 2,705 | 38 | Zimbabwe | 590 |
| 19 | Egypt | 2,524 | 39 | Bangladesh | 582 |
| 20 | Pakistan | 2,311 | 40 | Kenya | 582 |

a  Foreign debt is debt owed to non-residents and repayable in foreign currency; the figures shown include liabilities of government, public and private sectors. Developed countries have been excluded.

b  Debt service is the sum of interest and principal repayments (amortization) due on outstanding foreign debt. The debt service ratio is debt service expressed as a percentage of the country's exports of goods and services.

## Highest foreign debt burden
*Foreign debt as % of GDP*

| | | | | | |
|---|---|---|---|---|---|
| 1 | Nicaragua | 822.6 | 21 | Bulgaria | 110.7 |
| 2 | Mozambique | 583.9 | | Nigeria | 110.7 |
| 3 | Zambia | 386.5 | 23 | Syria[d] | 104.1 |
| 4 | Guinea-Bissau | 289.6 | 24 | Ecuador | 102.1 |
| 5 | Somalia[c] | 283.9 | 25 | Papua New Guinea | 96.9 |
| 6 | Tanzania | 268.4 | 26 | Uganda | 96.6 |
| 7 | Sudan[d] | 220.7 | 27 | Malawi | 96.3 |
| 8 | Côte d'Ivoire | 207.1 | 28 | Peru | 95.4 |
| 9 | Mauritania | 205.6 | 29 | Burundi | 94.4 |
| 10 | Sierra Leone | 202.5 | 30 | Mali | 93.2 |
| 11 | Congo | 185.2 | 31 | Togo | 86.5 |
| 12 | Jordan | 179.1 | 32 | Yemen[d] | 86.2 |
| 13 | Laos | 165.5 | 33 | Guinea | 86.0 |
| 14 | Madagascar | 153.9 | 34 | Bolivia | 83.6 |
| 15 | Jamaica | 153.6 | 35 | Morocco | 77.8 |
| 16 | Angola | 140.5 | 36 | Kenya | 75.9 |
| 17 | Egypt | 116.8 | 37 | Zimbabwe | 74.1 |
| 18 | Honduras | 114.2 | 38 | Niger | 73.9 |
| 19 | Panama | 111.8 | 39 | Gabon | 70.9 |
| 20 | Zaire[e] | 111.5 | 40 | CAR | 68.4 |

## Highest debt service ratios[b]
*%*

| | | | | | |
|---|---|---|---|---|---|
| 1 | Guinea-Bissau | 93.4 | 21 | Guatemala | 28.1 |
| 2 | Algeria | 71.9 | 22 | Philippines | 27.7 |
| 3 | Mexico | 44.4 | 23 | Ecuador | 27.1 |
| 4 | Uganda | 41.0 | 24 | Syria[c] | 26.9 |
| 5 | Paraguay | 40.9 | 25 | Ghana | 26.7 |
| 6 | Burundi | 39.9 | 26 | Nicaragua | 26.5 |
| 7 | Bolivia | 39.1 | 27 | Morocco[d] | 25.9 |
| 8 | Hungary | 35.6 | 28 | India | 25.6 |
| 9 | Colombia | 35.3 | 29 | Trinidad & Tobago | 25.2 |
| 10 | Honduras | 35.0 | 30 | Jamaica | 24.8 |
| 11 | Argentina | 34.9 | 31 | Kenya | 24.5 |
| 12 | Tanzania | 32.5 | 32 | Brazil | 24.4 |
| 13 | Indonesia | 32.1 | 33 | Malawi | 24.3 |
| 14 | Zimbabwe | 31.9 | 34 | Pakistan | 23.3 |
| | Turkey | 31.9 | 35 | Peru | 23.0 |
| 16 | Côte d'Ivoire | 31.5 | 36 | Portugal[d] | 22.4 |
| 17 | Panama | 31.3 | 37 | Uruguay | 22.2 |
| 18 | Nigeria | 30.6 | 38 | Chile | 20.9 |
| 19 | Papua New Guinea | 30.3 | 39 | Madagascar | 20.7 |
| 20 | Zambia | 29.3 | | Costa Rica | 20.7 |

c  1990.
d  1991.
e  1989.

# Aid

## Largest bilateral and multilateral donors
*$m*

| # | Country | $m | # | Country | $m |
|---|---------|-----|----|---------|-----|
| 1 | United States | 11,709 | 13 | Switzerland | 1,139 |
| 2 | Japan | 11,151 | 14 | Australia | 973 |
| 3 | France[a] | 8,270 | 15 | Belgium | 865 |
| 4 | Germany | 7,572 | 16 | Saudi Arabia | 783 |
| 5 | Italy | 4,122 | 17 | Finland | 644 |
| 6 | United Kingdom | 3,217 | 18 | Austria | 556 |
| 7 | Netherlands | 2,753 | 19 | Portugal | 302 |
| 8 | Canada | 2,515 | 20 | Kuwait | 202 |
| 9 | Sweden | 2,460 | 21 | Taiwan | 121 |
| 10 | Spain | 1,518 | 22 | New Zealand | 97 |
| 11 | Denmark | 1,392 | 23 | Ireland | 69 |
| 12 | Norway | 1,273 | 24 | Luxembourg | 36 |

## Largest recipients of bilateral and multilateral aid
*$m*

| # | Country | $m | # | Country | $m |
|---|---------|-----|----|---------|-----|
| 1 | Egypt | 3,538 | 36 | Algeria | 412 |
| 2 | China | 3,065 | 37 | Tunisia | 407 |
| 3 | India | 2,435 | 38 | El Salvador | 399 |
| 4 | Indonesia | 2,080 | 39 | Albania | 389 |
| 5 | Israel | 2,066 | 40 | Jordan | 379 |
| 6 | Philippines | 1,738 | 41 | Niger | 362 |
| 7 | Bangladesh | 1,728 | 42 | Madagascar | 359 |
| 8 | Mozambique | 1,393 | 43 | Honduras | 355 |
| 9 | Tanzania | 1,344 | 44 | Rwanda | 352 |
| 10 | Ethiopia | 1,301 | 45 | Turkey | 323 |
| 11 | Pakistan | 1,169 | 46 | Angola | 322 |
| 12 | Ex-Yugoslavia | 1,148 | 47 | Mexico | 317 |
| 13 | Zambia | 1,016 | 48 | Burundi | 316 |
| 14 | Morocco | 996 | 49 | Argentina | 286 |
| 15 | Thailand | 789 | 50 | Benin | 269 |
| 16 | Kenya | 780 | | Zaire | 269 |
| 17 | Côte d'Ivoire | 763 | 52 | Nigeria | 265 |
| 18 | Zimbabwe | 735 | 53 | Yemen | 262 |
| 19 | Cameroon | 727 | 54 | Ecuador | 249 |
| 20 | Uganda | 718 | 55 | Chad | 248 |
| 21 | Bolivia | 679 | 56 | Colombia | 240 |
| 22 | Senegal | 673 | 57 | Togo | 225 |
| 23 | Nicaragua | 662 | 58 | Malaysia | 213 |
| 24 | Sri Lanka | 658 | 59 | Guatemala | 210 |
| 25 | Ghana | 626 | | Mauritania | 210 |
| 26 | Sudan | 608 | 61 | Iraq | 187 |
| 27 | Vietnam | 586 | 62 | CAR | 179 |
| 28 | Somalia | 577 | 63 | Afghanistan | 174 |
| 29 | Malawi | 521 | 64 | Laos | 173 |
| 30 | Papua New Guinea | 483 | 65 | Iran | 169 |
| 31 | Nepal | 467 | 66 | Syria | 163 |
| 32 | Guinea | 463 | 67 | Panama | 157 |
| 33 | Burkina Faso | 444 | 68 | Lesotho | 142 |
| 34 | Mali | 439 | 69 | Namibia | 140 |
| 35 | Peru | 419 | 70 | Chile | 137 |

## Largest bilateral and multilateral donors
*% of GDP*

| | | | | | |
|---|---|---|---|---|---|
| 1 | Norway | 1.16 | 13 | Portugal | 0.36 |
| 2 | Sweden | 1.03 | 14 | Australia | 0.35 |
| 3 | Denmark | 1.02 | 15 | Italy | 0.34 |
| 4 | Kuwait | 0.93 | 16 | United Kingdom | 0.31 |
| 5 | Netherlands | 0.86 | 17 | Austria | 0.30 |
| 6 | France | 0.63 | | Japan | 0.30 |
| 7 | Finland | 0.62 | 19 | Luxembourg | 0.26 |
| | Saudi Arabia | 0.62 | | New Zealand | 0.26 |
| 9 | Canada | 0.46 | | Spain | 0.26 |
| | Switzerland | 0.46 | 22 | United States | 0.20 |
| 11 | Belgium | 0.39 | 23 | Ireland | 0.16 |
| | Germany | 0.39 | 24 | UAE | 0.09 |

## Largest recipients of bilateral and multilateral aid
*$ per head*

| | | | | | |
|---|---|---|---|---|---|
| 1 | Netherlands Antilles | 485 | 35 | Tanzania | 52 |
| 2 | Israel | 404 | 36 | Mali | 49 |
| 3 | Suriname | 169 | 37 | Rwanda | 48 |
| 4 | Nicaragua | 169 | | Tunisia | 48 |
| 5 | Bahrain | 133 | 39 | Burkina Faso | 47 |
| 6 | Papua New Guinea | 119 | | Congo | 47 |
| 7 | Zambia | 118 | 41 | Mongolia | 45 |
| 8 | Albania | 117 | 42 | Niger | 44 |
| 9 | Ex-Yugoslavia | 108 | 43 | Liberia | 43 |
| 10 | Mauritania | 101 | | Mauritius | 43 |
| 11 | Jordan | 96 | 45 | Bhutan | 42 |
| 12 | Namibia | 92 | 46 | Chad | 41 |
| 13 | Bolivia | 90 | | Uganda | 41 |
| 14 | Senegal | 86 | 48 | Ghana | 40 |
| 15 | Fiji | 84 | 49 | Laos | 39 |
| | Mozambique | 84 | 50 | Morocco | 38 |
| 17 | Botswana | 83 | | Sri Lanka | 38 |
| 18 | Guinea | 77 | 52 | Angola | 33 |
| 19 | Lesotho | 76 | | Oman | 33 |
| 20 | El Salvador | 74 | 54 | Sierra Leone | 31 |
| 21 | Zimbabwe | 71 | 55 | Kenya | 30 |
| 22 | Somalia | 70 | 56 | Madagascar | 29 |
| 23 | Honduras | 66 | 57 | Philippines | 27 |
| 24 | Egypt | 65 | 58 | Ethiopia | 24 |
| 25 | Panama | 62 | 59 | Ecuador | 23 |
| 26 | Cameroon | 59 | | Nepal | 23 |
| | Côte d'Ivoire | 59 | | Sudan | 23 |
| 28 | Togo | 58 | 62 | Guatemala | 22 |
| 29 | CAR | 57 | | Malta | 22 |
| | Gabon | 57 | | Paraguay | 22 |
| | Malawi | 57 | | Uruguay | 22 |
| 32 | Burundi | 54 | 66 | Lebanon | 21 |
| 33 | Benin | 53 | 67 | Yemen | 20 |
| | Jamaica | 53 | 68 | Peru | 19 |

a Including overseas territories.

# Industry

## Largest industrial output

*$bn, 1991*

| | | | | | |
|---|---|---|---|---|---|
| 1 | United States | 1,627 | 21 | Saudi Arabia | 56 |
| 2 | Japan | 1,412 | 22 | Indonesia | 48 |
| 3 | Germany | 614 | 23 | Spain | 47 |
| 4 | Italy | 380 | 24 | Argentina | 46 |
| 5 | France | 348 | 25 | Poland | 39 |
| 6 | United Kingdom | 324 | 26 | Norway | 38 |
| 7 | Ex-Soviet Union | 250 | 27 | Finland | 37 |
| 8 | Brazil | 161 | 28 | Thailand | 36 |
| 9 | China | 155 | 29 | Turkey | 33 |
| 10 | South Korea | 127 | 30 | Denmark | 31 |
| 11 | Canada | 117 | 31 | Israel | 23 |
| 12 | Australia | 93 | 32 | Iran | 20 |
| | Netherlands | 93 | 33 | Ex-Czechoslovakia | 19 |
| 14 | Taiwan | 86 | 34 | Hong Kong | 17 |
| 15 | Mexico | 85 | | Portugal[a] | 17 |
| 16 | Sweden | 70 | 36 | Algeria | 16 |
| 17 | Switzerland[a] | 61 | | Greece | 16 |
| 18 | India | 60 | 38 | Colombia | 15 |
| 19 | Austria | 59 | | Philippines | 15 |
| | Belgium | 59 | | Singapore | 15 |

## Highest growth in industrial output

*Average annual real % growth, 1980-91*

| | | | | | |
|---|---|---|---|---|---|
| 1 | Bhutan | 14.8 | 11 | Chad | 7.1 |
| 2 | South Korea | 12.1 | 12 | Syria | 6.8 |
| 3 | China | 11.0 | 13 | India | 6.3 |
| 4 | Botswana | 10.7 | 14 | Turkey | 6.0 |
| 5 | Mauritius | 10.1 | 15 | Indonesia | 5.9 |
| 6 | Oman | 9.6 | 16 | Singapore | 5.8 |
| | Thailand | 9.6 | 17 | Norway | 5.2 |
| 8 | Kenya | 8.6 | 18 | Bangladesh | 4.9 |
| 9 | Malaysia | 7.7 | | Japan | 4.9 |
| 10 | Pakistan | 7.5 | | Mauritania | 4.9 |

## Lowest growth in industrial output

*Average annual real % growth, 1980-91*

| | | | | | |
|---|---|---|---|---|---|
| 1 | UAE[b] | -8.7 | 11 | Argentina | -1.4 |
| 2 | Trinidad & Tobago | -6.6 | 12 | Peru | -1.1 |
| 3 | Panama | -5.7 | 13 | Bolivia | -0.8 |
| 4 | Mozambique | -3.6 | | Romania | -0.8 |
| 5 | Saudi Arabia | -2.9 | | Sierra Leone | -0.8 |
| 6 | Tanzania | -2.4 | 16 | Philippines | -0.5 |
| 7 | Namibia | -2.0 | 17 | Nigeria | -0.4 |
| 8 | Nicaragua | -1.7 | 18 | Guatemala | -0.2 |
| 9 | Côte d'Ivoire | -1.6 | | Jordan | -0.2 |
| | Hungary | -1.6 | 20 | South Africa | 0.0 |

a  1989.
b  1980-90.

## Largest chemicals output
*$bn, 1990*

| | | | | | |
|---|---|---|---|---|---|
| 1 | United States | 90.02 | 11 | Netherlands | 10.47 |
| 2 | Japan | 84.93 | 12 | India | 8.32 |
| 3 | Germany | 55.32 | 13 | Mexico | 7.79 |
| 4 | Italy | 24.29 | 14 | South Korea | 6.34 |
| 5 | France | 22.60 | 15 | Puerto Rico | 5.48 |
| 6 | United Kingdom | 17.58 | 16 | Belgium | 4.76 |
| 7 | China | 17.18 | 17 | Sweden | 4.05 |
| 8 | Canada | 13.79 | 18 | Australia | 3.57 |
| 9 | Brazil | 13.05 | 19 | Saudi Arabia | 3.11 |
| 10 | Spain | 12.45 | 20 | Austria | 2.91 |

## Largest machinery and transport output
*$bn, 1990*

| | | | | | |
|---|---|---|---|---|---|
| 1 | Japan | 331.23 | 11 | South Korea | 22.56 |
| 2 | United States | 315.08 | 12 | Netherlands | 14.54 |
| 3 | Germany | 193.61 | 13 | Sweden | 14.41 |
| 4 | Italy | 80.16 | 14 | India | 12.72 |
| 5 | France | 77.85 | 15 | Austria | 11.63 |
| 6 | United Kingdom | 46.88 | 16 | Belgium | 9.95 |
| 7 | Canada | 35.86 | 17 | Australia | 8.47 |
| 8 | China | 31.71 | 18 | Mexico | 8.34 |
| 9 | Spain | 31.11 | 19 | Finland | 6.54 |
| 10 | Brazil | 25.02 | 20 | Singapore | 5.49 |

## Largest textiles and clothing output
*$bn, 1990*

| | | | | | |
|---|---|---|---|---|---|
| 1 | United States | 45.01 | 11 | Canada | 8.28 |
| 2 | Japan | 42.47 | 12 | India | 5.87 |
| 3 | Italy | 31.58 | 13 | Thailand | 5.23 |
| 4 | China | 19.82 | 14 | Mexico | 5.01 |
| 5 | Germany | 18.44 | 15 | Hong Kong | 4.33 |
| 6 | France | 15.07 | 16 | Belgium | 3.46 |
| 7 | Brazil | 13.05 | 17 | Turkey | 3.18 |
| 8 | Spain | 9.96 | 18 | Australia | 3.12 |
| 9 | South Korea | 9.16 | 19 | Indonesia | 3.04 |
| 10 | United Kingdom | 8.79 | 20 | Austria | 2.49 |

## Largest processed food output
*$bn, 1990*

| | | | | | |
|---|---|---|---|---|---|
| 1 | United States | 108.03 | 11 | Mexico | 12.24 |
| 2 | Japan | 76.44 | 12 | Netherlands | 9.30 |
| 3 | Germany | 41.49 | 13 | Australia | 8.03 |
| 4 | France | 32.65 | 14 | South Korea | 7.75 |
| 5 | Spain | 22.40 | 15 | Belgium | 7.35 |
| 6 | China | 19.82 | 16 | Austria | 6.23 |
| 7 | Italy | 19.43 | 17 | Thailand | 6.07 |
| 8 | Canada | 19.31 | 18 | India | 5.87 |
| 9 | United Kingdom | 19.05 | 19 | Indonesia | 5.21 |
| 10 | Brazil | 14.14 | 20 | Sweden | 4.50 |

# Agriculture

## Most economically dependent on agriculture
*% of GDP from agriculture*

| | | | | | | |
|---|---|---|---|---|---|---|
| 1 | Mozambique | 64.0 | | Sierra Leone | 37.0 |
| 2 | Somalia | 62.0 | 22 | Togo | 36.0 |
| | Tanzania | 62.0 | | Uzbekistan | 36.0 |
| 4 | Myanmar | 59.0 | 24 | Nigeria | 35.1 |
| 5 | Uganda | 57.0 | 25 | Zaire | 35.0 |
| 6 | Burundi | 54.0 | 26 | Moldova | 34.0 |
| 7 | Nepal | 52.0 | 27 | Papua New Guinea | 33.9 |
| 8 | Côte d'Ivoire | 49.7 | 28 | Guinea | 33.0 |
| 9 | Chad | 48.0 | | Madagascar | 33.0 |
| | Ethiopia | 48.0 | 30 | India | 30.9 |
| 11 | Ghana | 46.0 | 31 | Sudan | 30.4 |
| 12 | Burkina Faso | 44.0 | 32 | Mongolia | 30.0 |
| | CAR | 44.0 | | Nicaragua | 30.0 |
| 14 | Bhutan | 42.0 | 34 | Bolivia | 29.2 |
| | Mali | 42.0 | 35 | Mauritania | 29.0 |
| 16 | Rwanda | 41.0 | 36 | Kenya | 28.5 |
| 17 | Bangladesh | 39.3 | 37 | Azerbaijan | 28.0 |
| 18 | Albania | 37.0 | | Kirgizstan | 28.0 |
| | Benin | 37.0 | 39 | Cameroon | 27.3 |
| | Niger | 37.0 | 40 | China | 26.7 |

## Least economically dependent on agriculture
*% of GDP from agriculture*

| | | | | | | |
|---|---|---|---|---|---|---|
| 1 | Singapore | 0.3 | 21 | France | 3.3 |
| 2 | Hong Kong | 0.4 | 22 | Canada | 3.4 |
| 3 | Kuwait | 0.8 | 23 | Venezuela | 3.5 |
| | Qatar | 0.8 | 24 | Iceland | 3.9 |
| 5 | Netherlands Antilles | 0.9 | 25 | Australia | 4.0 |
| 6 | Bahrain | 1.1 | 26 | Netherlands | 4.5 |
| 7 | Germany | 1.2 | 27 | Taiwan | 4.7 |
| 8 | Luxembourg | 1.6 | 28 | Israel | 5.4 |
| 9 | United Kingdom | 1.7 | 29 | Spain | 5.6 |
| 10 | UAE | 1.9 | 30 | Trinidad & Tobago | 5.7 |
| 11 | Belgium | 2.2 | 31 | Finland | 6.1 |
| | Brunei[a] | 2.2 | 32 | Libya | 6.2 |
| 13 | United States | 2.3 | 33 | Denmark | 6.4 |
| 14 | Japan | 2.5 | | South Africa | 6.4 |
| 15 | Austria | 2.7 | 35 | Barbados | 7.0 |
| 16 | Norway | 2.8 | 36 | Mexico | 7.6 |
| 17 | Botswana | 3.0 | 37 | South Korea | 7.9 |
| | Sweden | 3.0 | 38 | Gabon | 8.0 |
| 19 | Italy | 3.1 | | Jamaica | 8.0 |
| | Oman | 3.1 | 40 | Jordan | 8.4 |

a  Latest available.

## Fastest growth
*% average annual growth per head, 1980-92*

| | | | | | | |
|---|---|---|---|---|---|---|
| 1 | Saudi Arabia | 8.8 | | China | 2.5 |
| 2 | Lebanon | 3.4 | 9 | Cambodia | 2.3 |
| 3 | Burkina Faso | 3.0 | 10 | Nigeria | 2.1 |
| | Malaysia | 3.0 | | Vietnam | 2.1 |
| 5 | Indonesia | 2.6 | 12 | Brazil | 2.0 |
| 6 | Algeria | 2.5 | 13 | Morocco | 1.9 |
| | Benin | 2.5 | 14 | Nepal | 1.8 |

## Slowest growth
*% average annual growth per head, 1980-92*

| | | | | | | |
|---|---|---|---|---|---|---|
| 1 | Singapore | -6.9 | | Suriname | -2.8 |
| 2 | Somalia | -5.8 | 11 | Sudan | -2.6 |
| 3 | Liberia | -5.1 | 12 | Angola | -2.5 |
| 4 | Nicaragua | -4.6 | | Syria | -2.5 |
| 5 | Netherlands Antilles | -3.8 | 14 | Botswana | -2.4 |
| 6 | Afghanistan | -3.7 | | Cameroon | -2.4 |
| 7 | Macao | -3.6 | | Iceland | -2.4 |
| 8 | Hong Kong | -3.1 | | Lesotho | -2.4 |
| 9 | Malawi | -2.8 | | | |

## Biggest producers
*'000 tonnes*

### Cereals

| | | | | | |
|---|---|---|---|---|---|
| 1 | China | 400,409 | 6 | Indonesia | 55,757 |
| 2 | United States | 353,353 | 7 | Canada | 49,147 |
| 3 | India | 199,585 | 8 | Brazil | 44,165 |
| 4 | Russia | 102,117 | 9 | Germany | 34,749 |
| 5 | France | 60,420 | 10 | Kazakhstan | 29,427 |

### Meat

| | | | | | |
|---|---|---|---|---|---|
| 1 | China | 34,900 | 6 | France | 5,890 |
| 2 | United States | 30,876 | 7 | Italy | 3,923 |
| 3 | Russia | 8,151 | 8 | India | 3,899 |
| 4 | Brazil | 7,188 | 9 | Spain | 3,654 |
| 5 | Germany | 6,214 | 10 | Mexico | 3,563 |

### Fruit

| | | | | | |
|---|---|---|---|---|---|
| 1 | Brazil | 32,279 | 6 | Spain | 14,524 |
| 2 | India | 30,037 | 7 | Mexico | 14,199 |
| 3 | United States | 26,956 | 8 | France | 12,495 |
| 4 | China | 23,102 | 9 | Turkey | 9,350 |
| 5 | Italy | 19,820 | 10 | Uganda | 8,714 |

### Vegetables

| | | | | | |
|---|---|---|---|---|---|
| 1 | China | 119,786 | 6 | Japan | 13,737 |
| 2 | India | 59,194 | 7 | Russia | 11,900 |
| 3 | United States | 30,438 | 8 | Spain | 10,106 |
| 4 | Turkey | 19,054 | 9 | South Korea | 9,938 |
| 5 | Italy | 14,120 | 10 | Egypt | 9,358 |

# Commodities

## Wheat

*Top 10 producers*
*'000 tonnes*

| | | | | | |
|---|---|---|---|---|---|
| 1 | China | 100,500 | 1 | China | 109,000 |
| 2 | Ex-Soviet Union | 90,100 | 2 | Ex-Soviet Union | 105,000 |
| 3 | EU | 84,900 | 3 | EU | 61,700 |
| 4 | United States | 66,900 | 4 | India | 56,600 |
| 5 | India | 55,100 | 5 | United States | 30,400 |
| 6 | Canada | 29,900 | 6 | Pakistan | 17,800 |
| 7 | Turkey | 17,300 | 7 | Turkey | 15,000 |
| 8 | Australia | 16,200 | 8 | Iran | 11,700 |
| 9 | Pakistan | 15,700 | 9 | Egypt | 10,200 |
| 10 | Argentina | 9,700 | 10 | Poland | 8,600 |

*Top 10 consumers*
*'000 tonnes*

## Rice

*Top 10 producers[a]*
*'000 tonnes*

*Top 10 consumers[b]*
*'000 tonnes*

| | | | | | |
|---|---|---|---|---|---|
| 1 | China | 186,200 | 1 | China | 129,000 |
| 2 | India | 108,700 | 2 | India | 75,500 |
| 3 | Indonesia | 47,300 | 3 | Indonesia | 30,200 |
| 4 | Bangladesh | 27,000 | 4 | Bangladesh | 18,300 |
| 5 | Vietnam | 21,500 | 5 | Vietnam | 12,300 |
| 6 | Thailand | 19,900 | 6 | Japan | 9,500 |
| 7 | Myanmar | 13,400 | 7 | Thailand | 8,600 |
| 8 | Japan | 13,200 | 8 | Myanmar | 8,100 |
| 9 | Brazil | 9,900 | 9 | Brazil | 7,800 |
| 10 | Philippines | 9,500 | 10 | Philippines | 6,400 |

## Sugar[c]

*Top 10 producers*
*'000 tonnes*

*Top 10 consumers*
*'000 tonnes*

| | | | | | |
|---|---|---|---|---|---|
| 1 | EU | 16,811 | 1 | EU | 13,683 |
| 2 | India | 13,873 | 2 | India | 12,936 |
| 3 | Brazil | 9,925 | 3 | Ex-Soviet Union | 11,465 |
| 4 | China | 8,864 | 4 | United States | 8,098 |
| 5 | Cuba | 7,000 | 5 | China | 7,615 |
| 6 | United States | 6,805 | 6 | Brazil | 7,349 |
| 7 | Ex-Soviet Union | 6,705 | 7 | Mexico | 4,520 |
| 8 | Thailand | 5,076 | 8 | Japan | 3,029 |
| 9 | Australia | 4,363 | 9 | Pakistan | 2,720 |
| 10 | Mexico | 3,744 | 10 | Indonesia | 2,700 |

## Coarse grains[d]

*Top 5 producers*
*'000 tonnes*

*Top 5 consumers*
*'000 tonnes*

| | | | | | |
|---|---|---|---|---|---|
| 1 | United States | 277,900 | 1 | United States | 199,000 |
| 2 | China | 109,600 | 2 | China | 105,000 |
| 3 | Ex-Soviet Union | 97,400 | 3 | Ex-Soviet Union | 102,000 |
| 4 | EU | 83,100 | 4 | EU | 75,000 |
| 5 | India | 36,800 | 5 | India | 37,000 |

## Tea

| | Top 10 producers | | | Top 10 consumers | |
|---|---|---|---|---|---|
| | *'000 tonnes* | | | *'000 tonnes* | |
| 1 | India | 704 | 1 | India | 535 |
| 2 | China | 560 | 2 | China | 388 |
| 3 | Kenya | 188 | 3 | United Kingdom | 145 |
| 4 | Sri Lanka | 179 | 4 | Japan | 133 |
| 5 | Turkey | 156 | 5 | Turkey | 130 |
| 6 | Indonesia | 146 | 6 | Ex-Soviet Union | 128 |
| 7 | Japan | 92 | 7 | Pakistan | 119 |
| 8 | Ex-Soviet Union | 55 | 8 | Iran | 96 |
| 9 | Bangladesh | 48 | 9 | United States | 91 |
| 10 | Iran | 45 | 10 | Egypt | 76 |

## Coffee

| | Top 10 producers | | | Top 10 consumers | |
|---|---|---|---|---|---|
| | *'000 tonnes* | | | *'000 tonnes* | |
| 1 | Brazil | 1,497 | 1 | United States | 1,085 |
| 2 | Colombia | 830 | 2 | Germany | 672 |
| 3 | Indonesia | 513 | 3 | Brazil | 540 |
| 4 | Guatemala | 205 | 4 | Japan | 341 |
| 5 | El Salvador | 182 | 5 | France | 326 |
| 6 | Mexico | 178 | 6 | Italy | 283 |
| 7 | Costa Rica | 176 | 7 | Spain | 176 |
| 8 | Vietnam | 140 | 8 | Netherlands | 147 |
| 9 | Uganda | 136 | 9 | United Kingdom | 140 |
| 10 | Côte d'Ivoire | 123 | 10 | Canada | 120 |

## Cocoa

| | Top 10 producers | | | Top 10 consumers | |
|---|---|---|---|---|---|
| | *'000 tonnes* | | | *'000 tonnes* | |
| 1 | Côte d'Ivoire | 747 | 1 | United States | 593 |
| 2 | Brazil | 290 | 2 | Germany | 264 |
| 3 | Ghana | 243 | 3 | United Kingdom | 180 |
| 4 | Malaysia | 220 | 4 | France | 160 |
| 5 | Indonesia | 180 | 5 | Japan | 111 |
| 6 | Nigeria | 110 | 6 | Brazil | 73 |
| 7 | Cameroon | 105 | | Italy | 73 |
| 8 | Ecuador | 85 | 8 | Spain | 60 |
| 9 | Colombia | 50 | 9 | Belgium | 57 |
| 10 | Dominican Republic | 48 | 10 | Canada | 49 |

a  Paddy (unmilled rice, in the husk).
b  Milled rice.
c  Raw value.
d  Includes: maize (corn), barley, sorghum, rye, oats and millet.

# Commodities

## Copper

| Top 10 producers[a] '000 tonnes | | Top 10 consumers[b] '000 tonnes | |
|---|---|---|---|
| 1 Chile | 1,933 | 1 United States | 2,176 |
| 2 United States | 1,761 | 2 Japan | 1,411 |
| 3 Ex-Soviet Union | 840 | 3 Germany | 1,046 |
| 4 Canada | 764 | 4 China | 882 |
| 5 Zambia | 433 | 5 Ex-Soviet Union | 880 |
| 6 Australia | 378 | 6 Italy | 502 |
| 7 Peru | 368 | 7 France | 488 |
| 8 Poland | 332 | 8 Taiwan | 416 |
| 9 China | 309 | 9 Belgium | 372 |
| 10 Indonesia | 292 | 10 South Korea | 354 |

## Lead

| Top 10 producers[a] '000 tonnes | | Top 10 consumers[b] '000 tonnes | |
|---|---|---|---|
| 1 Australia | 572 | 1 United States | 1,244 |
| 2 United States | 408 | 2 Germany | 412 |
| 3 Canada | 343 | 3 Japan | 402 |
| 4 China | 287 | 4 United Kingdom | 264 |
| 5 Ex-Soviet Union | 225 | 5 Ex-Soviet Union | 260 |
| 6 Peru | 194 | 6 China | 250 |
| 7 Mexico | 173 | 7 Italy | 247 |
| 8 Sweden | 104 | 8 France | 246 |
| 9 South Africa | 75 | 9 Mexico | 165 |
| 10 Morocco | 70 | 10 South Korea | 164 |

## Zinc

| Top 10 producers[a] '000 tonnes | | Top 10 consumers[c] '000 tonnes | |
|---|---|---|---|
| 1 Canada | 1,312 | 1 United States | 1,038 |
| 2 Australia | 1,008 | 2 Japan | 784 |
| 3 China | 706 | 3 China | 540 |
| 4 Peru | 603 | 4 Germany | 532 |
| 5 United States | 552 | 5 Ex-Soviet Union | 380 |
| 6 Ex-Soviet Union | 550 | 6 Italy | 300 |
| 7 Mexico | 341 | 7 South Korea | 266 |
| 8 Spain | 206 | 8 France | 258 |
| 9 Ireland | 194 | 9 Australia | 191 |
| 10 Sweden | 164 | 10 United Kingdom | 190 |

## Tin

| Top 5 producers[a] '000 tonnes | | Top 5 consumers[b] '000 tonnes | |
|---|---|---|---|
| 1 China | 38.7 | 1 United States | 33.5 |
| 2 Indonesia | 29.4 | 2 Japan | 31.0 |
| 3 Brazil | 21.7 | 3 Germany | 20.3 |
| 4 Bolivia | 16.5 | 4 Ex-Soviet Union | 15.5 |
| 5 Malaysia | 14.3 | 5 China | 12.8 |

## Nickel

| Top 10 producers[a] | | Top 10 consumers[b] | |
| --- | --- | --- | --- |
| '000 tonnes | | '000 tonnes | |
| 1 Canada | 192.1 | 1 Japan | 148.1 |
| 2 Ex-Soviet Union | 180.0 | 2 United States | 118.6 |
| 3 New Caledonia | 100.5 | 3 Germany | 74.0 |
| 4 Indonesia | 78.1 | 4 Ex-Soviet Union | 70.0 |
| 5 Australia | 57.7 | 5 Italy | 36.9 |
| 6 Cuba | 32.2 | 6 China | 35.7 |
| 7 China | 30.0 | 7 France | 35.0 |
| 8 South Africa | 28.4 | 8 United Kingdom | 28.5 |
| 9 Dominican Republic | 27.5 | 9 Finland | 23.5 |
| 10 Colombia | 20.2 | 10 Belgium | 21.4 |

## Aluminium

| Top 10 producers[d] | | Top 10 consumers[b] | |
| --- | --- | --- | --- |
| '000 tonnes | | '000 tonnes | |
| 1 United States | 4,042 | 1 United States | 4,617 |
| 2 Ex-Soviet Union | 3,220 | 2 Japan | 2,298 |
| 3 Canada | 1,972 | 3 Ex-Soviet Union | 2,150 |
| 4 Australia | 1,236 | 4 Germany | 1,458 |
| 5 Brazil | 1,193 | 5 China | 1,254 |
| 6 China | 1,000 | 6 France | 716 |
| 7 Norway | 861 | 7 Italy | 660 |
| 8 Germany | 603 | 8 United Kingdom | 483 |
| 9 Venezuela | 566 | 9 Canada | 420 |
| 10 India | 496 | 10 India | 414 |

## Precious metals

| Gold[a] | | Silver[a] | |
| --- | --- | --- | --- |
| Top 10 producers | | Top 10 producers | |
| tonnes | | tonnes | |
| 1 South Africa | 614.1 | 1 Mexico | 2,325 |
| 2 United States | 329.1 | 2 United States | 1,741 |
| 3 Australia | 243.5 | 3 Peru | 1,570 |
| 4 Ex-Soviet Union | 237.0 | 4 Australia | 1,248 |
| 5 Canada | 159.1 | 5 Canada | 1,207 |
| 6 China | 118.0 | 6 Chile | 1,043 |
| 7 Brazil | 76.5 | 7 Ex-Soviet Union | 1,010 |
| 8 Papua New Guinea | 71.2 | 8 Poland | 798 |
| 9 Indonesia | 40.4 | 9 Bolivia | 282 |
| 10 Chile | 39.5 | Sweden | 282 |

a  Mine production.
b  Refined consumption.
c  Slab consumption.
d  Primary refined production.

# Commodities

## Rubber (natural and synthetic)

| Top 10 producers '000 tonnes | | Top 10 consumers '000 tonnes | |
|---|---|---|---|
| 1 United States | 2,340 | 1 United States | 2,905 |
| 2 Ex-Soviet Union | 1,870 | 2 Ex-Soviet Union | 1,830 |
| 3 Thailand | 1,531 | 3 Japan | 1,766 |
| 4 Japan | 1,388 | 4 China | 1,125 |
| 5 Indonesia | 1,387 | 5 Germany | 720 |
| 6 Malaysia | 1,218 | 6 South Korea | 551 |
| 7 China | 681 | 7 France | 539 |
| 8 Germany | 557 | 8 India | 515 |
| 9 France | 500 | 9 Brazil | 417 |
| 10 India | 471 | 10 Italy | 410 |

## Raw wool

| Top 10 producers [a] '000 tonnes | | Top 10 consumers [b] '000 tonnes | |
|---|---|---|---|
| 1 Australia | 869 | 1 China | 332 |
| 2 Ex-Soviet Union | 377 | 2 Ex-Soviet Union | 170 |
| 3 New Zealand | 256 | 3 Italy | 164 |
| 4 China | 247 | 4 Japan | 113 |
| 5 Argentina | 114 | 5 United Kingdom | 80 |
| 6 Uruguay | 83 | 6 Germany | 61 |
| 7 South Africa | 75 | United States | 61 |
| Turkey | 75 | 8 South Korea | 58 |
| 9 United Kingdom | 70 | 9 Turkey | 55 |
| 10 Pakistan | 66 | 10 India | 50 |

## Cotton

| Top 10 producers '000 tonnes | | Top 10 consumers '000 tonnes | |
|---|---|---|---|
| 1 China | 4,508 | 1 China | 4,425 |
| 2 United States | 3,531 | 2 United States | 2,160 |
| 3 India | 2,329 | 3 India | 2,013 |
| 4 Pakistan | 1,540 | 4 Pakistan | 1,440 |
| 5 Uzbekistan | 1,296 | 5 Russia | 758 |
| 6 Turkey | 574 | 6 Brazil | 742 |
| 7 Brazil | 413 | 7 Turkey | 605 |
| 8 Turkmenistan | 378 | 8 Japan | 568 |
| 9 Australia | 373 | 9 Indonesia | 414 |
| 10 Egypt | 357 | 10 South Korea | 397 |

## Major oil seeds [c]

| Top 5 producers '000 tonnes | | Top 5 consumers '000 tonnes | |
|---|---|---|---|
| 1 United States | 68,320 | 1 United States | 42,578 |
| 2 China | 32,950 | 2 China | 29,000 |
| 3 Brazil | 23,400 | 3 EU | 24,070 |
| 4 India | 19,190 | 4 Brazil | 18,365 |
| 5 Argentina | 13,930 | 5 India | 16,735 |

## Oil[d]

### Top 15 producers
*'000 barrels per day, 1992*

| | | |
|---|---|---|
| 1 | United States | 8,850 |
| 2 | Saudi Arabia[e] | 8,735 |
| 3 | Russia | 7,995 |
| 4 | Iran[e] | 3,455 |
| 5 | Mexico | 3,155 |
| 6 | China | 2,850 |
| 7 | Venezuela[e] | 2,500 |
| 8 | UAE[e] | 2,490 |
| 9 | Norway | 2,170 |
| 10 | Canada | 2,065 |
| 11 | United Kingdom | 1,950 |
| 12 | Nigeria[e] | 1,850 |
| 13 | Indonesia[e] | 1,540 |
| 14 | Libya[e] | 1,520 |
| 15 | Algeria[e] | 1,325 |

### Top 15 consumers
*'000 barrels per day, 1992*

| | | |
|---|---|---|
| 1 | United States | 16,240 |
| 2 | Japan | 5,545 |
| 3 | Russia | 4,405 |
| 4 | Germany | 2,850 |
| 5 | China | 2,615 |
| 6 | France | 2,010 |
| 7 | Italy | 1,945 |
| 8 | United Kingdom | 1,745 |
| 9 | Canada | 1,665 |
| 10 | Mexico | 1,605 |
| 11 | South Korea | 1,500 |
| 12 | Brazil | 1,305 |
| 13 | India | 1,285 |
| 14 | Spain | 1,065 |
| 15 | Netherlands | 785 |

## Natural gas

### Top 10 producers
*'000 terajoules, 1991*

| | | |
|---|---|---|
| 1 | Ex-Soviet Union | 27,412 |
| 2 | United States | 19,509 |
| 3 | Canada | 4,374 |
| 4 | Netherlands | 2,847 |
| 5 | Indonesia | 1,819 |
| 6 | United Kingdom | 1,779 |
| 7 | Algeria | 1,738 |
| 8 | Saudi Arabia | 1,452 |
| 9 | Norway | 1,105 |
| 10 | Venezuela | 1,054 |

### Top 10 consumers
*'000 terajoules, 1991*

| | | |
|---|---|---|
| 1 | Ex-Soviet Union | 23,839 |
| 2 | United States | 21,388 |
| 3 | Germany | 2,685 |
| 4 | Canada | 2,599 |
| 5 | Japan | 2,160 |
| 6 | United Kingdom | 2,028 |
| 7 | Italy | 1,984 |
| 8 | Netherlands | 1,578 |
| 9 | Saudi Arabia | 1,452 |
| 10 | France | 1,265 |

## Coal

### Top 10 producers
*Million tonnes, 1991*

| | | |
|---|---|---|
| 1 | China | 1,087.4 |
| 2 | United States | 901.9 |
| 3 | Ex-Soviet Union | 592.0 |
| 4 | Germany | 458.1 |
| 5 | India | 224.5 |
| 6 | Australia | 214.0 |
| 7 | Poland | 209.8 |
| 8 | South Africa | 176.2 |
| 9 | Ex-Czechoslovakia | 100.3 |
| 10 | United Kingdom | 96.1 |

### Top 10 consumers
*Million tonnes, 1991*

| | | |
|---|---|---|
| 1 | China | 1,058.2 |
| 2 | United States | 806.5 |
| 3 | Ex-Soviet Union | 565.5 |
| 4 | Germany | 469.1 |
| 5 | India | 227.9 |
| 6 | Poland | 168.8 |
| 7 | South Africa | 133.5 |
| 8 | Japan | 117.9 |
| 9 | United Kingdom | 108.2 |
| 10 | Ex-Czechoslovakia | 101.4 |

a  Greasy basis.
b  Clean basis.
c  Soybeans, sunflower seed, cottonseed, groundnuts and rapeseed.
d  Includes crude oil, shale oil, oil sands and natural gas liquids.
e  Opec members.

# Energy

## Largest producers
*Million tonnnes coal equivalent, 1991*

| | | | | | | |
|---|---|---:|---|---|---|---:|
| 1 | United States | 2,317.5 | | 16 | Algeria | 149.9 |
| 2 | Ex-Soviet Union | 2,217.7 | | 17 | France | 148.9 |
| 3 | China | 1,014.0 | | 18 | Nigeria | 141.4 |
| 4 | Saudi Arabia | 660.7 | | 19 | South Africa | 135.3 |
| 5 | Canada | 404.3 | | 20 | Poland | 132.1 |
| 6 | United Kingdom | 299.2 | | 21 | Libya | 116.6 |
| 7 | Iran | 284.3 | | 22 | Japan | 104.8 |
| 8 | Mexico | 274.7 | | 23 | Netherlands | 103.8 |
| 9 | Germany | 272.9 | | 24 | North Korea | 84.1 |
| 10 | India | 250.0 | | 25 | Brazil | 83.0 |
| 11 | Venezuela | 226.3 | | 26 | Egypt | 79.2 |
| 12 | Australia | 218.5 | | 27 | Argentina | 73.2 |
| 13 | UAE | 203.6 | | 28 | Malaysia | 66.5 |
| 14 | Norway | 185.5 | | 29 | Colombia | 61.7 |
| 15 | Indonesia | 180.5 | | 30 | Ex-Czechoslovakia | 60.7 |

## Largest consumers
*Million tonnes coal equivalent, 1991*

| | | | | | | |
|---|---|---:|---|---|---|---:|
| 1 | United States | 2,757.8 | | 16 | Spain | 119.6 |
| 2 | Ex-Soviet Union | 1,867.3 | | 17 | Netherlands | 109.1 |
| 3 | China | 933.0 | | 18 | South Africa | 107.4 |
| 4 | Japan | 589.6 | | 19 | Saudi Arabia | 106.5 |
| 5 | Germany | 509.2 | | 20 | Iran | 99.1 |
| 6 | France | 311.0 | | 21 | North Korea | 93.1 |
| 7 | United Kingdom | 309.3 | | 22 | Ex-Czechoslovakia | 88.9 |
| 8 | Canada | 299.5 | | 23 | Romania | 70.4 |
| 9 | India | 273.3 | | 24 | Belgium | 68.9 |
| 10 | Italy | 230.9 | | | Venezuela | 68.9 |
| 11 | Mexico | 164.9 | | 26 | Indonesia | 65.3 |
| 12 | South Korea | 130.4 | | 27 | Argentina | 64.7 |
| 13 | Australia | 127.0 | | 28 | Sweden | 59.3 |
| 14 | Poland | 121.3 | | 29 | Turkey | 59.2 |
| 15 | Brazil | 121.2 | | 30 | Thailand | 43.7 |

## Energy efficiency

| Most efficient | | | Least efficient | | |
|---|---|---:|---|---|---:|
| *GDP per kg of energy, 1991, $* | | | *GDP per kg of energy, 1991, $* | | |
| 1 | Burkina Faso | 17.5 | 1 | Bulgaria | 0.4 |
| 2 | CAR | 14.3 | | Romania | 0.4 |
| 3 | Chad | 13.1 | 3 | China | 0.5 |
| 4 | Mali | 12.2 | 4 | Poland | 0.6 |
| 5 | Bhutan | 11.5 | 5 | Bahrain | 0.7 |
| 6 | Hong Kong | 10.0 | 6 | Mongolia | 0.8 |
| 7 | Togo | 9.2 | | Trinidad & Tobago | 0.8 |
| 8 | Switzerland | 8.7 | 8 | Algeria | 0.9 |
| 9 | Burundi | 8.6 | | India | 0.9 |
| 10 | Benin | 8.4 | | Vietnam | 0.9 |

**Note:** Consumption data for small countries, especially oil producers, can be unreliable, often leading to unrealistically high consumption per head rates.

## Largest exporters
*Million tonnes coal equivalent, 1991*

| | | | | | |
|---|---|---|---|---|---|
| 1 | Saudi Arabia | 520.8 | 14 | Mexico | 107.8 |
| 2 | Ex-Soviet Union | 285.5 | 15 | United Kingdom | 104.5 |
| 3 | Iran | 186.1 | 16 | Libya | 93.7 |
| 4 | Canada | 173.2 | 17 | China | 55.5 |
| 5 | UAE | 164.5 | 18 | Malaysia | 52.7 |
| 6 | Norway | 159.9 | 19 | Oman | 47.7 |
| 7 | Venezuela | 151.7 | 20 | Singapore | 47.1 |
| 8 | United States | 143.4 | 21 | South Africa | 43.4 |
| 9 | Indonesia | 122.7 | 22 | Egypt | 37.4 |
| 10 | Algeria | 117.8 | 23 | Angola | 33.4 |
| 11 | Nigeria | 115.9 | 24 | Colombia | 32.9 |
| 12 | Netherlands | 114.5 | 25 | Italy | 29.2 |
| 13 | Australia | 113.0 | | | |

## Largest importers
*Million tonnes coal equivalent, 1991*

| | | | | | |
|---|---|---|---|---|---|
| 1 | United States | 605.9 | 14 | India | 50.1 |
| 2 | Japan | 527.9 | 15 | Sweden | 38.8 |
| 3 | Germany | 277.4 | 16 | Turkey | 38.4 |
| 4 | Italy | 215.6 | 17 | Ex-Czechoslovakia | 37.7 |
| 5 | France | 205.5 | 18 | Greece | 29.1 |
| 6 | Netherlands | 133.0 | 19 | Thailand | 28.8 |
| 7 | South Korea | 125.7 | 20 | Poland | 28.5 |
| 8 | United Kingdom | 125.1 | 21 | Finland | 26.9 |
| 9 | Spain | 103.9 | 22 | Austria | 26.4 |
| 10 | Belgium | 90.3 | 23 | Romania | 25.7 |
| 11 | Singapore | 89.2 | 24 | Denmark | 25.4 |
| 12 | Brazil | 57.1 | 25 | Switzerland | 24.8 |
| 13 | Canada | 55.8 | | | |

## Largest consumption per head
*Kg coal equivalent, 1991*

| | | | | | |
|---|---|---|---|---|---|
| 1 | Qatar | 29,161 | 16 | Norway | 6,818 |
| 2 | UAE | 22,379 | 17 | Iceland | 6,486 |
| 3 | Brunei | 16,136 | 18 | Ex-Soviet Union | 6,415 |
| 4 | Bahrain | 15,608 | 19 | Germany | 6,375 |
| 5 | Luxembourg | 13,757 | 20 | Singapore | 5,821 |
| 6 | Canada | 11,095 | 21 | Ex-Czechoslovakia | 5,666 |
| 7 | United States | 10,921 | 22 | France | 5,457 |
| 8 | Netherlands Antilles | 9,486 | 23 | United Kingdom | 5,353 |
| 9 | Trinidad & Tobago | 8,063 | 24 | New Zealand | 5,304 |
| 10 | Australia | 7,321 | 25 | Denmark | 5,084 |
| 11 | Netherlands | 7,248 | 26 | Japan | 4,754 |
| 12 | Saudi Arabia | 6,922 | 27 | Switzerland | 4,701 |
| 13 | Belgium | 6,900 | 28 | Libya | 4,328 |
| 14 | Sweden | 6,892 | 29 | North Korea | 4,196 |
| 15 | Finland | 6,845 | 30 | Austria | 4,195 |

# Workers of the world

## Highest % of population in labour force
*1991-92 or latest*

| | | | | | |
|---|---|---|---|---|---|
| 1 | Singapore | 57.6 | 26 | Moldova | 48.8 |
| 2 | Denmark | 56.6 | 27 | Barbados | 48.2 |
| 3 | Thailand | 56.3 | | CAR | 48.2 |
| 4 | Latvia | 55.1 | | Cyprus | 48.2 |
| 5 | Burundi | 52.9 | | Portugal | 48.2 |
| | Japan | 52.9 | 31 | Slovenia | 48.1 |
| 7 | Russia | 52.6 | 32 | New Zealand | 47.9 |
| 8 | Belorussia | 52.5 | 33 | Panama | 47.5 |
| 9 | Sweden | 52.3 | 34 | Bangladesh | 46.9 |
| 10 | Lithuania | 51.7 | 35 | Rwanda | 46.3 |
| 11 | Ex-Czechoslovakia | 51.6 | 36 | Netherlands | 46.2 |
| 12 | Switzerland | 51.5 | 37 | Austria | 46.1 |
| 13 | Burkina Faso | 51.1 | 38 | Poland | 45.7 |
| 14 | Bahamas | 51.0 | 39 | Colombia | 45.2 |
| 15 | Ukraine | 50.8 | | Romania | 45.2 |
| 16 | Estonia | 50.5 | 41 | Uruguay | 44.7 |
| 17 | United States | 50.4 | 42 | Bahrain | 44.6 |
| 18 | Germany | 50.2 | 43 | France | 44.5 |
| 19 | Finland | 50.1 | | Jamaica | 44.5 |
| | Macao | 50.1 | 45 | South Korea | 44.4 |
| 21 | United Kingdom | 49.9 | 46 | Brazil | 43.8 |
| 22 | Norway | 49.8 | 47 | Luxembourg | 43.5 |
| 23 | Canada | 49.6 | 48 | Malawi | 43.3 |
| 24 | Hong Kong | 49.5 | | Paraguay | 43.3 |
| 25 | Australia | 49.2 | 50 | Cambodia | 43.1 |

## Most male workforce
*% male workers, 1991-92 or latest*

| | | | | | |
|---|---|---|---|---|---|
| 1 | Iran | 90.4 | 21 | Ireland | 68.4 |
| 2 | Pakistan | 86.3 | 22 | Honduras | 68.3 |
| 3 | Bahrain | 82.5 | 23 | Chile | 68.0 |
| 4 | Syria | 82.0 | 24 | Côte d'Ivoire | 67.7 |
| 5 | Tunisia | 79.1 | 25 | Sri Lanka | 67.4 |
| 6 | Mexico | 76.5 | 26 | Nigeria | 66.7 |
| 7 | Kuwait | 75.7 | 27 | Nicaragua | 65.9 |
| 8 | Malta | 74.6 | 28 | Brazil | 64.5 |
| 9 | Senegal | 74.4 | 29 | Malaysia | 64.5 |
| 10 | Guatemala | 74.2 | 30 | Trinidad & Tobago | 64.1 |
| 11 | Morocco | 73.9 | 31 | Spain | 63.8 |
| 12 | Ecuador | 73.6 | 32 | Luxembourg | 63.5 |
| 13 | Argentina | 72.1 | 33 | Greece | 63.2 |
| 14 | Egypt | 71.2 | 34 | Philippines | 63.1 |
| 15 | India | 71.0 | 35 | Italy | 62.9 |
| 16 | Panama | 70.8 | 36 | Cyprus | 62.1 |
| 17 | Costa Rica | 70.1 | 37 | Hong Kong | 62.0 |
| 18 | Mauritius | 69.8 | 38 | Switzerland | 61.7 |
| 19 | Turkey | 69.3 | 39 | Botswana | 61.6 |
| 20 | Venezuela | 69.0 | 40 | Peru | 60.7 |

## Lowest % of population in labour force
*1991-92 or latest*

| | | | | | |
|---|---|---|---|---|---|
| 1 | Suriname | 21.2 | | Malaysia | 37.6 |
| 2 | Iran | 26.0 | 27 | Zimbabwe | 37.7 |
| 3 | Syria | 27.8 | 28 | Ireland | 37.8 |
| 4 | Pakistan | 28.0 | 29 | Argentina | 38.1 |
| 5 | Tunisia | 29.8 | | Bolivia | 38.1 |
| 6 | Egypt | 30.7 | 31 | Kuwait | 38.9 |
| 7 | Nigeria | 31.1 | 32 | Spain | 39.0 |
| 8 | Puerto Rico | 32.4 | 33 | Trinidad & Tobago | 39.3 |
| 9 | Morocco | 32.5 | 34 | Côte d'Ivoire | 39.4 |
| 10 | Botswana | 33.4 | 35 | Netherlands Antilles | 39.4 |
| 11 | Guatemala | 33.5 | 36 | Greece | 39.6 |
| 12 | Senegal | 34.0 | 37 | Peru | 39.9 |
| 13 | Nicaragua | 34.7 | 38 | El Salvador | 40.6 |
| 14 | Ecuador | 34.8 | 39 | Mauritius | 40.9 |
| | Honduras | 34.8 | 40 | Sri Lanka | 40.9 |
| 16 | Fiji | 35.2 | 41 | Hungary | 41.0 |
| 17 | Israel | 36.3 | 42 | Ethiopia | 41.3 |
| 18 | Turkey | 36.5 | 43 | Belgium | 41.9 |
| 19 | Costa Rica | 37.0 | 44 | Philippines | 42.0 |
| 20 | Malta | 37.2 | 45 | Taiwan | 42.2 |
| 21 | Venezuela | 37.3 | 46 | Italy | 42.5 |
| 22 | Chile | 37.5 | 47 | Cambodia | 43.1 |
| | Mexico | 37.5 | 48 | Malawi | 43.3 |
| | South Africa | 37.5 | | Paraguay | 43.3 |
| 25 | India | 37.6 | 50 | Luxembourg | 43.5 |

## Most female workforce
*% female workers, 1991-92 or latest*

| | | | | | |
|---|---|---|---|---|---|
| 1 | Cambodia | 55.7 | 21 | Slovenia | 46.7 |
| 2 | Rwanda | 53.5 | 22 | Denmark | 46.5 |
| 3 | Burundi | 52.6 | | Jamaica | 46.5 |
| 4 | Malawi | 51.0 | 24 | Poland | 45.9 |
| 5 | Latvia | 50.0 | 25 | United States | 45.5 |
| 6 | Estonia | 49.9 | 26 | El Salvador | 45.3 |
| 7 | Ukraine | 49.2 | | Norway | 45.3 |
| 8 | Belorussia | 49.0 | 28 | Canada | 45.0 |
| 9 | Burkina Faso | 48.9 | 29 | Hungary | 44.5 |
| 10 | Moldova | 48.8 | 30 | Portugal | 44.3 |
| 11 | Russia | 48.5 | | Romania | 44.3 |
| 12 | Lithuania | 48.3 | 32 | France | 44.1 |
| 13 | Barbados | 48.2 | 33 | New Zealand | 43.6 |
| 14 | Sweden | 48.0 | 34 | Colombia | 43.4 |
| 15 | Zimbabwe | 47.8 | 35 | United Kingdom | 43.4 |
| 16 | Bahamas | 47.5 | 36 | Germany | 42.3 |
| 17 | Ex-Czechoslovakia | 47.4 | 37 | Australia | 41.8 |
| 18 | Finland | 46.9 | | Israel | 41.8 |
| | Thailand | 46.9 | 39 | Belgium | 41.6 |
| 20 | CAR | 46.8 | 40 | Bangladesh | 41.4 |

# Banking and business

## Largest banks
*By capital, $m*

| | | | |
|---|---|---|---|
| 1 | Sumitomo Bank | Japan | 19,524 |
| 2 | Dai-Ichi Kangyo Bank | Japan | 17,377 |
| 3 | Sanwa Bank | Japan | 17,155 |
| 4 | Fuji Bank | Japan | 17,045 |
| 5 | Mitsubishi Bank | Japan | 15,982 |
| 6 | Sakura Bank | Japan | 15,608 |
| 7 | Crédit Agricole | France | 15,606 |
| 8 | Union Bank of Switzerland | Switzerland | 12,802 |
| 9 | Industrial Bank of Japan | Japan | 12,053 |
| 10 | HSBC Holdings | United Kingdom | 11,798 |
| 11 | Deutsche Bank | Germany | 11,303 |
| 12 | Crédit Lyonnais | France | 10,697 |
| 13 | Industrial & Commercial Bank of China | China | 10,624 |
| 14 | Banque Nationale de Paris | France | 10,221 |
| 15 | ABN-AMRO Bank | Netherlands | 9,531 |
| 16 | Long-Term Credit Bank of Japan | Japan | 9,433 |
| 17 | Tokai Bank | Japan | 9,364 |
| 18 | Compagnie Financière de Paribas | France | 9,316 |
| 19 | Bank of China | China | 9,216 |
| 20 | Asahi Bank | Japan | 9,172 |
| 21 | Barclays Bank | United Kingdom | 9,014 |
| 22 | Bank of Tokyo | Japan | 8,977 |
| 23 | Swiss Bank Corp | Switzerland | 8,847 |
| 24 | Internationale Nederland Group | Netherlands | 8,598 |
| 25 | BankAmerica Corp | United States | 8,580 |
| 26 | National Westminster Bank | United Kingdom | 8,428 |
| 27 | Société Générale | France | 7,983 |
| 28 | Rabobank Nederland | Netherlands | 7,760 |
| 29 | Citicorp | United States | 7,752 |
| 30 | Mitsubishi Trust & Banking Corporation | Japan | 7,508 |
| 31 | Chemical Banking Corp | United States | 7,400 |
| 32 | Crédit Suisse | Switzerland | 7,384 |
| 33 | Sumitomo Trust & Banking | Japan | 7,358 |
| 34 | Groupe des Caisses d'Epargne Ecureuil | France | 7,239 |
| 35 | NationsBank | United States | 7,174 |
| 36 | Banca di Roma | Italy | 6,847 |
| 37 | J.P. Morgan & Co | United States | 6,820 |
| 38 | Cariplo | Italy | 6,721 |
| 39 | People's Construction Bank of China | China | 6,380 |
| 40 | Dresdner Bank | Germany | 6,254 |

**Notes:** Capital is essentially equity and reserves.
Figures for Japanese banks refer to the year ended March 31, 1993. Figures for all
other countries refer to the year ended December 31, 1992.

## Largest businesses
*By sales, $bn*

| | | | |
|---|---|---|---|
| 1 | General Motors | United States | 132.8 |
| 2 | Exxon | United States | 103.5 |
| 3 | Ford Motor | United States | 100.8 |
| 4 | Royal Dutch/Shell Group | United Kingdom/Netherlands | 98.9 |
| 5 | Toyota Motor[a] | Japan | 79.1 |
| 6 | IRI[b] | Italy | 67.5 |
| 7 | IBM | United States | 65.1 |
| 8 | Daimler-Benz | Germany | 63.3 |
| 9 | General Electric | United States | 62.2 |
| 10 | Hitachi[c] | Japan | 61.5 |
| 11 | British Petroleum | United Kingdom | 59.2 |
| 12 | Matsushita Electrical Industrial[c] | Japan | 57.5 |
| 13 | Mobil | United States | 57.4 |
| 14 | Volkswagen | Germany | 56.7 |
| 15 | Siemens[d] | Germany | 51.4 |
| 16 | Nissan Motor[c] | Japan | 50.2 |
| | Philip Morris | United States | 50.2 |
| 18 | Samsung | South Korea | 49.6 |
| 19 | Fiat | Italy | 47.9 |
| 20 | Unilever | United Kingdom/Netherlands | 44.0 |
| 21 | ENI | Italy | 40.4 |
| 22 | Elf Aquitaine[b] | France | 39.7 |
| 23 | Nestlé | Switzerland | 39.1 |
| 24 | Chevron | United States | 38.5 |
| 25 | Toshiba[c] | Japan | 37.5 |
| 26 | E.I. Du Pont de Nemours | United States | 37.4 |
| 27 | Texaco | United States | 37.1 |
| 28 | Chrysler | United States | 36.9 |
| 29 | Renault[b] | France | 33.9 |
| 30 | Honda Motor[c] | Japan | 33.4 |
| 31 | Philips Electronics | Netherlands | 33.3 |
| 32 | Sony[c] | Japan | 31.5 |
| 33 | Asea Brown Boveri | Sweden/Switzerland | 30.5 |
| | Alcatel Alsthom | France | 30.5 |
| 35 | Boeing | United States | 30.4 |
| 36 | Procter & Gamble[a] | United States | 29.9 |
| 37 | Hoechst | Germany | 29.6 |
| 38 | Peugeot | France | 29.4 |
| 39 | BASF | Germany | 28.5 |
| 40 | NEC[c] | Japan | 28.4 |

a  Year ended June 30, 1992.
b  Government owned.
c  Year ended March 31, 1993.
d  Year ended September 30, 1992.

**Notes:** All companies shown have derived at least half of their sales from manufacturing and/or mining. Figures refer to the year ended December 31, 1992, except where specified. They include sales of consolidated subsidiaries but exclude excise taxes collected by manufacturers, thus differing, in some instances, from figures published by the companies themselves.

# Stockmarkets

## Largest market capitalisation
*$m, end 1992*

| | | | | | |
|---|---|---:|---|---|---:|
| 1 | United States | 4,757,879 | 26 | Israel | 29,634 |
| 2 | Japan | 2,399,004 | 27 | Austria | 21,750 |
| 3 | United Kingdom | 838,579 | 28 | Argentina | 18,633 |
| 4 | France | 350,858 | 29 | China | 18,314 |
| 5 | Germany | 348,138 | 30 | Norway | 17,821 |
| 6 | Canada | 243,018 | 31 | New Zealand | 15,348 |
| 7 | Switzerland | 195,285 | 32 | Philippines | 13,794 |
| 8 | Hong Kong | 172,106 | 33 | Finland | 12,202 |
| 9 | Netherlands | 171,435 | 34 | Indonesia | 12,038 |
| 10 | South Africa | 150,669 | 35 | Luxembourg | 11,936 |
| 11 | Mexico | 139,061 | 36 | Turkey | 9,931 |
| 12 | Australia | 135,451 | 37 | Greece | 9,489 |
| 13 | Italy | 115,258 | 38 | Portugal | 9,213 |
| 14 | South Korea | 107,448 | 39 | Kuwait | 9,115 |
| 15 | Taiwan | 101,124 | 40 | Pakistan | 8,028 |
| 16 | Spain | 98,969 | 41 | Venezuela | 7,600 |
| 17 | Malaysia | 94,004 | 42 | Colombia | 5,681 |
| 18 | Sweden | 76,622 | 43 | Jordan | 3,365 |
| 19 | India | 65,119 | 44 | Jamaica | 3,227 |
| 20 | Belgium | 64,172 | 45 | Peru | 2,630 |
| 21 | Thailand | 58,259 | 46 | Egypt | 2,594 |
| 22 | Singapore | 48,818 | 47 | Morocco | 1,876 |
| 23 | Brazil | 45,261 | 48 | Sri Lanka | 1,439 |
| 24 | Denmark | 39,451 | 49 | Nigeria | 1,243 |
| 25 | Chile | 29,644 | 50 | Iran | 1,157 |

## Highest growth in market capitalisation, $ terms
*% increase, 1985-92*

| | | | | | |
|---|---|---:|---|---|---:|
| 1 | Indonesia | 10,189 | 21 | Austria | 373 |
| 2 | Portugal | 4,698 | 22 | India | 353 |
| 3 | Mexico | 3,545 | 23 | France | 344 |
| 4 | Thailand | 3,039 | 24 | Singapore | 341 |
| 5 | Uruguay | 2,353 | 25 | Sri Lanka | 294 |
| 6 | Philippines | 1,962 | 26 | Israel | 289 |
| 7 | Chile | 1,373 | 27 | Peru | 246 |
| 8 | South Korea | 1,356 | 28 | Belgium | 207 |
| 9 | Colombia | 1,266 | 29 | Netherlands | 189 |
| 10 | Greece | 1,140 | 30 | Bangladesh | 179 |
| 11 | Jamaica | 1,113 | 31 | South Africa | 172 |
| 12 | Turkey[a] | 962 | 32 | Denmark | 161 |
| 13 | Taiwan | 869 | 33 | United Kingdom | 156 |
| 14 | Argentina | 815 | 34 | Costa Rica | 145 |
| 15 | Morocco | 636 | | Japan | 145 |
| 16 | Venezuela | 574 | 36 | Australia | 123 |
| 17 | Pakistan | 486 | 37 | Switzerland | 117 |
| 18 | Malaysia | 479 | 38 | Finland | 108 |
| 19 | Spain | 421 | 39 | Sweden | 105 |
| 20 | Hong Kong | 399 | | United States | 105 |

## Highest growth in value traded, $ terms
*% increase, 1985-92*

| | | | | | |
|---|---|---|---|---|---|
| 1 | Indonesia | 130,000 | 24 | Hong Kong | 831 |
| 2 | Portugal | 69,000 | | Malaysia | 831 |
| 3 | Turkey[a] | 62,908 | 26 | France | 752 |
| 4 | Thailand | 12,587 | 27 | Jordan | 708 |
| 5 | Greece | 9,341 | 28 | United Kingdom | 460 |
| 6 | Venezuela | 8,387 | 29 | Norway | 441 |
| 7 | Taiwan | 4,813 | 30 | Morocco | 438 |
| 8 | Sri Lanka | 3,700 | 31 | Netherlands | 433 |
| 9 | Chile | 3,460 | 32 | Finland | 357 |
| 10 | Philippines | 2,696 | 33 | Belgium | 331 |
| 11 | South Korea | 2,690 | 34 | India | 315 |
| 12 | Argentina | 2,385 | | Pakistan | 315 |
| 13 | Israel | 1,864 | 36 | Côte d'Ivoire | 300 |
| 14 | Mexico | 1,789 | 37 | New Zealand | 250 |
| 15 | Colombia | 1,747 | 38 | Luxembourg | 228 |
| 16 | Jamaica | 1,738 | 39 | Egypt | 202 |
| 17 | Denmark | 1,379 | 40 | Sweden | 195 |
| 18 | Austria | 1,338 | 41 | Australia | 191 |
| 19 | Germany | 1,146 | 42 | South Africa | 174 |
| 20 | Spain | 1,082 | 43 | United States | 169 |
| 21 | Bangladesh | 1,000 | 44 | Zimbabwe | 122 |
| 22 | Peru | 947 | 45 | Canada | 109 |
| 23 | Singapore | 918 | 46 | Italy | 104 |

## Highest growth in number of listed companies[b]
*% increase, 1985-92*

| | | | | | |
|---|---|---|---|---|---|
| 1 | Portugal | 696 | | South Africa | 41 |
| 2 | Indonesia | 546 | 22 | Switzerland | 37 |
| 3 | Turkey[a] | 263 | 23 | Netherlands | 35 |
| 4 | Thailand | 205 | 24 | Singapore | 34 |
| 5 | Bangladesh | 110 | 25 | Jamaica | 26 |
| 6 | Egypt | 107 | 26 | Finland | 24 |
| 7 | Taiwan | 102 | | Mexico | 24 |
| 8 | South Korea | 101 | 28 | Canada | 23 |
| 9 | Costa Rica | 82 | | Philippines | 23 |
| 10 | Peru | 81 | 30 | Spain | 19 |
| 11 | Austria | 75 | 31 | Japan | 16 |
| 12 | Pakistan | 73 | 32 | Greece | 13 |
| 13 | Malaysia | 65 | | Zimbabwe | 13 |
| 14 | France | 61 | 34 | Sri Lanka | 11 |
| 15 | Hong Kong | 59 | 35 | Denmark | 10 |
| | Nigeria | 59 | 36 | Chile | 7 |
| 17 | Italy | 55 | 37 | Kenya | 6 |
| 18 | India | 54 | 38 | Brazil | 4 |
| 19 | Israel | 42 | 39 | Australia | 3 |
| 20 | Germany | 41 | | | |

a 1986-92.
b Only 39 stockmarkets experienced an increase in number of listed domestic
companies 1985-92.

# Transport: *roads and cars*

## Longest road networks
*Km, 1988-92*

| | | | | | |
|---|---|---|---|---|---|
| 1 | United States | 6,257,882 | 16 | Mexico | 242,294 |
| 2 | India | 1,843,420 | 17 | South Africa | 182,329 |
| 3 | Brazil | 1,661,850 | 18 | Pakistan | 177,410 |
| 4 | Japan | 1,124,843 | 19 | Ukraine | 169,964 |
| 5 | Canada | 849,404 | 20 | Kazakhstan | 166,864 |
| 6 | France | 811,200 | 21 | Philippines | 160,709 |
| 7 | Australia | 810,264 | 22 | Hungary | 158,711 |
| 8 | Germany | 636,282 | 23 | Saudi Arabia | 151,532 |
| 9 | Romania | 461,880 | 24 | Zaire | 145,000 |
| 10 | Turkey | 386,704 | 25 | Belgium | 137,876 |
| 11 | Poland | 367,000 | 26 | Sweden | 135,859 |
| 12 | United Kingdom | 360,047 | 27 | Greece | 130,000 |
| 13 | Spain | 331,961 | 28 | Ex-Yugoslavia | 122,571 |
| 14 | Italy | 305,388 | 29 | Austria | 110,000 |
| 15 | Indonesia | 244,164 | 30 | Colombia | 107,377 |

## Densest road networks
*Km of road per km² land area, 1988-92*

| | | | | | |
|---|---|---|---|---|---|
| 1 | Belgium | 4.50 | 16 | Ireland | 1.31 |
| 2 | Singapore | 4.42 | 17 | Austria | 1.30 |
| 3 | Bahrain | 4.30 | 18 | Poland | 1.17 |
| 4 | Japan | 2.98 | 19 | Cyprus | 1.13 |
| 5 | Netherlands | 2.80 | 20 | Italy | 1.02 |
| 6 | Ukraine | 2.79 | 21 | Latvia | 1.00 |
| 7 | Luxembourg | 1.98 | 22 | Greece | 0.98 |
| 8 | Romania | 1.94 | | Mauritius | 0.98 |
| 9 | Germany | 1.80 | 24 | Portugal | 0.79 |
| 10 | Hungary | 1.70 | 25 | Lithuania | 0.68 |
| | Switzerland | 1.70 | 26 | Albania | 0.64 |
| 12 | Denmark | 1.65 | | Spain | 0.64 |
| 13 | United Kingdom | 1.56 | | United States | 0.64 |
| 14 | France | 1.47 | 29 | El Salvador | 0.60 |
| 15 | Hong Kong | 1.45 | 30 | Ex-Czechoslovakia | 0.59 |

## Highest car ownership
*Number of cars per 100 people, 1988-92*

| | | | | | |
|---|---|---|---|---|---|
| 1 | United States | 56 | 11 | Sweden | 42 |
| 2 | Luxembourg | 52 | 12 | Austria | 41 |
| 3 | Italy | 50 | 13 | Belgium | 39 |
| 4 | Canada | 49 | 14 | Finland | 38 |
| 5 | Germany | 47 | | Norway | 38 |
| 6 | Iceland | 46 | 16 | Netherlands | 37 |
| 7 | Australia | 45 | 17 | United Kingdom | 35 |
| | New Zealand | 45 | 18 | Cyprus | 34 |
| | Switzerland | 45 | | Spain | 34 |
| 10 | France | 42 | 20 | Japan | 31 |

## Most crowded road networks
*Number of vehicles per km of road network, 1988-92*

| | | | | | |
|---|---|---|---|---|---|
| 1 | Hong Kong | 279 | 16 | Spain | 46 |
| 2 | Taiwan | 150 | 17 | Slovenia | 44 |
| 3 | Singapore | 145 | 18 | Luxembourg | 42 |
| 4 | Kuwait | 140 | 19 | Bulgaria | 39 |
| 5 | Brunei | 96 | 20 | Jordan | 37 |
| 6 | Italy | 91 | | Mauritius | 37 |
| 7 | Israel | 84 | 22 | France | 36 |
| 8 | Netherlands | 66 | 23 | Mexico | 35 |
| 9 | United Kingdom | 65 | 24 | Saudi Arabia | 34 |
| 10 | Germany | 62 | 25 | Austria | 32 |
| 11 | Thailand | 58 | | CAR | 32 |
| 12 | Japan | 55 | | Egypt | 32 |
| 13 | Ex-Czechoslovakia | 52 | 28 | Belgium | 31 |
| 14 | Bahrain | 50 | 29 | Portugal | 30 |
| 15 | Switzerland | 48 | | United States| | 30 |

## Most used road networks
*'000 vehicle-km per year per km of road network, 1988-92*

| | | | | | |
|---|---|---|---|---|---|
| 1 | Hong Kong | 5,876.8 | 16 | France | 543.6 |
| 2 | Kuwait | 3,474.6 | 17 | Denmark | 534.9 |
| 3 | Israel | 1,654.5 | 18 | South Korea | 458.2 |
| 4 | Germany | 1,260.9 | 19 | Portugal | 392.2 |
| 5 | Madagascar | 1,194.2 | 20 | Belgium | 384.2 |
| 6 | Italy | 1,187.5 | 21 | Colombia | 383.4 |
| 7 | Thailand | 1,173.7 | 22 | Bulgaria | 356.0 |
| 8 | United Kingdom | 1,128.1 | 23 | Ex-Czechoslovakia | 347.9 |
| 9 | Netherlands | 885.2 | 24 | Spain | 303.4 |
| 10 | Luxembourg | 755.5 | 25 | Poland | 302.5 |
| 11 | Iraq | 745.0 | 26 | Ireland | 276.5 |
| 12 | Sweden | 700.7 | 27 | Ecuador | 251.1 |
| 13 | Japan | 584.4 | 28 | Honduras | 231.5 |
| 14 | United States | 556.2 | 29 | Tunisia | 219.5 |
| 15 | Finland | 551.8 | 30 | Hungary | 216.5 |

## Most accidents
*Number of people injured per 100m vehicle-km, 1988-92*

| | | | | | |
|---|---|---|---|---|---|
| 1 | Rwanda | 1,764 | | Morocco | 207 |
| 2 | South Korea | 1,126 | 12 | Israel | 166 |
| 3 | Jordan | 658 | 13 | Portugal | 147 |
| 4 | Costa Rica | 404 | 14 | Belgium | 143 |
| 5 | Turkey | 331 | 15 | South Africa | 141 |
| 6 | Kenya | 330 | 16 | Japan | 128 |
| 7 | Honduras | 317 | 17 | Latvia | 125 |
| 8 | Hong Kong | 219 | 18 | Ex-Czechoslovakia | 115 |
| 9 | Egypt | 217 | 19 | Spain | 104 |
| 10 | Canada | 207 | 20 | United States | 98 |

# Transport: *planes and trains*

## Most air passenger-km
*Million passenger-km[a] per year, 1991*

| | | | | | |
|---|---|---|---|---|---|
| 1 | United States | 720,753 | 21 | Saudi Arabia | 14,881 |
| 2 | Ex-Soviet Union | 224,947 | 22 | Malaysia | 14,226 |
| 3 | Japan | 100,431 | 23 | New Zealand | 11,299 |
| 4 | United Kingdom | 99,856 | 24 | Philippines | 11,028 |
| 5 | France | 48,725 | 25 | Argentina | 9,207 |
| 6 | Australia | 44,276 | 26 | Pakistan | 9,062 |
| 7 | Germany | 43,270 | 27 | South Africa | 8,413 |
| 8 | Singapore | 33,452 | 28 | Sweden | 8,163 |
| 9 | China | 30,132 | 29 | Israel | 7,527 |
| 10 | Canada | 30,042 | 30 | Portugal | 7,072 |
| 11 | Brazil | 28,537 | 31 | Norway | 6,291 |
| 12 | Netherlands | 28,197 | 32 | Belgium | 6,223 |
| 13 | Spain | 23,200 | 33 | Greece | 6,193 |
| 14 | Italy | 22,653 | 34 | Venezuela | 5,939 |
| 15 | South Korea | 20,716 | 35 | Iran | 5,551 |
| 16 | Mexico | 18,267 | 36 | Egypt | 5,230 |
| 17 | Thailand | 18,246 | 37 | UAE | 4,861 |
| 18 | Indonesia | 15,965 | 38 | Finland | 4,719 |
| 19 | India | 15,677 | 39 | Colombia | 4,465 |
| 20 | Switzerland | 15,327 | 40 | Denmark | 4,400 |

## Busiest airports
*Number of passengers '000, 1991*

| | | | |
|---|---|---|---|
| 1 | Chicago | O'Hare | 59,852 |
| 2 | Dallas | Dallas/Ft.Worth | 48,198 |
| 3 | Los Angeles | Los Angeles Intl. | 45,668 |
| 4 | Tokyo | Haneda | 41,981 |
| 5 | London | Heathrow | 40,245 |
| 6 | Atlanta | Hartsfield | 37,915 |
| 7 | San Francisco | San Francisco Intl. | 31,197 |
| 8 | Denver | Stapleton | 28,285 |
| 9 | New York | Kennedy | 27,442 |
| 10 | Frankfurt | Frankfurt/Main | 27,272 |

## Busiest international airports
*Number of international passengers '000, 1991*

| | | | |
|---|---|---|---|
| 1 | London | Heathrow | 33,531 |
| 2 | Frankfurt | Frankfurt/Main | 20,861 |
| 3 | Paris | Charles de Gaulle | 19,384 |
| 4 | Hong Kong | Hong Kong Intl. | 19,158 |
| 5 | Tokyo | Narita | 17,743 |
| 6 | London | Gatwick | 17,679 |
| 7 | New York | Kennedy | 16,670 |
| 8 | Amsterdam | Schipol | 16,082 |
| 9 | Singapore | Changi | 14,983 |
| 10 | Zurich | Zurich | 11,185 |

a  Air passenger–km data refer to the distance travelled by each aircraft of national origin.

## Longest railway networks
*'000 km*

| | | | | | |
|---|---|---|---|---|---|
| 1 | United States | 242.7 | 21 | Sweden | 9.8 |
| 2 | Russia | 87.5 | 22 | Ex-Yugoslavia[d] | 9.4 |
| 3 | India | 62.4 | 23 | Pakistan | 8.8 |
| 4 | China | 53.5 | 24 | Turkey | 8.4 |
| 5 | Germany | 41.0 | 25 | Hungary | 7.8 |
| 6 | Australia[a] | 35.8 | 26 | Chile[e] | 6.3 |
| 7 | Argentina[b] | 34.2 | 27 | Finland | 5.9 |
| 8 | France | 32.7 | 28 | Austria | 5.6 |
| 9 | Mexico[a] | 26.5 | 29 | Belorussia | 5.4 |
| 10 | Poland | 25.2 | 30 | Zaire[a] | 5.1 |
| 11 | South Africa | 23.8 | 31 | Philippines[a] | 4.9 |
| 12 | Ukraine | 22.6 | 32 | Cuba[c] | 4.8 |
| 13 | Canada | 22.4 | | Iran | 4.8 |
| 14 | Brazil[c] | 22.1 | | Sudan[a] | 4.8 |
| 15 | Japan | 20.1 | 35 | North Korea[a] | 4.5 |
| 16 | United Kingdom | 16.5 | 36 | Bulgaria | 4.3 |
| 17 | Italy | 16.1 | | New Zealand | 4.3 |
| 18 | Ex-Czechoslovakia | 13.1 | 38 | Indonesia[d] | 4.2 |
| 19 | Spain | 13.0 | 39 | Belgium | 4.1 |
| 20 | Romania | 11.4 | | Egypt | 4.1 |

## Most rail passengers
*Km per year per person*

| | | | | | |
|---|---|---|---|---|---|
| 1 | Japan | 1,992 | 11 | Netherlands | 1,018 |
| 2 | Switzerland | 1,762 | 12 | Egypt | 955 |
| 3 | Belorussia | 1,740 | 13 | Denmark | 893 |
| 4 | Russia | 1,707 | 14 | Italy | 857 |
| 5 | Ukraine | 1,458 | 15 | Poland | 847 |
| 6 | Latvia | 1,400 | 16 | South Korea | 737 |
| 7 | Austria | 1,210 | 17 | Lithuania | 730 |
| 8 | France | 1,095 | 18 | Germany | 693 |
| 9 | Ex-Czechoslovakia | 1,081 | 19 | Belgium | 676 |
| 10 | Romania | 1,066 | 20 | Hungary | 668 |

## Most rail freight
*Million tonnes-km per year*

| | | | | | |
|---|---|---|---|---|---|
| 1 | Russia | 1,967,064 | 11 | Belorussia | 56,441 |
| 2 | United States | 1,557,470 | 12 | Australia[a] | 50,670 |
| 3 | China | 1,154,900 | 13 | France | 49,536 |
| 4 | Ukraine | 337,760 | 14 | Ex-Czechoslovakia | 44,046 |
| 5 | India | 250,238 | 15 | Mexico[a] | 32,988 |
| 6 | Canada | 101,806 | 16 | Japan | 26,300 |
| 7 | Brazil[b] | 92,838 | 17 | Romania | 24,230 |
| 8 | South Africa | 89,248 | 18 | Italy | 20,162 |
| 9 | Germany | 69,518 | 19 | Sweden | 19,053 |
| 10 | Poland | 56,951 | 20 | United Kingdom | 15,509 |

| | | | |
|---|---|---|---|
| a | 1989. | d | 1990. |
| b | 1987. | e | 1991. |
| c | 1988. | | |

# Transport: *sail away*

## Largest merchant fleets
*Number of vessels over 100 GRT [a], mid-1993*

| | | | | | | |
|---|---|---|---|---|---|---|
| 1 | Japan | 9,895 | | 21 | Singapore | 1,068 |
| 2 | United States | 5,782 | | 22 | Honduras | 1,057 |
| 3 | Panama | 5,510 | | 23 | Netherlands | 1,018 |
| 4 | Russia | 5,131 | | 24 | Malta | 1,009 |
| 5 | China | 2,407 | | 25 | Turkey | 920 |
| 6 | Norway | 2,365 | | 26 | India | 875 |
| 7 | South Korea | 2,107 | | 27 | France | 866 |
| 8 | Indonesia | 2,047 | | 28 | Australia | 642 |
| 9 | Spain | 2,030 | | 29 | Mexico | 635 |
| 10 | Greece | 1,908 | | 30 | Sweden | 629 |
| 11 | United Kingdom | 1,689 | | 31 | Peru | 624 |
| 12 | Liberia | 1,662 | | 32 | Poland | 604 |
| 13 | Italy | 1,575 | | 33 | Brazil | 582 |
| 14 | Philippines | 1,559 | | 34 | Malaysia | 571 |
| 15 | Cyprus | 1,528 | | 35 | Morocco | 492 |
| 16 | Germany | 1,255 | | 36 | Romania | 472 |
| 17 | Denmark | 1,253 | | 37 | Argentina | 433 |
| 18 | Canada | 1,129 | | 38 | Iran | 428 |
| 19 | Bahamas | 1,127 | | 39 | Hong Kong | 417 |
| 20 | Ukraine | 1,112 | | 40 | Chile | 403 |

## Largest ports
*Total cargo traffic, '000 tonnes [b]*

| | | | | | | |
|---|---|---|---|---|---|---|
| 1 | Rotterdam | 293,100 | | 21 | Hampton Roads | 68,530 |
| 2 | Singapore | 238,400 | | 22 | Pusan[d] | 66,547 |
| 3 | Chiba | 191,650 | | 23 | Hamburg | 65,084 |
| 4 | Kobe | 169,645 | | 24 | Vancouver | 63,306 |
| 5 | Shanghai[c] | 139,590 | | 25 | Philadelphia[d] | 58,831 |
| 6 | Nagoya | 130,857 | | 26 | Le Havre | 53,110 |
| 7 | Yokohama | 121,386 | | 27 | Yokkaichi | 51,919 |
| 8 | Antwerp | 103,628 | | 28 | Newcastle | 50,870 |
| 9 | Kitakyushu | 95,831 | | 29 | Tampa | 49,157 |
| 10 | Osaka | 95,109 | | 30 | London | 44,524 |
| 11 | Marseilles | 90,417 | | 31 | Tees & Hartlepool | 43,392 |
| 12 | Houston | 86,747 | | 32 | Port Hedland | 42,612 |
| 13 | Ulsan | 84,576 | | 33 | Sullom Voe | 41,430 |
| 14 | Hong Kong | 84,222 | | 34 | Genoa | 41,381 |
| 15 | Kaohsiung | 79,497 | | 35 | Arzew | 40,629 |
| 16 | Tokyo[c] | 79,335 | | 36 | Dunkirk | 40,205 |
| 17 | Corpus Christi | 72,558 | | 37 | Grimsby-Immingham | 39,083 |
| 18 | Long Beach[d] | 72,398 | | 38 | New York | 38,024 |
| 19 | Inchon[d] | 70,959 | | 39 | Warri | 37,101 |
| 20 | Los Angeles[d] | 70,910 | | 40 | Trieste | 36,677 |

a   Gross Tonnage (GRT) = total volume within the hull and above deck. 1 GRT=100 cu ft.
b   Total cargo loaded and discharged.
c   1990.
d   1991.

# Tourism

## Most tourist arrivals
*Number of arrivals, '000*

| | | | | | |
|---|---|---|---|---|---|
| 1 | France | 59,590 | 21 | Singapore | 5,446 |
| 2 | United States | 44,647 | 22 | Thailand | 5,136 |
| 3 | Spain | 39,638 | 23 | Morocco | 4,390 |
| 4 | Italy | 26,113 | 24 | Poland | 4,000 |
| 5 | Hungary | 20,188 | 25 | Bulgaria | 3,750 |
| 6 | Austria | 19,098 | 26 | Ireland | 3,666 |
| 7 | United Kingdom | 18,535 | 27 | Tunisia | 3,540 |
| 8 | Mexico | 17,271 | 28 | South Korea | 3,231 |
| 9 | China | 16,512 | 29 | Belgium | 3,220 |
| 10 | Germany | 15,147 | 30 | Macao | 3,180 |
| 11 | Canada | 14,741 | 31 | Indonesia | 3,064 |
| 12 | Switzerland | 12,800 | 32 | Argentina | 3,031 |
| 13 | Greece | 9,331 | 33 | Egypt | 2,944 |
| 14 | Portugal | 8,921 | 34 | South Africa | 2,892 |
| 15 | Czechoslovakia | 8,000 | 35 | Puerto Rico | 2,640 |
| 16 | Hong Kong | 6,986 | 36 | Australia | 2,603 |
| 17 | Turkey | 6,549 | 37 | Norway | 2,375 |
| 18 | Romania | 6,280 | 38 | Japan | 2,103 |
| 19 | Netherlands | 6,049 | 39 | Cyprus | 1,991 |
| 20 | Malaysia | 6,016 | 40 | Taiwan | 1,873 |

## Biggest tourist spending
*$m*

| | | | | | |
|---|---|---|---|---|---|
| 1 | United States | 39,872 | 11 | Sweden | 6,794 |
| 2 | Germany | 37,309 | 12 | Belgium | 6,603 |
| 3 | Japan | 26,837 | 13 | Mexico | 6,108 |
| 4 | United Kingdom | 19,831 | 14 | Switzerland | 6,068 |
| 5 | Italy | 16,617 | 15 | Spain | 5,542 |
| 6 | France | 13,910 | 16 | Australia | 3,994 |
| 7 | Canada | 11,265 | 17 | Norway | 3,870 |
| 8 | Netherlands | 9,330 | 18 | South Korea | 3,794 |
| 9 | Taiwan | 7,098 | 19 | Denmark | 3,779 |
| 10 | Austria | 6,895 | 20 | Finland | 2,403 |

## Largest tourist receipts
*$m*

| | | | | | |
|---|---|---|---|---|---|
| 1 | United States | 53,861 | 11 | Canada | 5,679 |
| 2 | France | 25,000 | 12 | Singapore | 5,204 |
| 3 | Spain | 22,181 | 13 | Netherlands | 5,004 |
| 4 | Italy | 21,577 | 14 | Thailand | 4,829 |
| 5 | United Kingdom | 13,683 | 15 | Belgium | 4,053 |
| 6 | Austria | 13,250 | 16 | Australia | 3,992 |
| 7 | Germany | 10,982 | 17 | China | 3,948 |
| 8 | Switzerland | 7,650 | 18 | Denmark | 3,784 |
| 9 | Hong Kong | 6,037 | 19 | Portugal | 3,721 |
| 10 | Mexico | 5,997 | 20 | Turkey | 3,639 |

# Education

## Highest primary enrolment
*Number enrolled as % of relevant age group, 1990*

| | | | | | |
|---|---|---|---|---|---|
| 1 | China | 135 | | Syria | 109 |
| 2 | Gabon[a] | 134 | 22 | Brazil | 108 |
| 3 | Peru | 126 | | Honduras | 108 |
| 4 | Portugal | 119 | | South Korea | 108 |
| 5 | Ecuador[b] | 118 | 25 | Lesotho | 107 |
| 6 | Indonesia | 117 | | Panama | 107 |
| | Netherlands | 117 | | Paraguay | 107 |
| | Zimbabwe | 117 | | Sri Lanka | 107 |
| 9 | Tunisia | 116 | | Sweden | 107 |
| 10 | Iran | 112 | | United Kingdom | 107 |
| | Mexico | 112 | 31 | Hong Kong | 106 |
| 12 | Argentina | 111 | | Mauritius | 106 |
| | France | 111 | | New Zealand | 106 |
| | Philippines | 111 | | Uruguay | 106 |
| | UAE[b] | 111 | 35 | Australia | 105 |
| 16 | Botswana | 110 | | Canada | 105 |
| | Colombia | 110 | | Germany | 105 |
| | Singapore | 110 | | Jamaica | 105 |
| | Turkey | 110 | | United States | 105 |
| 20 | Spain | 109 | 40 | Laos | 104 |

## Lowest primary enrolment
*Number enrolled as % of relevant age group, 1990*

| | | | | | |
|---|---|---|---|---|---|
| 1 | Afghanistan[b] | 24 | 21 | Malawi | 71 |
| | Mali | 24 | | Papua New Guinea | 71 |
| 3 | Bhutan | 26 | 23 | Burundi | 72 |
| 4 | Niger | 29 | | Nigeria | 72 |
| 5 | Liberia[a] | 35 | 25 | Bangladesh | 73 |
| 6 | Burkina Faso | 36 | 26 | Ghana | 75 |
| 7 | Guinea | 37 | 27 | Uganda | 76 |
| | Pakistan | 37 | 28 | El Salvador | 78 |
| 9 | Ethiopia | 38 | | Saudi Arabia | 78 |
| 10 | Sierra Leone | 48 | 30 | Guatemala | 79 |
| 11 | Sudan | 49 | 31 | Bolivia | 82 |
| 12 | Mauritania | 51 | 32 | Thailand | 85 |
| 13 | Chad | 57 | 33 | Nepal | 86 |
| 14 | Mozambique | 58 | 34 | Romania | 91 |
| | Senegal | 58 | 35 | Madagascar | 92 |
| 16 | Benin | 61 | | Venezuela | 92 |
| 17 | Tanzania | 63 | 37 | Ex-Czechoslovakia | 93 |
| 18 | CAR | 67 | | Israel | 93 |
| 19 | Morocco | 68 | | Malaysia | 93 |
| 20 | Rwanda | 69 | | Zambia | 93 |

**Notes:** The gross enrolment ratios shown are the actual number enrolled as a percentage of the number of children in the official primary age group. They may exceed 100 when children outside the primary age group are receiving primary education either because they have not moved on to secondary education or because they have started primary education early.

## Most literate
*% adult literacy rate, 1990*

| | | | | | |
|---|---|---|---|---|---|
| 1 | Australia | 99.0 | | Luxembourg | 99.0 |
| | Austria | 99.0 | | Netherlands | 99.0 |
| | Bahamas | 99.0 | | New Zealand | 99.0 |
| | Barbados | 99.0 | | Norway | 99.0 |
| | Belgium | 99.0 | | Sweden | 99.0 |
| | Canada | 99.0 | | Switzerland | 99.0 |
| | Denmark | 99.0 | | United Kingdom | 99.0 |
| | Finland | 99.0 | | United States | 99.0 |
| | France | 99.0 | 22 | Jamaica | 98.4 |
| | Germany | 99.0 | 23 | Spain | 97.5 |
| | Iceland | 99.0 | 24 | Italy | 97.1 |
| | Ireland | 99.0 | 25 | Ex-Czechoslovakia | 97.0 |
| | Japan | 99.0 | | Hungary | 97.0 |

## Least literate
*% adult literacy rate, 1990*

| | | | | | |
|---|---|---|---|---|---|
| 1 | Burkina Faso | 18.2 | 14 | Pakistan | 34.8 |
| 2 | Sierra Leone | 20.7 | 15 | Oman | 35.0 |
| 3 | Benin | 23.4 | 16 | Cambodia | 35.2 |
| 4 | Guinea | 24.0 | 17 | Bangladesh | 35.3 |
| 5 | Somalia | 24.1 | 18 | CAR | 37.7 |
| 6 | Nepal | 25.6 | 19 | Senegal | 38.3 |
| 7 | Sudan | 27.1 | 20 | Bhutan | 38.4 |
| 8 | Niger | 28.4 | 21 | Yemen | 38.6 |
| 9 | Afghanistan | 29.4 | 22 | Liberia | 39.5 |
| 10 | Chad | 29.8 | 23 | Namibia | 40.0 |
| 11 | Mali | 32.0 | 24 | Angola | 41.7 |
| 12 | Mozambique | 32.9 | 25 | Togo | 43.3 |
| 13 | Mauritania | 34.0 | 26 | Malawi | 47.0 |

## Highest tertiary enrolment[c]
*Number enrolled as % of relevant age group, 1990*

| | | | | | |
|---|---|---|---|---|---|
| 1 | United States | 75 | 15 | Austria | 33 |
| 2 | Canada | 70 | | Israel | 33 |
| 3 | Uruguay | 50 | | Sweden | 33 |
| 4 | Finland | 47 | 18 | Denmark | 32 |
| 5 | Norway | 43 | | Germany | 32 |
| 6 | Argentina[b] | 41 | 20 | Bulgaria | 31 |
| | New Zealand | 41 | | Italy | 31 |
| 8 | France | 40 | | Japan | 31 |
| 9 | South Korea | 39 | 23 | Greece | 29 |
| 10 | Belgium | 37 | | Venezuela | 29 |
| 11 | Peru | 36 | 25 | Philippines | 27 |
| 12 | Australia | 35 | 26 | Costa Rica | 26 |
| 13 | Netherlands | 34 | | Ireland | 26 |
| | Spain | 34 | | Switzerland | 26 |

a  1988.                          b  1989.
c  Tertiary education includes all levels of post-secondary education including
   courses leading to awards not equivalent to a university degree, courses leading to
   a first university degree and postgraduate courses.

# Life: *the chances*

## Highest life expectancy
*Years, 1990-95*

| | | | | | |
|---|---|---:|---|---|---:|
| 1 | Japan | 79 | 34 | Brunei | 74 |
| 2 | Greece | 78 | | Jamaica | 74 |
| | Hong Kong | 78 | 36 | Albania | 73 |
| | Iceland | 78 | | Ex-Czechoslovakia | 73 |
| | Spain | 78 | | Lithuania | 73 |
| | Sweden | 78 | | Panama | 73 |
| | Switzerland | 78 | | Uruguay | 73 |
| 8 | Australia | 77 | 41 | Bahamas | 72 |
| | Canada | 77 | | Bulgaria | 72 |
| | Cyprus | 77 | | Chile | 72 |
| | France | 77 | | Estonia | 72 |
| | Israel | 77 | | Fiji | 72 |
| | Italy | 77 | | Poland | 72 |
| | Netherlands | 77 | | Sri Lanka | 72 |
| | Norway | 77 | | Ex-Yugoslavia | 72 |
| 16 | Austria | 76 | 49 | Argentina | 71 |
| | Barbados | 76 | | Bahrain | 71 |
| | Belgium | 76 | | China | 71 |
| | Costa Rica | 76 | | Latvia | 71 |
| | Cuba | 76 | | Malaysia | 71 |
| | Denmark | 76 | | North Korea | 71 |
| | Finland | 76 | | South Korea | 71 |
| | Germany | 76 | | Trinidad & Tobago | 71 |
| | Luxembourg | 76 | | UAE | 71 |
| | Malta | 76 | 58 | Hungary | 70 |
| | New Zealand | 76 | | Mauritius | 70 |
| | United Kingdom | 76 | | Mexico | 70 |
| | United States | 76 | | Oman | 70 |
| 29 | Ireland | 75 | | Qatar | 70 |
| | Kuwait | 75 | | Romania | 70 |
| | Portugal | 75 | | Suriname | 70 |
| | Puerto Rico | 75 | | Venezuela | 70 |
| | Singapore | 75 | | | |

## Highest male life expectancy
*Years, 1990-95*

| | | | | | |
|---|---|---:|---|---|---:|
| 1 | Japan | 75.9 | 6 | Cyprus | 74.8 |
| 2 | Iceland | 75.8 | 7 | Switzerland | 74.7 |
| 3 | Sweden | 75.2 | 8 | Israel | 74.6 |
| 4 | Hong Kong | 75.1 | | Spain | 74.6 |
| 5 | Greece | 74.9 | 10 | Netherlands | 74.3 |

## Highest female life expectancy
*Years, 1990-95*

| | | | | | |
|---|---|---:|---|---|---:|
| 1 | Japan | 81.6 | 6 | Canada | 80.7 |
| 2 | Switzerland | 81.2 | 7 | Netherlands | 80.5 |
| 3 | France | 80.8 | | Norway | 80.5 |
| | Iceland | 80.8 | | Spain | 80.5 |
| | Sweden | 80.8 | 10 | Hong Kong | 80.4 |

## Lowest life expectancy
*Years, 1990-95*

| | | | | | | |
|---|---|---|---|---|---|---|
| 1 | Uganda | 42 | | Nepal | 54 |
| 2 | Afghanistan | 43 | 34 | Liberia | 55 |
| | Sierra Leone | 43 | 35 | Togo | 55 |
| 4 | Malawi | 44 | 36 | Cameroon | 56 |
| | Zambia | 44 | | Ghana | 56 |
| 6 | Benin | 46 | | Madagascar | 56 |
| | CAR | 46 | | Papua New Guinea | 56 |
| | Guinea | 46 | | Zimbabwe | 56 |
| | Mali | 46 | 41 | Haiti | 57 |
| | Rwanda | 46 | 42 | Myanmar | 58 |
| 11 | Angola | 47 | 43 | Kenya | 59 |
| | Ethiopia | 47 | | Namibia | 59 |
| | Mozambique | 47 | | Pakistan | 59 |
| | Niger | 47 | 46 | India | 60 |
| | Somalia | 47 | 47 | Bolivia | 61 |
| 16 | Burkina Faso | 48 | | Botswana | 61 |
| | Burundi | 48 | | Lesotho | 61 |
| | Chad | 48 | 50 | Egypt | 62 |
| | Mauritania | 48 | 51 | Indonesia | 63 |
| 20 | Bhutan | 49 | | Libya | 63 |
| | Senegal | 49 | | Morocco | 63 |
| 22 | Cambodia | 51 | | South Africa | 63 |
| | Laos | 51 | 55 | Mongolia | 64 |
| | Tanzania | 51 | | Vietnam | 64 |
| 25 | Congo | 52 | 57 | Guatemala | 65 |
| | Côte d'Ivoire | 52 | | Peru | 65 |
| | Sudan | 52 | | Philippines | 65 |
| | Zaire | 52 | 60 | Algeria | 66 |
| 29 | Bangladesh | 53 | | Brazil | 66 |
| | Nigeria | 53 | | El Salvador | 66 |
| | Yemen | 53 | | Honduras | 66 |
| 32 | Gabon | 54 | | Iraq | 66 |

## Lowest male life expectancy
*Years, 1990-95*

| | | | | | |
|---|---|---|---|---|---|
| 1 | Uganda | 40.8 | 6 | Guinea | 44.0 |
| 2 | Sierra Leone | 41.4 | 7 | Mali | 44.4 |
| 3 | Afghanistan | 43.0 | 8 | CAR | 44.7 |
| 4 | Malawi | 43.5 | 9 | Benin | 44.8 |
| 5 | Zambia | 43.5 | 10 | Angola | 44.9 |

## Lowest female life expectancy
*Years, 1990-95*

| | | | | | |
|---|---|---|---|---|---|
| 1 | Uganda | 42.9 | 6 | Guinea | 45.0 |
| 2 | Afghanistan | 44.0 | 7 | Mali | 47.6 |
| 3 | Sierra Leone | 44.6 | 8 | Benin | 48.0 |
| 4 | Zambia | 44.8 | 9 | Angola | 48.1 |
| 5 | Malawi | 44.9 | 10 | CAR | 49.4 |

# Death: *the chances*

## Highest death rates
*Number of deaths per 1,000 population*

| | | | | | | |
|---|---|---|---|---|---|---|
| 1 | Sierra Leone | 21.6 | | 51 | Belgium | 10.9 |
| 2 | Malawi | 21.5 | | 52 | Norway | 10.8 |
| 3 | Uganda | 21.0 | | 53 | Cameroon | 10.7 |
| 4 | Guinea | 20.3 | | | Luxembourg | 10.7 |
| 5 | Afghanistan | 20.1 | | | Namibia | 10.7 |
| 6 | Mali | 19.1 | | | Papua New Guinea | 10.7 |
| 7 | Niger | 18.7 | | 57 | Austria | 10.6 |
| 8 | Ethiopia | 18.5 | | 58 | Pakistan | 10.5 |
| 9 | Somalia | 18.5 | | 59 | Kenya | 10.3 |
| 10 | CAR | 18.4 | | | Uruguay | 10.3 |
| 11 | Mozambique | 18.2 | | 61 | Finland | 10.2 |
| | Rwanda | 18.2 | | | Portugal | 10.2 |
| 13 | Chad | 18.0 | | 63 | Poland | 10.1 |
| | Zambia | 18.0 | | 64 | India | 10.0 |
| 15 | Mauritania | 17.5 | | | Italy | 10.0 |
| 16 | Angola | 16.9 | | | Lithuania | 10.0 |
| 17 | Burkina Faso | 16.4 | | 67 | Switzerland | 9.9 |
| 18 | Benin | 16.0 | | 68 | France | 9.8 |
| 19 | Burundi | 16.0 | | | Greece | 9.8 |
| | Senegal | 16.0 | | 70 | Lesotho | 9.7 |
| 21 | Gabon | 15.9 | | 71 | Ex-Yugoslavia | 9.5 |
| 22 | Laos | 15.2 | | 72 | Ireland | 9.2 |
| 23 | Congo | 14.7 | | | Spain | 9.2 |
| | Côte d'Ivoire | 14.7 | | 74 | Egypt | 9.1 |
| 25 | Tanzania | 14.6 | | 75 | United States | 8.9 |
| | Zaire | 14.6 | | 76 | Barbados | 8.8 |
| 27 | Bhutan | 14.4 | | 77 | Netherlands | 8.7 |
| 28 | Sudan | 14.3 | | 78 | Argentina | 8.6 |
| 29 | Liberia | 14.2 | | | South Africa | 8.6 |
| 30 | Nigeria | 13.9 | | 80 | Indonesia | 8.5 |
| 31 | Hungary | 13.8 | | | Vietnam | 8.5 |
| 32 | Yemen | 13.7 | | 82 | Bolivia | 8.4 |
| 33 | Nepal | 13.0 | | 83 | Morocco | 8.3 |
| 34 | Togo | 12.8 | | 84 | New Zealand | 8.2 |
| 35 | Madagascar | 12.7 | | 85 | Libya | 8.1 |
| 36 | Cambodia | 12.3 | | 86 | Malta | 8.0 |
| 37 | Bangladesh | 12.2 | | 87 | Botswana | 7.9 |
| | Bulgaria | 12.2 | | 88 | Canada | 7.8 |
| 39 | Latvia | 12.1 | | 89 | Australia | 7.7 |
| 40 | Haiti | 11.9 | | | Guatemala | 7.7 |
| 41 | Estonia | 11.7 | | | Mongolia | 7.7 |
| | Ghana | 11.7 | | 92 | Cyprus | 7.6 |
| 43 | Denmark | 11.6 | | | Peru | 7.6 |
| 44 | Sweden | 11.5 | | 94 | Japan | 7.5 |
| | United Kingdom | 11.5 | | 95 | Brazil | 7.2 |
| 46 | Germany | 11.4 | | | Honduras | 7.2 |
| 47 | Ex-Czechoslavakia | 11.3 | | 97 | El Salvador | 7.1 |
| 48 | Romania | 11.2 | | | Lebanon | 7.1 |
| 49 | Myanmar | 11.1 | | | Turkey | 7.1 |
| 50 | Zimbabwe | 11.0 | | 100 | Iceland | 7.0 |

## Highest infant mortality
*Number of deaths per 1,000 live births*

| | | | | | | |
|---|---|---|---|---|---|---|
| 1 | Afghanistan | 162 | 27 | Laos | 97 |
| 2 | Mali | 159 | 28 | Bangladesh | 96 |
| 3 | Mozambique | 147 | | Nigeria | 96 |
| 4 | Sierra Leone | 143 | 30 | Gabon | 94 |
| 5 | Malawi | 142 | 31 | Zaire | 93 |
| 6 | Guinea | 134 | 32 | Côte d'Ivoire | 91 |
| 7 | Liberia | 126 | 33 | India | 88 |
| 8 | Niger | 124 | 34 | Haiti | 86 |
| 9 | Chad | 122 | 35 | Togo | 85 |
| | Ethiopia | 122 | | Bolivia | 85 |
| | Somalia | 122 | 37 | Zambia | 84 |
| 12 | Mauritania | 117 | 38 | Congo | 82 |
| 13 | Angola | 112 | 39 | Benin | 81 |
| 14 | Bhutan | 111 | | Ghana | 81 |
| 15 | Madagascar | 110 | | Myanmar | 81 |
| | Rwanda | 110 | 42 | Senegal | 80 |
| 17 | Burkina Faso | 109 | 43 | Lesotho | 79 |
| 18 | Yemen | 106 | 44 | Peru | 76 |
| 19 | CAR | 105 | 45 | Namibia | 70 |
| 20 | Uganda | 104 | 46 | Libya | 68 |
| 21 | Cambodia | 102 | | Morocco | 68 |
| | Tanzania | 102 | 48 | Kenya | 66 |
| 23 | Nepal | 99 | 49 | Indonesia | 65 |
| | Sudan | 99 | 50 | Honduras | 60 |
| 25 | Burundi | 98 | | Mongolia | 60 |
| | Pakistan | 98 | | | |

## Lowest death rates
*Number of deaths per 1,000 pop.*

| 1 | Kuwait | 2.2 |
|---|---|---|
| 2 | Bahrain | 3.6 |
| 3 | Costa Rica | 3.7 |
| 4 | Qatar | 3.9 |
| | UAE | 3.9 |
| 6 | Brunei | 4.4 |
| 7 | Fiji | 4.5 |
| 8 | Oman | 4.9 |
| | Saudi Arabia | 4.9 |
| 10 | Malaysia | 5.1 |

## Lowest infant mortality
*Number of deaths per 1,000 pop*

| 1 | Iceland | 5 |
|---|---|---|
| | Japan | 5 |
| 3 | Austria | 6 |
| | Canada | 6 |
| | Finland | 6 |
| | Hong Kong | 6 |
| | Spain | 6 |
| | Sweden | 6 |
| 9 | Australia | 7 |
| | Belgium | 7 |
| | Brunei | 7 |
| | Denmark | 7 |
| | France | 7 |
| | Germany | 7 |
| | Ireland | 7 |
| | Netherlands | 7 |
| | Singapore | 7 |
| | Switzerland | 7 |
| | United Kingdom | 7 |

**Notes:** The data for the number of deaths per 1,000 population are crude rates, i.e. not adjusted for differences in age structure. Thus a country with a high proportion of older people will have a higher rate than one with a younger population. This explains why a number of developed countries have apparently high death rates.

Both death and, in particular, infant mortality rates can be underestimated in certain countries where not all deaths are officially recorded.

All rates refer to 1990-95.

# Death: *the causes*

## Cancer
%

| | | |
|---|---|---|
| 1 | Netherlands | 25.9 |
| 2 | Switzerland | 25.2 |
| 3 | France | 24.8 |
| 4 | Canada | 24.6 |
| | Denmark | 24.6 |
| 6 | Belgium | 24.5 |
| | United Kingdom | 24.5 |
| 8 | Italy | 24.0 |
| 9 | Luxembourg | 23.7 |
| 10 | New Zealand | 23.2 |
| 11 | Iceland | 23.1 |
| 12 | Austria | 22.8 |
| 13 | Australia | 22.3 |
| | Costa Rica | 22.3 |
| 15 | Germany | 22.0 |
| | Ireland | 22.0 |
| | Japan | 22.0 |
| 18 | United States | 21.9 |
| | Uruguay | 21.9 |
| 20 | Norway | 20.8 |

## Heart attack
%

| | | |
|---|---|---|
| 1 | Belorussia | 36.2 |
| 2 | Sweden | 36.0 |
| 3 | Iceland | 35.8 |
| 4 | United States | 35.6 |
| 5 | Malta | 35.0 |
| 6 | Austria | 34.6 |
| | Bahrain | 34.6 |
| | Finland | 34.6 |
| | Ex-Yugoslavia | 34.6 |
| 10 | Australia | 34.1 |
| 11 | Israel | 33.2 |
| 12 | Ireland | 32.7 |
| 13 | Ex-Soviet Union[a] | 32.5 |
| 14 | Argentina | 32.4 |
| 15 | New Zealand | 32.0 |
| 16 | Cuba | 31.8 |
| 17 | Ex-Czechoslovakia | 31.7 |
| 18 | Germany | 31.4 |
| | Greece | 31.4 |
| | Norway | 31.4 |

## Infectious disease
%

| | | |
|---|---|---|
| 1 | Guatemala | 16.5 |
| 2 | Mexico | 5.7 |
| 3 | Venezuela | 4.4 |
| 4 | Sri Lanka | 3.9 |
| 5 | Suriname | 3.8 |
| 6 | Brazil | 3.4 |
| | Kuwait | 3.4 |
| 8 | Chile | 3.3 |
| 9 | Jamaica | 3.2 |
| 10 | Argentina | 2.9 |
| 11 | Bahamas | 2.7 |
| | Singapore | 2.7 |
| 13 | Barbados | 2.4 |
| | Costa Rica | 2.4 |
| | Puerto Rico | 2.4 |
| 16 | Israel | 1.9 |
| 17 | Trinidad & Tobago | 1.7 |
| 18 | Mauritius | 1.5 |
| | Uruguay | 1.5 |
| 20 | Japan | 1.4 |
| | United States | 1.4 |

## Motor accident
%

| | | |
|---|---|---|
| 1 | Kuwait | 2.8 |
| 2 | Suriname | 2.4 |
| 3 | Venezuela | 2.3 |
| 4 | Portugal | 2.2 |
| 5 | Brazil | 2.1 |
| 6 | Greece | 1.7 |
| | Mauritius | 1.7 |
| | Mexico | 1.7 |
| | Poland | 1.7 |
| 10 | Belorussia | 1.6 |
| | Luxembourg | 1.6 |
| | New Zealand | 1.6 |
| | Ex Soviet Union[a] | 1.6 |
| | Spain | 1.6 |
| | Ukraine | 1.6 |
| 16 | Belgium | 1.5 |
| | Costa Rica | 1.5 |
| | Hungary | 1.5 |
| 19 | Australia | 1.4 |
| | France | 1.4 |
| | United States | 1.4 |

a  Includes all republics.

**Notes:** Data refer to the chances a newborn baby has of eventually dying from one of the causes shown. Statistics are only available for a limited number of countries and many less developed countries are excluded.

## Stroke
%

| | | |
|---|---|---|
| 1 | Portugal | 25.2 |
| 2 | Bulgaria | 21.7 |
| 3 | Greece | 20.8 |
| 4 | Ex-Soviet Union[a] | 19.9 |
| 5 | Jamaica | 19.3 |
| 6 | Ukraine | 17.6 |
| 7 | Ex-Czechoslovakia | 16.8 |
| | Romania | 16.8 |
| 9 | Mauritius | 16.5 |
| 10 | Luxembourg | 16.1 |
| 11 | Japan | 15.7 |
| 12 | Ex-Yugoslavia | 15.5 |
| 13 | Spain | 14.9 |
| 14 | Hungary | 14.7 |
| | Italy | 14.7 |
| 16 | Belorussia | 14.2 |
| 17 | Trinidad & Tobago | 13.9 |
| 18 | Austria | 13.8 |
| 19 | Singapore | 13.7 |
| 20 | Malta | 13.6 |

## Injury and poisoning
%

| | | |
|---|---|---|
| 1 | Hungary | 8.7 |
| | Suriname | 8.7 |
| 3 | Ex-Soviet Union[a] | 8.3 |
| 4 | France | 8.0 |
| 5 | Cuba | 7.9 |
| 6 | Ukraine | 7.7 |
| 7 | Mexico | 7.6 |
| 8 | Finland | 7.5 |
| 9 | Belorussia | 7.4 |
| 10 | Chile | 7.2 |
| | Switzerland | 7.2 |
| 12 | Brazil | 6.6 |
| | Ex-Czechoslovakia | 6.6 |
| 14 | Poland | 6.4 |
| | Sri Lanka | 6.4 |
| 16 | Bahamas | 6.3 |
| | Venezuela | 6.3 |
| 18 | Costa Rica | 6.2 |
| 19 | Denmark | 5.8 |
| 20 | Puerto Rico | 5.7 |

## AIDS
*Cases per 100,000 inhabitants[b]*

| | | | | | |
|---|---|---|---|---|---|
| 1 | Bahamas | 415.21 | 21 | Togo | 50.09 |
| 2 | Bermuda | 400.00 | 22 | Spain | 46.54 |
| 3 | Malawi | 296.70 | 23 | Haiti | 45.96 |
| 4 | Congo | 216.75 | 24 | Honduras | 44.13 |
| 5 | Uganda | 198.06 | 25 | Switzerland | 43.62 |
| 6 | Zimbabwe | 180.93 | 26 | France | 41.46 |
| 7 | Tanzania | 149.12 | 27 | Gabon | 32.64 |
| 8 | Kenya | 136.54 | 28 | Burkina Faso | 30.25 |
| 9 | Rwanda | 129.77 | 29 | Canada | 29.50 |
| 10 | Barbados | 126.92 | 30 | Italy | 28.37 |
| 11 | United States | 121.98 | 31 | Dominican Republic | 27.87 |
| 12 | CAR | 117.81 | 32 | Suriname | 27.23 |
| 13 | Burundi | 116.20 | 33 | Brazil | 25.75 |
| 14 | Côte d'Ivoire | 114.14 | 34 | Australia | 22.96 |
| 15 | Trinidad & Tobago | 97.00 | 35 | Denmark | 22.07 |
| 16 | Zambia | 82.94 | 36 | Namibia | 20.34 |
| 17 | Ghana | 65.00 | 37 | Panama | 18.46 |
| 18 | Botswana | 59.49 | 38 | Jamaica | 18.12 |
| 19 | Netherlands Antilles | 57.89 | 39 | Cameroon | 17.75 |
| 20 | Zaire | 52.79 | 40 | Netherlands | 16.68 |

b   AIDS data refer to the total number of cases reported to the World Health
Organisation up to the end of 1992. The number of cases diagnosed and reported
depends on the quality of medical practice and administration and is likely to be
under-recorded in a number of countries.

# Till death us do part

## Highest marriage rates[a]
*Number of marriages per 1,000 population*

| | | | | | | |
|---|---|---|---|---|---|---|
| 1 | Bermuda | 15.0 | | Jordan | 8.1 |
| 2 | Cuba | 15.0 | 32 | Barbados | 8.0 |
| 3 | Bangladesh | 11.3 | 33 | Turkey | 7.9 |
| 4 | Mauritius | 10.6 | 34 | Costa Rica | 7.6 |
| 5 | Azerbaijan | 10.1 | 35 | Chile | 7.5 |
| 6 | Kazakhstan | 10.0 | | Estonia | 7.5 |
| | Uzbekistan | 10.0 | | Mongolia | 7.5 |
| 8 | Cyprus | 9.9 | | Syria | 7.5 |
| 9 | Turkmenistan | 9.8 | 39 | Malta | 7.4 |
| 10 | Kirgizstan | 9.7 | | Mexico | 7.4 |
| 11 | Belorussia | 9.6 | 41 | Canada | 7.3 |
| 12 | Russia | 9.4 | | South Korea | 7.3 |
| | United States | 9.4 | 43 | Brunei | 7.2 |
| 14 | Fiji | 9.3 | 44 | Georgia | 7.0 |
| | Ukraine | 9.3 | | Israel | 7.0 |
| 16 | Lithuania | 9.2 | | Uruguay | 7.0 |
| | Moldova | 9.2 | 47 | Switzerland | 6.9 |
| | Puerto Rico | 9.2 | | Tunisia | 6.9 |
| | Tajikistan | 9.2 | 49 | Australia | 6.8 |
| 20 | Latvia | 9.1 | | New Zealand | 6.8 |
| 21 | Singapore | 9.0 | | Portugal | 6.8 |
| 22 | Albania | 8.6 | | United Kingdom | 6.8 |
| | Bahamas | 8.6 | 53 | Ex-Czechoslovakia | 6.7 |
| 24 | Iraq | 8.5 | | Ecuador | 6.7 |
| 25 | Sri Lanka | 8.4 | | Netherlands Antilles | 6.7 |
| 26 | Armenia | 8.3 | 56 | Germany | 6.5 |
| | Iran | 8.3 | 57 | Netherlands | 6.3 |
| | Romania | 8.3 | | Ex-Yugoslavia | 6.3 |
| 29 | Thailand | 8.2 | 59 | Belgium | 6.2 |
| 30 | Hong Kong | 8.1 | | Luxembourg | 6.2 |

## Youngest brides[a]
*Average age, years*

| | | |
|---|---|---|
| 1 | Niger | 15.8 |
| 2 | Guinea | 16.0 |
| 3 | Chad | 16.5 |
| 4 | Bangladesh | 16.7 |
| 5 | Gabon | 17.7 |
| | Uganda | 17.7 |
| 7 | Afghanistan | 17.8 |
| | Malawi | 17.8 |
| | Yemen | 17.8 |
| 10 | Angola | 17.9 |
| | Nepal | 17.9 |

## Oldest brides[a]
*Average age, years*

| | | |
|---|---|---|
| 1 | Jamaica | 32.2 |
| 2 | Barbados | 30.4 |
| 3 | Iceland | 28.3 |
| 4 | Netherlands | 26.7 |
| 5 | Hong Kong | 26.6 |
| 6 | Botswana | 26.4 |
| 7 | Singapore | 26.2 |
| 8 | Finland | 26.1 |
| | South Africa | 26.1 |
| 10 | Denmark | 25.6 |

a   Latest available year.

**Note:** Marriage rates refer to registered marriages only and, therefore, reflect the customs surrounding registry and efficiency of administration. The data are based on latest available figures and hence will be affected by the population age structure at the time.

## Highest divorce rates[a]
*Number of divorces per 1,000 population*

| | | | | | |
|---|---|---|---|---|---|
| **1** | United States | 4.7 | | Kirgizstan | 1.9 |
| **2** | Latvia | 4.2 | | Netherlands | 1.9 |
| **3** | Cuba | 4.1 | **33** | Azerbaijan | 1.6 |
| **4** | Russia | 3.9 | | Barbados | 1.6 |
| **5** | Puerto Rico | 3.8 | | Singapore | 1.6 |
| **6** | Estonia | 3.7 | | Tunisia | 1.6 |
| | Ukraine | 3.7 | **37** | Kuwait | 1.5 |
| **8** | Belorussia | 3.4 | | Tajikistan | 1.5 |
| **9** | Lithuania | 3.3 | | Uzbekistan | 1.5 |
| **10** | Canada | 3.1 | **40** | Georgia | 1.4 |
| **11** | Denmark | 3.0 | | Romania | 1.4 |
| **12** | Bermuda | 2.9 | | Turkmenistan | 1.4 |
| | Finland | 2.9 | **43** | Armenia | 1.3 |
| | Moldova | 2.9 | | Bulgaria | 1.3 |
| | United Kingdom | 2.9 | | Israel | 1.3 |
| **16** | Kazakhstan | 2.8 | | Japan | 1.3 |
| **17** | New Zealand | 2.7 | **47** | Bahrain | 1.2 |
| **18** | Australia | 2.5 | | Jordan | 1.2 |
| **19** | Ex-Czechoslovakia | 2.4 | | Venezuela | 1.2 |
| | Hungary | 2.4 | **50** | Bahamas | 1.1 |
| | Norway | 2.4 | | Costa Rica | 1.1 |
| **22** | Iceland | 2.3 | **52** | Hong Kong | 1.0 |
| | Luxembourg | 2.3 | | Portugal | 1.0 |
| **24** | Germany | 2.2 | **54** | Poland | 0.9 |
| | Netherlands Antilles | 2.2 | | Trinidad & Tobago | 0.9 |
| | Sweden | 2.2 | **56** | Albania | 0.8 |
| **27** | Austria | 2.1 | | Brunei | 0.8 |
| | Uruguay | 2.1 | | Ex-Yugoslavia | 0.8 |
| **29** | Switzerland | 2.0 | | Panama | 0.8 |
| **30** | France | 1.9 | | South Korea | 0.8 |

## Youngest grooms[a]
*Average age, years*

| | | |
|---|---|---|
| **1** | Nepal | 21.5 |
| | Niger | 21.5 |
| **3** | Yemen | 22.2 |
| **4** | Mozambique | 22.6 |
| | Rwanda | 22.6 |
| **6** | Malawi | 22.9 |
| **7** | Chad | 23.0 |
| **8** | CAR | 23.3 |
| **9** | India | 23.4 |
| **10** | Cuba | 23.5 |
| | Madagascar | 23.5 |

## Oldest grooms[a]
*Average age, years*

| | | |
|---|---|---|
| **1** | Jamaica | 33.8 |
| **2** | Barbados | 32.7 |
| **3** | Botswana | 30.8 |
| **4** | Iceland | 29.9 |
| **5** | Japan | 29.6 |
| | Macao | 29.6 |
| **7** | Netherlands | 29.3 |
| **8** | Hong Kong | 29.2 |
| **9** | Finland | 28.5 |
| **10** | Denmark | 28.4 |
| | Singapore | 28.4 |

# Households and prices

## Biggest households[a]
*Population per dwelling*

| | | | | | |
|---|---|---|---|---|---|
| 1 | Gabon | 8.3 | | Sudan | 5.6 |
| 2 | Iraq | 7.1 | 25 | India | 5.5 |
| 3 | Algeria | 7.0 | | Mauritania | 5.5 |
| 4 | Yemen | 6.8 | | Tunisia | 5.5 |
| 5 | Guinea | 6.7 | 28 | Benin | 5.4 |
| | Jordan | 6.7 | | Zaire | 5.4 |
| | Pakistan | 6.7 | 30 | Congo | 5.3 |
| 8 | Bahrain | 6.6 | | Philippines | 5.3 |
| 9 | Kuwait | 6.5 | | Tanzania | 5.3 |
| 10 | Niger | 6.4 | 33 | Cameroon | 5.2 |
| 11 | Syria | 6.3 | | Colombia | 5.2 |
| 12 | Burkina Faso | 6.2 | | Guatemala | 5.2 |
| | Liberia | 6.2 | | Iran | 5.2 |
| 14 | Côte d'Ivoire | 6.0 | | Malaysia | 5.2 |
| 15 | Afghanistan | 5.9 | | Myanmar | 5.2 |
| | Morocco | 5.9 | | Paraguay | 5.2 |
| 17 | Brunei | 5.8 | | Sri Lanka | 5.2 |
| | Fiji | 5.8 | | Turkey | 5.2 |
| | Nepal | 5.8 | 42 | Ecuador | 5.1 |
| 20 | Bangladesh | 5.7 | | Kenya | 5.1 |
| | Togo | 5.7 | | Peru | 5.1 |
| 22 | Mali | 5.6 | | Venezuela | 5.1 |
| | Qatar | 5.6 | | | |

## Highest cost of living[b]
*September 1993 USA=100*

| | | | | | |
|---|---|---|---|---|---|
| 1 | Japan | 213 | | Russia | 104 |
| 2 | Libya | 147 | | United Kingdom | 104 |
| 3 | Congo | 144 | 19 | China | 103 |
| 4 | Gabon | 138 | | Netherlands | 103 |
| 5 | Côte d'Ivoire | 134 | | Sweden | 103 |
| 6 | Switzerland | 132 | | Taiwan | 103 |
| 7 | Norway | 131 | 23 | Israel | 102 |
| 8 | France | 123 | 24 | Singapore | 101 |
| 9 | Austria | 119 | 25 | United States | 100 |
| 10 | Senegal | 118 | 26 | Togo | 97 |
| 11 | Cameroon | 115 | 27 | Luxembourg | 96 |
| 12 | Denmark | 109 | 28 | Ireland | 94 |
| 13 | Hong Kong | 108 | | Papua New Guinea | 94 |
| | South Korea | 108 | 30 | Argentina | 93 |
| 15 | Germany | 107 | | Finland | 93 |
| 16 | Belgium | 104 | | Spain | 93 |

a  Latest available year.
b  The cost of living index shown is compiled by The Economist Inteligence Unit for
   use by companies in determining expatriate compensation: it is a comparison of the
   cost of maintaining a typical international lifestyle in the country rather than a
   comparison of the purchasing power of a citizen of the country. The index is based
   on typical urban prices an international executive and family will face abroad. The
   prices are for products of international comparable quality found in a supermarket

## Smallest households[a]
*Population per dwelling*

| | | | | | | |
|---|---|---|---|---|---|---|
| 1 | Denmark | 2.2 | 24 | Australia | 3.0 |
| | Sweden | 2.2 | | Japan | 3.0 |
| 3 | Western Germany | 2.3 | 26 | Greece | 3.1 |
| 4 | Latvia | 2.4 | | Poland | 3.1 |
| | Norway | 2.4 | | Romania | 3.1 |
| 6 | Finland | 2.5 | 29 | Malta | 3.2 |
| | Netherlands | 2.5 | | Ukraine | 3.2 |
| | Switzerland | 2.5 | 31 | Puerto Rico | 3.3 |
| 9 | Bermuda | 2.6 | | Uruguay | 3.3 |
| | France | 2.6 | 33 | Hong Kong | 3.4 |
| | United States | 2.6 | 34 | Cyprus | 3.5 |
| 12 | Austria | 2.7 | | Israel | 3.5 |
| | Belgium | 2.7 | | Spain | 3.5 |
| | Canada | 2.7 | 37 | Barbados | 3.6 |
| | Hungary | 2.7 | | Ex-Yugoslavia | 3.6 |
| 16 | Ex-Czechoslovakia | 2.8 | | Ireland | 3.6 |
| | Italy | 2.8 | | Macao | 3.6 |
| | Luxembourg | 2.8 | 41 | Bahamas | 3.8 |
| | New Zealand | 2.8 | | Belorussia | 3.8 |
| | United Kingdom | 2.8 | | Bolivia | 3.8 |
| 21 | Bulgaria | 2.9 | | South Korea | 3.8 |
| | Portugal | 2.9 | 45 | Argentina | 3.9 |
| | Russia | 2.9 | | | |

## Lowest cost of living[b]
*September 1993 USA=100*

| | | | | | |
|---|---|---|---|---|---|
| 1 | India | 38 | 18 | Ecuador | 64 |
| 2 | Iran | 41 | | Peru | 64 |
| 3 | Ex-Yugoslavia | 42 | 20 | Chile | 65 |
| 4 | Kenya | 45 | | South Africa | 65 |
| | Zimbabwe | 45 | 22 | Algeria | 67 |
| 6 | Czech Republic | 52 | 23 | Tunisia | 70 |
| | Pakistan | 52 | 24 | Kuwait | 71 |
| | Venezuela | 52 | 25 | Brunei | 72 |
| 9 | Paraguay | 57 | | Guatemala | 72 |
| 10 | Philippines | 58 | 27 | Morocco | 73 |
| 11 | Hungary | 59 | | Panama | 73 |
| 12 | Poland | 60 | 29 | Saudi Arabia | 75 |
| 13 | Nigeria | 61 | 30 | New Zealand | 76 |
| | Turkey | 61 | 31 | Brazil | 77 |
| 15 | Bangladesh | 62 | | Malaysia | 77 |
| | Sri Lanka | 62 | | Thailand | 77 |
| 17 | Colombia | 63 | | UAE | 77 |

or department store. Prices found in local markets and bazaars are not used unless the available merchandise is of the specified quality and the shopping area itself is safe for executive and family members. New York City prices are used as the base, so USA = 100. Francophone countries in Sub-Saharan Africa using the CFA Franc appear expensive because their currencies were over-valued before the January 12th 1994 devaluation.

# **Consumer goods:** *ownership*

## TV

*Number of people per receiver, 1991*

| | | | | | |
|---|---|---|---|---|---|
| 1 | Bermuda | 0.9 | | Switzerland | 2.5 |
| 2 | United States | 1.2 | 27 | Latvia | 2.6 |
| 3 | Malta | 1.4 | | Qatar | 2.6 |
| | Oman | 1.4 | 29 | Lithuania | 2.7 |
| 5 | Canada | 1.6 | | Russia | 2.7 |
| | Japan | 1.6 | | Singapore | 2.7 |
| 7 | Germany | 1.8 | 32 | Estonia | 2.8 |
| 8 | Denmark | 1.9 | 33 | Netherlands Antilles | 3.0 |
| 9 | Finland | 2.0 | | Ukraine | 3.0 |
| 10 | Australia | 2.1 | 35 | Iceland | 3.2 |
| | Austria | 2.1 | | Trinidad & Tobago | 3.2 |
| | Ex-Czechoslovakia | 2.1 | 37 | Ireland | 3.4 |
| | Netherlands | 2.1 | | Poland | 3.4 |
| 14 | Belgium | 2.2 | 39 | Hong Kong | 3.6 |
| | Sweden | 2.2 | 40 | Belorussia | 3.7 |
| 16 | New Zealand | 2.3 | 41 | Barbados | 3.8 |
| | United Kingdom | 2.3 | | Puerto Rico | 3.8 |
| 18 | Hungary | 2.4 | 43 | Israel | 3.9 |
| | Italy | 2.4 | | Luxembourg | 3.9 |
| | Kuwait | 2.4 | | Saudi Arabia | 3.9 |
| | Norway | 2.4 | 46 | Bulgaria | 4.0 |
| 22 | Bahrain | 2.5 | 47 | Lebanon | 4.2 |
| | France | 2.5 | 48 | Uruguay | 4.3 |
| | South Korea | 2.5 | 49 | Brunei | 4.4 |
| | Spain | 2.5 | 50 | Bahamas | 4.5 |

## Telephone[a]

*Number of people per telephone*

| | | | | | |
|---|---|---|---|---|---|
| 1 | Bermuda | 1.0 | | Japan | 1.9 |
| | Denmark | 1.0 | 24 | Australia | 2.0 |
| | Sweden | 1.0 | | Malta | 2.0 |
| | United States | 1.0 | 26 | Israel | 2.1 |
| 5 | Switzerland | 1.1 | 27 | Barbados | 2.2 |
| 6 | Norway | 1.3 | | Greece | 2.2 |
| | United Kingdom | 1.3 | 29 | Ex-Yugoslavia | 2.3 |
| 8 | Canada | 1.4 | | Singapore | 2.3 |
| | Finland | 1.4 | | Spain | 2.3 |
| | New Zealand | 1.4 | 32 | Ex-Czechoslovakia | 2.4 |
| 11 | Iceland | 1.5 | | UAE | 2.4 |
| | Luxembourg | 1.5 | 34 | Ireland | 2.9 |
| 13 | Netherlands | 1.6 | | Taiwan | 2.9 |
| | South Korea | 1.6 | 36 | Bulgaria | 3.4 |
| 15 | Austria | 1.7 | 37 | Bahrain | 3.5 |
| | France | 1.7 | 38 | Portugal | 3.6 |
| 17 | Belgium | 1.8 | 39 | Qatar | 3.8 |
| | Germany | 1.8 | 40 | Kuwait | 3.9 |
| | Hong Kong | 1.8 | 41 | Macao | 4.4 |
| | Italy | 1.8 | 42 | Hungary | 5.4 |
| 21 | Bahamas | 1.9 | | Libya | 5.4 |
| | Cyprus | 1.9 | | Uruguay | 5.4 |

## Home computer[a]
*% of households owning*

| | | | | | |
|---|---|---|---|---|---|
| 1 | Netherlands | 25 | 11 | Ireland | 12 |
| 2 | United Kingdom | 18 | | Italy | 12 |
| 3 | Finland | 16 | | Japan | 12 |
| | Norway | 16 | | Luxembourg | 12 |
| | United States | 16 | | Sweden | 12 |
| | Western Germany | 16 | 16 | Austria | 11 |
| 7 | Belgium | 15 | 17 | Spain | 8 |
| 8 | Denmark | 14 | 18 | Portugal | 7 |
| | France | 14 | 19 | Greece | 6 |
| | Switzerland | 14 | | | |

## Video cassette recorder
*% of households owning*

| | | | | | |
|---|---|---|---|---|---|
| 1 | Japan | 98 | | Sweden | 56 |
| 2 | United Kingdom | 72 | 11 | France | 54 |
| 3 | Canada | 70 | 12 | Belgium | 48 |
| | United States | 70 | | Ireland | 48 |
| 5 | Switzerland | 68 | 14 | South Korea | 46 |
| 6 | Austria | 59 | 15 | Denmark | 45 |
| | Finland | 59 | | Spain | 45 |
| 8 | Netherlands | 58 | 17 | Norway | 43 |
| 9 | Germany | 56 | 18 | Italy | 38 |

## Dishwasher[a]
*% of households owning*

| | | | | | |
|---|---|---|---|---|---|
| 1 | United States | 51 | 11 | Belgium | 26 |
| 2 | Luxembourg | 50 | | Denmark | 26 |
| 3 | Iceland | 45 | 13 | Italy | 18 |
| 4 | Norway | 37 | 14 | Ireland | 15 |
| 5 | Austria | 35 | 15 | Portugal | 14 |
| 6 | Western Germany | 34 | 16 | Greece | 11 |
| 7 | France | 33 | | Netherlands | 11 |
| 8 | Switzerland | 32 | | Spain | 11 |
| 9 | Finland | 31 | | United Kingdom | 11 |
| | Sweden | 31 | | | |

## Microwave[a]
*% of households owning*

| | | | | | |
|---|---|---|---|---|---|
| 1 | United States | 80 | 11 | Belgium | 21 |
| 2 | Japan | 79 | 12 | Ireland | 20 |
| 3 | Finland | 53 | 13 | Luxembourg | 16 |
| 4 | United Kingdom | 48 | 14 | Switzerland | 15 |
| 5 | Sweden | 37 | 15 | Denmark | 14 |
| 6 | Western Germany | 36 | 16 | Spain | 9 |
| 7 | Norway | 34 | 17 | Italy | 6 |
| 8 | Austria | 31 | 18 | Portugal | 4 |
| 9 | France | 25 | 19 | Greece | 2 |
| 10 | Netherlands | 22 | | | |

a Latest available year up to 1992.
**Note:** A number of difficulties arise when dealing with household penetration data. Definitions of articles may vary.

# Culture and crime

## Books published[a]
*Per year*

| | | |
|---|---|---|
| 1 | United Kingdom | 86,573 |
| 2 | Ex-Soviet Union | 76,711 |
| 3 | China | 73,923 |
| 4 | Germany | 67,890 |
| 5 | France | 43,682 |
| 6 | Spain | 39,082 |
| 7 | South Korea | 29,432 |
| 8 | Italy | 27,751 |
| 9 | Switzerland | 14,886 |
| 10 | India | 13,937 |
| 11 | Belgium | 13,913 |
| 12 | Netherlands | 13,691 |
| 13 | Sweden | 11,866 |
| 14 | Finland | 11,208 |
| 15 | Australia | 10,723 |
| 16 | Poland | 10,688 |
| 17 | Denmark | 10,198 |
| 18 | Ex-Yugoslavia | 9,797 |
| 19 | Ex-Czechoslovakia | 9,362 |
| 20 | Hungary | 8,133 |

## Library book loans[a]
*'000 per year*

| | | |
|---|---|---|
| 1 | United Kingdom | 564,525 |
| 2 | Ukraine | 519,600 |
| 3 | Germany | 324,857 |
| 4 | Japan | 203,133 |
| 5 | China | 180,660 |
| 6 | Canada | 176,185 |
| 7 | Netherlands | 174,182 |
| 8 | Poland | 154,891 |
| 9 | France | 120,000 |
| 10 | Ex-Czechoslovakia | 96,074 |
| 11 | Finland | 85,700 |
| 12 | Denmark | 78,280 |
| 13 | Sweden | 73,307 |
| 14 | Romania | 54,025 |
| 15 | Hungary | 47,996 |
| 16 | Mexico | 45,701 |
| 17 | Bulgaria | 24,088 |
| 18 | Norway | 19,130 |
| 19 | Spain | 16,981 |
| 20 | South Korea | 13,911 |

## Cinema attendances[a]
*Per head per year*

| | | |
|---|---|---|
| 1 | China | 14.1 |
| 2 | Ukraine | 11.9 |
| 3 | Hong Kong | 10.3 |
| | Ex-Soviet Union[b] | 10.3 |
| 5 | Mongolia | 9.4 |
| 6 | Romania | 5.6 |
| 7 | Iceland | 5.2 |
| 8 | India | 5.0 |
| 9 | United States | 3.9 |
| 10 | Vietnam | 3.8 |
| 11 | Ex-Czechoslovakia | 3.2 |
| 12 | Canada | 3.0 |
| 13 | Bulgaria | 2.9 |
| 14 | Cuba | 2.8 |
| 15 | Norway | 2.5 |
| 16 | Australia | 2.4 |
| 17 | Switzerland | 2.3 |
| 18 | Albania | 2.2 |
| 19 | Hungary | 2.1 |
| | France | 2.1 |

## Most translated authors[c]

| 1987 | | No. of translations |
|---|---|---|
| 1 | A. Christie | 366 |
| 2 | W. Disney Productions | 309 |
| 3 | V.I. Lenin | 251 |
| 4 | J. Verne | 229 |
| 5 | M.S. Gorbachev | 186 |
| 6 | E. Blyton | 175 |
| 7 | B. Cartland | 167 |
| 8 | I. Asimov | 128 |
| 9 | A. Maclean | 114 |
| 10 | R. Goscinny | 113 |
| 11 | G. Simenon | 111 |
| 12 | H.C. Andersen | 106 |
| | A.C. Doyle | 106 |
| | S. King | 106 |
| 15 | V. Holt | 94 |
| 16 | J. London | 89 |
| 17 | M. Twain | 87 |
| 18 | W. Vandersteen | 86 |
| 19 | W. Shakespeare | 83 |
| 20 | K. Marx | 81 |

a  Data for books, libraries and cinemas are for 1991 or the latest available year.
b  Excluding Ukraine
c  The Bible was translated 73 times in 14 countries in 1987.

## Biggest wine drinkers
*Average annual consumption of litres per head*

| | | |
|---|---|---|
| 1 | Italy | 69.6 |
| 2 | France | 65.4 |
| 3 | Portugal | 55.7 |
| 4 | Switzerland | 44.5 |
| 5 | Austria | 35.9 |
| 6 | Argentina | 35.6 |
| 7 | Spain | 35.5 |
| 8 | Malta | 27.9 |
| 9 | Ex-Yugoslavia | 27.6 |
| 10 | Romania | 26.5 |
| 11 | Bulgaria | 26.3 |
| 12 | Belgium | 25.8 |
| 13 | Hungary | 25.7 |
| 14 | Germany | 25.4 |
| 15 | Greece | 23.9 |
| 16 | Denmark | 21.7 |
| 17 | Chile | 19.0 |
| 18 | Australia | 18.3 |
| 19 | New Zealand | 16.2 |
| 20 | Netherlands | 16.1 |

## Biggest smokers
*Average annual consumption of cigarettes per head, per day*

| | | |
|---|---|---|
| 1 | Malta | 8.2 |
| 2 | Austria | 8.0 |
| 3 | Hungary | 7.9 |
| 4 | Greece | 7.8 |
| 5 | Poland | 7.5 |
| 6 | Japan[a] | 7.2 |
| 7 | Switzerland | 6.5 |
| 8 | Spain | 6.1 |
| 9 | South Korea[a] | 5.9 |
| 10 | Australia[a] | 5.8 |
| 11 | United States[a] | 5.5 |
| 12 | Luxembourg | 5.2 |
| | Ex-Yugoslavia | 5.2 |
| 14 | Ex-Czechoslovakia | 5.1 |
| | Germany | 5.1 |
| 16 | Belgium | 4.7 |
| | France | 4.7 |
| | Ireland | 4.7 |
| 19 | Taiwan[a] | 4.6 |
| 20 | Portugal | 4.4 |

## Murders[b]
*Number per 100,000 pop., 1990*

| | | |
|---|---|---|
| 1 | Bahamas | 52.61 |
| 2 | Philippines | 30.12 |
| 3 | Guatemala | 27.40 |
| 4 | Jamaica | 20.85 |
| 5 | Botswana | 19.50 |
| 6 | Zimbabwe | 17.88 |
| 7 | Peru | 12.01 |
| 8 | Barbados | 11.67 |
| 9 | Sri Lanka | 11.60 |
| 10 | Malta | 10.44 |
| 11 | Paraguay | 10.00 |
| 12 | Thailand | 9.50 |
| 13 | United States | 9.40 |
| 14 | Ex-Soviet Union | 8.67 |
| 15 | Trinidad & Tobago | 8.42 |
| 16 | Papua New Guinea | 7.78 |
| 17 | Sweden | 7.02 |
| 18 | Taiwan | 6.40 |

## Drug offences[b]
*Number per 100,000 pop., 1990*

| | | |
|---|---|---|
| 1 | Bahamas | 460.2 |
| 2 | Sweden | 326.1 |
| 3 | Switzerland | 279.7 |
| 4 | Denmark | 271.2 |
| 5 | Canada[c] | 258.9 |
| 6 | Trinidad & Tobago | 236.6 |
| 7 | Barbados | 216.0 |
| 8 | Norway | 213.9 |
| 9 | Jamaica | 212.8 |
| 10 | Luxembourg | 201.9 |
| 11 | Germany | 165.3 |
| 12 | Israel | 161.8 |
| 13 | France | 99.9 |
| 14 | Mauritius | 89.5 |
| 15 | Botswana[c] | 85.5 |
| 16 | Brunei | 80.3 |
| 17 | Sri Lanka | 71.2 |
| 18 | Austria | 69.5 |

a   1991.
b   Crime statistics are based on offences recorded by the police. The number will therefore depend partly on the efficiency of police administration systems, the definition of offences, and the proportion of crimes reported, and therefore may not be strictly comparable.
c   1988.

# Environment: *trees and disasters*

## Top deforesters

*Average annual rate, km² 1981-90*

| | | | | | |
|---|---|---|---|---|---|
| 1 | Brazil | -36,710 | 22 | Vietnam | -1,370 |
| 2 | Indonesia | -12,120 | 23 | Madagascar | -1,350 |
| 3 | Zaire | -7,320 | | Mozambique | -1,350 |
| 4 | Mexico | -6,780 | 25 | Cambodia | -1,310 |
| 5 | Bolivia | -6,250 | 26 | CAR | -1,290 |
| 6 | Venezuela | -5,990 | | Laos | -1,290 |
| 7 | Thailand | -5,150 | 27 | Nicaragua | -1,240 |
| 8 | Sudan | -4,820 | 28 | Cameroon | -1,220 |
| 9 | Tanzania | -4,380 | 29 | Côte d'Ivoire | -1,190 |
| 10 | Paraguay | -4,030 | | Nigeria | -1,190 |
| 11 | Myanmar | -4,010 | 31 | Gabon | -1,160 |
| 12 | Malaysia | -3,960 | 32 | Papua New Guinea | -1,130 |
| 13 | Colombia | -3,670 | 33 | Honduras | -1,120 |
| 14 | Zambia | -3,630 | 34 | Mali | -1,060 |
| 15 | India | -3,390 | 35 | Chad | -890 |
| 16 | United States | -3,170 | 36 | Guinea | -870 |
| 17 | Philippines | -3,160 | 37 | Guatemala | -810 |
| 18 | Peru | -2,710 | 38 | Botswana | -770 |
| 19 | Ecuador | -2,380 | | Pakistan | -770 |
| 20 | Angola | -1,740 | 40 | Benin | -700 |
| 21 | Ghana | -1,380 | | | |

## Top reafforesters

*Average annual rate, km² 1980s*

| | | | | | |
|---|---|---|---|---|---|
| 1 | China | 45,520 | 6 | Japan | 2,400 |
| 2 | Ex-Soviet Union | 45,400 | 7 | Sweden | 2,070 |
| 3 | United States | 17,750 | 8 | North Korea | 2,000 |
| 4 | Canada | 7,200 | 9 | Finland | 1,580 |
| 5 | Brazil | 4,490 | 10 | India | 1,380 |

## Fastest forest depletion

*% average annual decrease in forested area, 1981-90*

| | | | | | |
|---|---|---|---|---|---|
| 1 | Jamaica | 5.3 | | Nicaragua | 1.7 |
| 2 | Haiti | 3.9 | | Panama | 1.7 |
| 3 | Bangladesh | 3.3 | 17 | Guatemala | 1.6 |
| 4 | Pakistan | 2.9 | 18 | Togo | 1.4 |
| | Philippines | 2.9 | | Vietnam | 1.4 |
| | Thailand | 2.9 | 20 | Ghana | 1.3 |
| 7 | Costa Rica | 2.6 | | Ireland | 1.3 |
| 8 | Dominican Republic | 2.5 | | Malawi | 1.3 |
| 9 | Paraguay | 2.4 | | Sri Lanka | 1.3 |
| 10 | El Salvador | 2.1 | 24 | Benin | 1.2 |
| 11 | Honduras | 1.9 | | Mexico | 1.2 |
| | Trinidad & Tobago | 1.9 | | Myanmar | 1.2 |
| 13 | Malaysia | 1.8 | | Tanzania | 1.2 |
| 14 | Ecuador | 1.7 | | Venezuela | 1.2 |

## Most forested countries
*% of total area covered with forest, 1991*

| | | | | | |
|---|---|---|---|---|---|
| 1 | Suriname | 91 | | Sweden | 62 |
| 2 | Papua New Guinea | 83 | 13 | Guinea | 59 |
| 3 | Cambodia | 74 | 14 | Brazil | 58 |
| | Gabon | 74 | | Malaysia | 58 |
| | North Korea | 74 | 16 | CAR | 57 |
| | Zaire | 74 | | Indonesia | 57 |
| 7 | Finland | 69 | 18 | Bhutan | 55 |
| 8 | Japan | 67 | 19 | Laos | 53 |
| 9 | Fiji | 65 | | Peru | 53 |
| | South Korea | 65 | | Senegal | 53 |
| 11 | Congo | 62 | | | |

## Oil tanker spills

| | Country affected | Oil spilled ('000 tonnes) | Name | Flag | Year |
|---|---|---|---|---|---|
| 1 | Trinidad & Tobago | 276 | Atlantic Express | Greece | 1979 |
| 2 | South Africa | 256 | Castello de Belvar | Spain | 1983 |
| 3 | France | 228 | Amoco Cadiz | Liberia | 1978 |
| 4 | Canada | 140 | Odyssey | Liberia | 1988 |
| 5 | United Kingdom | 121 | Torrey Canyon | Liberia | 1967 |
| 6 | Oman | 120 | Sea Star | South Korea | 1972 |
| 7 | Greece | 102 | Irenes Serenade | Greece | 1980 |
| 8 | Spain | 101 | Urquiola | Spain | 1976 |
| 9 | United States | 99 | Hawaiian Patriot | Liberia | 1977 |
| 10 | Turkey | 95 | Independenta | Romania | 1979 |

## Industrial disasters, 1983-92[a]

| | Location | Origin of accident | Deaths |
|---|---|---|---|
| 1983 | Nile, Egypt | gas explosion | 317 |
| 1984 | St J Ixhuatepec | gas explosion | 503 |
| | Bhopal, India | chemical leakage | 2,800 |
| | Cubatao, Brazil | pipeline explosion | 508 |
| 1986 | Chernobyl, Ex-Soviet Union | reactor explosion | 31 |
| | Miamisburg, USA | rail accident | ... |
| 1987 | Shangsi, China | fertiliser misuse | ... |
| 1988 | Islamabad, Pakistan | explosives | 100 |
| | Arzamas, Ex-Soviet Union | explosives | 73 |
| | Tours, France | chemical leakage | ... |
| | North Sea, UK | oil explosion | 167 |
| | Sverdlosk, Ex-Soviet Union | explosives | 5 |
| 1989 | Ionava, Ex-Soviet Union | chemical explosion | 6 |
| | Acha Ufa, Ex-Soviet Union | gas explosion | 575 |
| 1990 | Ufa, Ex-Soviet Union | chemical explosion | ... |
| | Bangkok, Thailand | explosion (lorry) | 54 |
| | Patna, India | explosion (train) | 100 |
| 1991 | Thailand | explosives | 171 |
| | Livorno, Italy | oil explosion | 140 |
| | Sterlington, USA | gas explosion | 8 |
| 1992 | Kozlu, Turkey | gas explosion | 270 |

a Not ranked due to difficulties in comparing the effects of each.

# Environment: *pollution and waste*

## Carbon dioxide emissions
*Kg per head*

| | | | | | | |
|---|---|---|---|---|---|---|
| 1 | Qatar | 44,700 | | 21 | Ireland | 9,230 |
| 2 | UAE | 36,490 | | | Netherlands | 9,230 |
| 3 | Iraq | 27,860 | | 23 | Libya | 9,120 |
| 4 | Luxembourg | 27,500 | | 24 | Japan | 8,790 |
| 5 | United States | 19,530 | | 25 | Poland | 8,060 |
| 6 | Bahrain | 19,400 | | 26 | Austria | 7,800 |
| 7 | Canada | 15,210 | | 27 | Oman | 7,400 |
| 8 | Australia | 15,100 | | 28 | Israel | 7,290 |
| 9 | Singapore | 15,060 | | 29 | Greece | 7,180 |
| 10 | Trinidad & Tobago | 14,730 | | | South Africa | 7,180 |
| 11 | Saudi Arabia | 13,960 | | 31 | Iceland | 7,000 |
| 12 | Norway | 13,740 | | 32 | Italy | 6,960 |
| 13 | Ex-Soviet Union | 12,310 | | | New Zealand | 6,960 |
| 14 | Denmark | 12,240 | | 34 | France | 6,560 |
| 15 | Ex-Czechoslovakia | 12,200 | | | Bulgaria | 6,300 |
| 16 | Germany | 12,130 | | 36 | Sweden | 6,230 |
| 17 | North Korea | 10,960 | | 37 | Switzerland | 6,160 |
| 18 | Finland | 10,410 | | | Venezuela | 6,160 |
| 19 | Belgium | 10,220 | | 39 | Hungary | 6,050 |
| 20 | United Kingdom | 10,000 | | | South Korea | 6,050 |

## Nitrogen oxide emissions
*Kg per head*

| | | | | | | |
|---|---|---|---|---|---|---|
| 1 | United States | 73.4 | | 11 | Ireland | 36.2 |
| 2 | Canada | 69.1 | | 12 | Italy[a] | 34.5 |
| 3 | Luxembourg | 56.6 | | 13 | Belgium | 29.9 |
| 4 | Finland | 56.5 | | 14 | Austria | 27.3 |
| 5 | Denmark | 54.8 | | 15 | France | 26.3 |
| 6 | Norway | 50.9 | | 16 | Switzerland | 25.5 |
| 7 | United Kingdom | 47.6 | | 17 | Spain | 23.4 |
| 8 | Sweden | 44.7 | | 18 | Portugal | 14.4 |
| 9 | Germany | 40.1 | | 19 | Japan | 10.5 |
| 10 | Netherlands | 36.3 | | | | |

## Sulphur dioxide emissions
*Kg per head*

| | | | | | | |
|---|---|---|---|---|---|---|
| 1 | Canada | 118.7 | | 11 | Luxembourg | 25.7 |
| 2 | United States | 81.2 | | 12 | France | 22.9 |
| 3 | Germany | 70.7 | | 13 | Portugal | 21.4 |
| 4 | United Kingdom | 61.8 | | 14 | Netherlands | 13.5 |
| 5 | Spain | 56.1 | | 15 | Sweden | 12.2 |
| 6 | Ireland | 52.9 | | 16 | Norway | 10.7 |
| 7 | Belgium | 41.8 | | 17 | Austria | 10.6 |
| 8 | Finland | 38.3 | | 18 | Switzerland | 8.9 |
| 9 | Denmark | 35.0 | | 19 | Japan | 7.0 |
| 10 | Italy[a] | 34.4 | | | | |

## Solid hazardous waste generated
*Kg per head*

| | | | | | |
|---|---|---|---|---|---|
| 1 | Luxembourg | 1,989 | 11 | France | 69 |
| 2 | United States | 705 | | Netherlands | 69 |
| 3 | Ex-Czechoslovakia | 701 | 13 | Finland | 62 |
| 4 | Hungary | 392 | 14 | Sweden | 57 |
| 5 | Canada | 218 | 15 | Italy | 56 |
| 6 | Portugal | 106 | 16 | Norway | 47 |
| 7 | Belgium | 93 | 17 | United Kingdom | 44 |
| 8 | Austria | 78 | | Spain | 44 |
| 9 | Switzerland | 76 | 19 | Greece | 43 |
| 10 | Germany | 74 | 20 | New Zealand | 32 |

## Solid industrial waste generated
*Kg per head*

| | | | | | |
|---|---|---|---|---|---|
| 1 | Luxembourg | 3,485 | 11 | Italy | 701 |
| 2 | United States | 3,049 | 12 | Norway[b] | 519 |
| 3 | Belgium | 2,712 | 13 | Sweden | 474 |
| 4 | Japan | 2,529 | 14 | Denmark | 467 |
| 5 | Canada | 2,300 | 15 | Netherlands | 447 |
| 6 | Finland | 2,111 | 16 | Greece | 428 |
| 7 | Austria | 1,748 | 17 | Ireland | 425 |
| 8 | Western Germany | 1,002 | 18 | Ex-Yugoslavia | 301 |
| 9 | France | 891 | 19 | Spain | 130 |
| 10 | United Kingdom | 874 | 20 | Portugal | 64 |

## Solid municipal waste generated
*Kg per head*

| | | | | | |
|---|---|---|---|---|---|
| 1 | United States | 721 | 11 | Sweden | 374 |
| 2 | Finland | 624 | 12 | Germany | 350 |
| 3 | Canada | 601 | 13 | United Kingdom | 348 |
| 4 | Netherlands | 497 | | Italy | 348 |
| 5 | Denmark | 475 | 15 | Belgium | 343 |
| 6 | Norway | 472 | 16 | Poland | 338 |
| 7 | Hungary | 463 | 17 | France | 328 |
| 8 | Luxembourg | 445 | 18 | Austria | 325 |
| 9 | Switzerland | 441 | 19 | Spain | 322 |
| 10 | Japan | 411 | 20 | Iceland | 314 |

a   Excluding emissions from industrial processes.
b   Wastes from the chemical industry only.

The statistics for all tables (including those on page 82) except carbon dioxide
emissions, fresh water resources and water use cover OECD and emerging Eastern
European countries only. They normally refer to various years in the mid to late 1980s,
though some refer to an earlier period.

# Environment: *recycling and water*

## Glass recycling
*Recovery rates, %*

| | | | | | |
|---|---|---|---|---|---|
| 1 | Netherlands | 66.7 | 11 | Finland | 35.7 |
| 2 | Switzerland | 64.7 | 12 | Portugal | 30.0 |
| 3 | Denmark | 60.4 | 13 | France | 28.5 |
| 4 | Austria | 60.0 | 14 | Spain | 27.0 |
| 5 | Belgium | 55.0 | 15 | Ireland | 23.0 |
| 6 | Japan | 54.4 | 16 | United Kingdom | 21.0 |
| 7 | New Zealand[a] | 53.0 | 17 | United States | 19.9 |
| 8 | Italy | 48.0 | 18 | Greece | 15.0 |
| 9 | Germany | 45.0 | 19 | Canada | 12.0 |
| 10 | Sweden | 44.0 | 20 | Norway | 10.0 |

## Paper recycling
*Recovery rates, %*

| | | | | | |
|---|---|---|---|---|---|
| 1 | Spain | 51.0 | 11 | Austria | 36.8 |
| 2 | Netherlands | 50.3 | 12 | Denmark | 35.4 |
| 3 | Japan | 49.6 | 13 | United Kingdom | 31.0 |
| 4 | Switzerland | 49.4 | 14 | Greece | 30.0 |
| 5 | France | 45.7 | 15 | United States | 28.6 |
| 6 | Sweden | 42.9 | 16 | Norway | 26.0 |
| 7 | Finland | 40.8 | 17 | Canada | 20.0 |
| 8 | Germany | 39.6 | 18 | New Zealand | 19.0 |
| 9 | Portugal | 39.1 | 19 | Belgium | 14.7 |
| 10 | Italy | 38.0 | 20 | Ireland | 3.0 |

## Freshwater resources
*Cubic metres per head, '000*

| | | | | | |
|---|---|---|---|---|---|
| 1 | Iceland | 653.9 | 11 | Bhutan | 58.9 |
| 2 | Suriname | 456.6 | 12 | Panama | 57.3 |
| 3 | Papua New Guinea | 197.5 | 13 | CAR | 44.4 |
| 4 | Gabon | 132.6 | 14 | Nicaragua | 44.3 |
| 5 | New Zealand | 114.9 | 15 | Venezuela | 42.4 |
| 6 | Canada | 106.0 | 16 | Bolivia | 39.9 |
| 7 | Norway | 94.5 | 17 | Fiji | 38.6 |
| 8 | Liberia | 84.3 | 18 | Guinea | 37.0 |
| 9 | Congo | 76.4 | 19 | Sierra Leone | 36.6 |
| 10 | Laos | 64.4 | 20 | Chile | 34.4 |

## Water use
*Cubic metres per head, latest year*

| | | | | | |
|---|---|---|---|---|---|
| 1 | Iraq | 4,575 | 11 | Spain | 1,184 |
| 2 | Pakistan | 2,053 | 12 | Suriname | 1,155 |
| 3 | United States | 1,952 | 13 | Romania | 1,144 |
| 4 | Afghanistan | 1,706 | 14 | Sudan | 1,092 |
| 5 | Canada | 1,684 | 15 | Portugal | 1,075 |
| 6 | Madagascar | 1,642 | 16 | Australia | 1,060 |
| 7 | Chile | 1,623 | 17 | Argentina | 1,042 |
| 8 | Bulgaria | 1,600 | 18 | Netherlands | 993 |
| 9 | Iran | 1,362 | 19 | Italy | 984 |
| 10 | Egypt | 1,213 | 20 | Belgium | 917 |

a   Refillable glass bottles only.     See also note on page 81.

# ═══Part II═══
# COUNTRY PROFILES

# ALGERIA

| | | | |
|---|---|---|---|
| Area | 2,381,741sq km | Currency | Algerian dinar (AD) |
| Capital | Algiers | | |

## People

| | | | | |
|---|---|---|---|---|
| Population | 26.4m | Life expectancy: men | | 65 yrs |
| Pop. per sq km | 12 | women | | 67 yrs |
| Av. ann. growth | | Adult literacy | | 57.4% |
| in pop. 1985–92 | 2.7% | Fertility rate (per woman) | | 4.9 |
| Pop. under 15 | 41.3% | | | |
| Pop. over 65 | 3.4% | | *per 1,000 pop.* | |
| No. of men per 100 women | 100 | Crude birth rate | | 34.0 |
| Human Development Index | 53 | Crude death rate | | 7.0 |

## The economy

| | | | |
|---|---|---|---|
| GDP | AD1,048bn | GDP per head | $1,832 |
| GDP | $48bn | GDP per head in purchasing | |
| Av. ann. growth in real | | power parity (USA=100) | 14 |
| GDP 1985–92 | 1.1% | | |

| Origins of GDP | | Components of GDP | |
|---|---|---|---|
| | *% of total* | | *% of total* |
| Agriculture | 12.0 | Private consumption | 48.5 |
| Industry, of which: | 49.3 | Public consumption | 15.9 |
| manufacturing | 10.1 | Investment | 29.8 |
| Services | 17.9 | Exports | 30.7 |
| | | Imports | -25.0 |

## Structure of manufacturing

| | *% of total* | | *% of total* |
|---|---|---|---|
| Agric. & food processing | 20 | Other | 50 |
| Textiles & clothing | 17 | Av. ann. increase in industrial | |
| Metal products & machinery | 13 | output 1980–91 | 1.8% |

## Energy

| | *'000 TCE* | | |
|---|---|---|---|
| Total output | 149,880 | % output exported | 78.6 |
| Total consumption | 26,767 | % consumption imported | 6.6 |
| Consumption per head, | | | |
| kg coal equivalent | 1,044 | | |

## Inflation and finance

| | | | |
|---|---|---|---|
| Consumer price | | *av. ann. increase 1988–92* | |
| inflation 1993 | 25.0% | Narrow money (M1) | 11.0% |
| Av. ann. inflation 1988–93 | 17.5% | Broad money | 15.2% |

## Exchange rates

| | *end 1993* | | *end June 1993* |
|---|---|---|---|
| AD per $ | 24.12 | Effective rates | 1985 = 100 |
| AD per SDR | 33.13 | – nominal | ... |
| AD per Ecu | 27.01 | – real | ... |

## Principal exports[a]

| | $bn fob | | $bn fob |
|---|---|---|---|
| Energy & products | 12.0 | Total including others | **12.3** |

### Main export destinations

| | % of total | | % of total |
|---|---|---|---|
| Italy | 20.0 | Germany | 12.5 |
| France | 15.1 | Spain | 9.1 |
| United States | 13.7 | Netherlands | 5.0 |

## Principal imports[b]

| | $bn cif | | $bn cif |
|---|---|---|---|
| Machinery & industrial equipment | 3.7 | Semi-finished products | 1.8 |
| | | Consumer goods | 1.1 |
| Agric. products & foodstuffs | 2.1 | Total incl. others | **9.5** |

### Main origins of imports

| | % of total | | % of total |
|---|---|---|---|
| France | 29.2 | Spain | 9.0 |
| Italy | 13.8 | United States | 8.8 |
| Germany | 7.0 | Belgium/Luxembourg | 4.1 |

## Balance of payments[c], reserves and debt, $m

| | | | |
|---|---|---|---|
| Visible exports fob | 12,330 | Overall balance | 1,047 |
| Visible imports fob | -6,852 | Change in reserves | 436 |
| Trade balance | 5,478 | Level of reserves | |
| Invisibles inflows | 463 | end Dec. | 1,726 |
| Invisibles outflows | -3,790 | No. months import cover | 3.0 |
| Net transfers | 216 | Foreign debt | 26,349 |
| Current account balance | 2,367 | – as % of GDP | 61.0 |
| – as % of GDP | 4.5 | Debt service | 8,841 |
| Capital balance | -999 | Debt service ratio | 71.9 |

## Family life

| | | | |
|---|---|---|---|
| No. of households | 3.3m | Divorces per 1,000 pop. | ... |
| Av. no. per household | 7.0 | Cost of living, Sept. 1993 | |
| Marriages per 1,000 pop. | 5.7 | New York = 100 | 67 |

a  1991.
b  1990.

# ARGENTINA

| | | | |
|---|---|---|---|
| Area | 2,766,889 sq km | Currency | Peso (P) |
| Capital | Buenos Aires | | |

## People

| | | | |
|---|---|---|---|
| Population | 33.1m | Life expectancy: men | 68yrs |
| Pop. per sq km | 12 | women | 75yrs |
| Av. ann. growth | | Adult literacy | 95.3% |
| in pop. 1985–92 | 1.3% | Fertility rate (per woman) | 2.8 |
| Pop. under 15 | 28.3% | | |
| Pop. over 65 | 9.6% | | *per 1,000 pop.* |
| No. of men per 100 women | 98 | Crude birth rate | 20.3 |
| Human Development Index | 83 | Crude death rate | 8.6 |

## The economy

| | | | |
|---|---|---|---|
| GDP | P198bn | GDP per head | $6,051 |
| GDP | $200bn | GDP per head in purchasing | |
| Av. ann. growth in real | | power parity (USA=100) | 20 |
| GDP 1985–92 | 1.4% | | |

| **Origins of GDP** | | **Components of GDP** | |
|---|---|---|---|
| | *% of total* | | *% of total* |
| Agriculture | 6.0 | Private consumption* | 84.8 |
| Industry, of which: | 30.7 | Public consumption | ... |
| manufacturing | 21.9 | Investment | 16.7 |
| Services | 63.3 | Exports | 6.6 |
| | | Imports | -8.1 |

## Structure of manufacturing

| | *% of total* | | *% of total* |
|---|---|---|---|
| Food & agric. | 20 | Other | 57 |
| Textiles & clothing | 10 | Av. ann. increase in industrial | |
| Machinery & transport | 13 | output 1980–91 | -1.4% |

## Energy

| | *'000 TCE* | | |
|---|---|---|---|
| Total output | 73,187 | % output exported | 10.1 |
| Total consumption | 64,683 | % consumption imported | 7.8 |
| Consumption per head | | | |
| kg coal equivalent | 1,977 | | |

## Inflation and finance

| Consumer price | | *av. ann. increase 1988–92* | |
|---|---|---|---|
| inflation 1993 | 10.6% | Narrow money (M1) | 504% |
| Av. ann. inflation 1988–93 | 383.4% | Broad money | 470% |

## Exchange rates

| | *end 1993* | | *end June 1993* |
|---|---|---|---|
| P per $ | 1.00 | Effective rates, | *1985 = 100* |
| P per SDR | 1.37 | – nominal | ... |
| P per Ecu | 1.12 | – real | ... |

## Principal exports

| | $bn fob | | $bn fob |
|---|---|---|---|
| Agricultural products | 2.9 | Cattle & meat | 1.1 |
| Processed foods | 2.3 | Minerals | 0.8 |
| Oils | 1.1 | Total incl. others | **12.0** |

### Main export destinations

| | % of total | | % of total |
|---|---|---|---|
| United States | 10.7 | Netherlands | 10.4 |
| Brazil | 10.5 | Italy | 4.7 |
| Germany | 6.1 | | |

## Principal imports

| | $bn cif | | $bn cif |
|---|---|---|---|
| Machinery & industrial | | Metals | 1.1 |
| equipment | 4.8 | Plastics | 0.8 |
| Transport equipment | 2.3 | Total incl. others | **14.8** |
| Chemicals | 1.8 | | |

### Main origins of imports

| | % of total | | % of total |
|---|---|---|---|
| Brazil | 22.7 | Italy | 5.1 |
| United States | 20.3 | Japan | 4.6 |
| Germany | 7.5 | | |

## Balance of payments, reserves and debt, $bn

| | | | |
|---|---|---|---|
| Visible exports fob | 12.2 | Overall balance | 2.4 |
| Visible imports fob | -13.6 | Change in reserves | 4.3 |
| Trade balance | -1.4 | Level of reserves | |
| Invisibles inflows | 2.8 | end Dec.[b] | 11.4 |
| Invisibles outflows | -9.8 | No. months import cover | 9.9 |
| Net transfers | -0.03 | Foreign debt | 67.6 |
| Current account balance | -8.4 | – as % of GDP | 30.1 |
| – as % of GDP | -4.2 | Debt service | 5.2 |
| Capital balance | 8.6 | Debt service ratio | 34.9 |

## Family life

| | | | |
|---|---|---|---|
| No. of households | 7.1m | Divorces per 1,000 pop. | ... |
| Av. no. per household | 3.9 | Cost of living, Sept. 1993 | |
| Marriages per 1,000 pop. | 5.8 | New York = 100 | 93 |

a  Including public consumption.
b  Excluding gold.

# AUSTRALIA

| | | | |
|---|---|---|---|
| Area | 7,686,848 sq km | Currency | Australian dollar (A$) |
| Capital | Canberra | | |

## People

| | | | |
|---|---|---|---|
| Population | 17.5m | Life expectancy: men | 74 yrs |
| Pop. per sq km | 2 | women | 80 yrs |
| Av. ann. growth | | Adult literacy | 99.0% |
| in pop. 1985–92 | 1.6% | Fertility rate (per woman) | 1.9 |
| Pop. under 15 | 21.7% | | |
| Pop. over 65 | 11.6% | | *per 1,000 pop.* |
| No. of men per 100 women | 100 | Crude birth rate | 15.1 |
| Human Development Index | 97 | Crude death rate | 7.7 |

## The economy

| | | | |
|---|---|---|---|
| GDP | A$407bn | GDP per head | $17,065 |
| GDP | $299bn | GDP per head in purchasing | |
| Av. ann. growth in real | | power parity (USA=100) | 75 |
| GDP 1985–92 | 2.8% | | |

| Origins of GDP[a] | | Components of GDP[a] | |
|---|---|---|---|
| | *% of total* | | *% of total* |
| Agriculture & mining | 8.8 | Private consumption | 61.7 |
| Industry, of which: | 24.1 | Public consumption | 18.8 |
| manufacturing | 17.3 | Investment | 19.5 |
| Services | 67.1 | Exports | 18.7 |
| | | Imports | -19.2 |

## Structure of manufacturing

| | *% of total* | | *% of total* |
|---|---|---|---|
| Agric. & food processing | 18 | Other | 56 |
| Textiles & clothing | 7 | Av. ann. increase in industrial | |
| Machinery & transport | 19 | output 1980–91 | 3.0% |

## Energy

| | *'000 TCE* | | |
|---|---|---|---|
| Total output | 218,465 | % output exported | 51.7 |
| Total consumption | 126,984 | % consumption imported | 14.4 |
| Consumption per head, | | | |
| kg coal equivalent | 7,321 | | |

## Inflation and finance

| Consumer price | | *av. ann. increase 1988–92* | |
|---|---|---|---|
| inflation 1993 | 2.0% | Narrow money (M1) | 14.1% |
| Av. ann. inflation 1988–93 | 4.7% | Broad money | 13.6% |

## Exchange rates

| | *end 1993* | | *end June 1993* |
|---|---|---|---|
| A$ per $ | 1.48 | Effective rates | *1985 = 100* |
| A$ per SDR | 2.04 | – nominal | 99.2 |
| A$ per Ecu | 1.65 | – real | 84.8 |

## Principal exports[a]

|  | $bn fob |  | $bn fob |
|---|---|---|---|
| Ores & minerals | 9.2 | Wool | 3.0 |
| Coal & oil | 8.0 | Cereals | 2.6 |
| Gold | 3.2 | Total incl. others | **41.9** |

### Main export destinations

|  | % of total |  | % of total |
|---|---|---|---|
| Japan | 24.8 | United States | 8.1 |
| Asean[b] | 14.5 | Developing countries | 41.0 |
| EU | 11.6 |  |  |

## Principal imports[a]

|  | $bn cif |  | $bn cif |
|---|---|---|---|
| Machinery | 12.4 | Consumer goods | 3.4 |
| Motor vehicles & other |  | Energy & products | 2.6 |
| transport equipment | 5.7 |  |  |
| Chemicals | 4.6 | Total incl. others | **41.5** |

### Main origins of imports

|  | % of total |  | % of total |
|---|---|---|---|
| United States | 21.8 | Asean[b] | 8.0 |
| EU | 19.6 | Developing countries | 32.2 |
| Japan | 18.4 |  |  |

## Balance of payments, reserves and aid, $bn

|  |  |  |  |
|---|---|---|---|
| Visible exports fob | 42.4 | Capital balance | 10.2 |
| Visible imports fob | -40.8 | Overall balance | -4.8 |
| Trade balance | 1.6 | Change in reserves | -0.6 |
| Invisibles inflows | 13.5 | Level of reserves |  |
| Invisibles outflows | -26.9 | end Dec. | 13.8 |
| Net transfers | 1.2 | No. months import cover | 3.9 |
| Current account balance | -10.7 | Aid given | 1.0 |
| – as % of GDP | -3.6 | – as % of GDP | 0.35 |

## Family life

|  |  |  |  |
|---|---|---|---|
| No. of households | 5.3m | Divorces per 1,000 pop. | 2.5 |
| Av. no. per household | 3.0 | Cost of living, Sept. 1993 |  |
| Marriages per 1,000 pop. | 6.8 | New York = 100 | 83 |

a Year ending June 30, 1993.
b Brunei, Indonesia, Malaysia, Philippines, Singapore, Thailand.

# AUSTRIA

| | | | |
|---|---|---|---|
| Area | 83,849 sq km | Currency | Schilling (ASch) |
| Capital | Vienna | | |

## People

| | | | |
|---|---|---|---|
| Population | 7.9m | Life expectancy: men | 73 yrs |
| Pop. per sq km | 94 | women | 79 yrs |
| Av. ann. growth | | Adult literacy | 99.0% |
| in pop. 1985–92 | 0.6% | Fertility rate (per woman) | 1.5 |
| Pop. under 15 | 17.6% | | |
| Pop. over 65 | 15.4% | | *per 1,000 pop.* |
| No. of men per 100 women | 93 | Crude birth rate | 11.6 |
| Human Development Index | 95 | Crude death rate | 11.2 |

## The economy

| | | | |
|---|---|---|---|
| GDP | ASch1,923bn | GDP per head | $22,106 |
| GDP | $175bn | GDP per head in purchasing | |
| Av. ann. growth in real | | power parity (USA=100) | 77 |
| GDP 1985–92 | 2.8% | | |

| Origins of GDP | | Components of GDP | |
|---|---|---|---|
| | *% of total* | | *% of total* |
| Agriculture | 2.5 | Private consumption | 55.6 |
| Industry, of which: | 36.3 | Public consumption | 18.3 |
| manufacturing | 28.7 | Investment | 26.1 |
| Services | 61.2 | Exports | 39.6 |
| | | Imports | -38.4 |

## Structure of manufacturing

| | *% of total* | | *% of total* |
|---|---|---|---|
| Agric. & food processing | 15 | Other | 51 |
| Textiles & clothing | 6 | Av. ann. increase in industrial | |
| Machinery & transport | 28 | output 1980–91 | 2.0% |

## Energy

| | *'000 TCE* | | |
|---|---|---|---|
| Total output | 8,337 | % output exported | 26.1 |
| Total consumption | 32,487 | % consumption imported | 81.4 |
| Consumption per head, | | | |
| kg coal equivalent | 4,195 | | |

## Inflation and finance

| | | | |
|---|---|---|---|
| Consumer price | | *av. ann. increase 1988–92* | |
| inflation 1993 | 3.6% | Narrow money (M1) | 5.8% |
| Av. ann. inflation 1988–93 | 3.1% | Broad money | 7.4% |

## Exchange rates

| | *end 1993* | | *end June 1993* |
|---|---|---|---|
| ASch per $ | 12.14 | Effective rates | *1985 = 100* |
| ASch per SDR | 16.68 | – nominal | 114.3 |
| ASch per Ecu | 13.60 | – real | 101.8 |

## Principal exports

| | $bn fob | | $bn fob |
|---|---|---|---|
| Machinery & transport | | Chemicals | 3.8 |
| equipment | 17.3 | Raw materials | 1.8 |
| Manufactured goods | 13.1 | Food, drink & tobacco | 1.2 |
| Consumer goods | 6.2 | Total incl. others | **44.3** |

### Main export destinations

| | % of total | | % of total |
|---|---|---|---|
| Germany | 39.8 | United Kingdom | 3.6 |
| Italy | 8.8 | EU | 66.1 |
| Switzerland | 5.9 | Efta | 8.6 |
| France | 4.4 | Eastern Europe | 11.0 |

## Principal imports

| | $bn cif | | $bn cif |
|---|---|---|---|
| Machinery & transport | | Chemicals | 5.3 |
| equipment | 21.5 | Fuel & energy | 2.8 |
| Manufactured products | 10.0 | Food & drink | 2.4 |
| Consumer goods | 9.6 | Total incl. others | **54.1** |

### Main origins of imports

| | % of total | | % of total |
|---|---|---|---|
| Germany | 42.9 | Switzerland | 4.0 |
| Italy | 8.6 | EU | 67.9 |
| Japan | 4.7 | Efta | 6.8 |
| France | 4.4 | Eastern Europe | 7.3 |

## Balance of payments, reserves and aid, $bn

| | | | |
|---|---|---|---|
| Visible exports fob | 43.4 | Capital balance | 1.0 |
| Visible imports fob | -52.2 | Overall balance | 2.6 |
| Trade balance | -8.8 | Change in reserves | 2.0 |
| Invisibles inflows | 38.7 | Level of reserves | |
| Invisibles outflows | -29.6 | end Dec. | 15.7 |
| Net transfers | -0.9 | No. months import cover | 3.6 |
| Current account balance | -0.7 | Aid given | 0.6 |
| – as % of GDP | -0.4 | – as % of GDP | 0.30 |

## Family life

| | | | |
|---|---|---|---|
| No. of households | 2.8m | Divorces per 1,000 pop. | 2.1 |
| Av. no. per household | 2.7 | Cost of living, Sept. 1993 | |
| Marriages per 1,000 pop. | 5.6 | New York = 100 | 119 |

# BANGLADESH

| Area | 143,998 sq km | Currency | Taka (Tk) |
|---|---|---|---|
| Capital | Dhaka | | |

## People

| | | | |
|---|---|---|---|
| Population | 112.8m | Life expectancy: men | 53 yrs |
| Pop. per sq km | 891 | women | 53 yrs |
| Av. ann. growth | | Adult literacy | 35.3% |
| in pop. 1985–92 | 2.2% | Fertility rate (per woman) | 4.7 |
| Pop. under 15 | 40.3% | | |
| Pop. over 65 | 3.0% | | *per 1,000 pop.* |
| No. of men per 100 women | 106 | Crude birth rate | 38.5 |
| Human Development Index | 19 | Crude death rate | 13.6 |

## The economy

| | | | |
|---|---|---|---|
| GDP | Tk974bn | GDP per head | $219 |
| GDP | $25bn | GDP per head in purchasing | |
| Av. ann. growth in real | | power parity (USA=100) | 4 |
| GDP 1985–92 | 4.0% | | |

| Origins of GDP[a] | | Components of GDP[a] | |
|---|---|---|---|
| | *% of total* | | *% of total* |
| Agriculture | 33.5 | Private consumption | 84.6 |
| Industry, of which: | 15.3 | Public consumption | 11.3 |
| manufacturing | 9.4 | Investment | 10.4 |
| Services | 51.2 | Exports | 10.0 |
| | | Imports | -16.3 |

## Structure of manufacturing

| | *% of total* | | *% of total* |
|---|---|---|---|
| Agric. & food processing | 24 | Other | 35 |
| Textiles & clothing | 35 | Av. ann. increase in industrial | |
| Metal products & machinery | 5 | output 1980–91 | 4.9% |

## Energy

| | *'000 TCE* | | |
|---|---|---|---|
| Total output | 6,562 | % output exported | 0.0 |
| Total consumption | 8,965 | % consumption imported | 31.1 |
| Consumption per head, | | | |
| kg coal equivalent | 77 | | |

## Inflation and finance

| Consumer price | | *av. ann. increase 1988–92* | |
|---|---|---|---|
| inflation 1993 | 1.0% | Narrow money (M1) | 9.6% |
| Av. ann. inflation 1988–93 | 6.6% | Broad money | 13.6% |

## Exchange rates

| | *end 1993* | | *end June 1993* |
|---|---|---|---|
| Tk per $ | 39.85 | Effective rates | 1985 = 100 |
| Tk per SDR | 54.74 | – nominal | ... |
| Tk per Ecu | 44.63 | – real | ... |

## Principal exports

|  | $m fob |  | $m fob |
|---|---|---|---|
| Textiles & clothing | 1,040.0 | Leather | 139.7 |
| Jute goods | 288.8 | Raw jute | 105.6 |
| Fish & fish products | 163.9 | Total incl. others | **1,900** |

### Main export destinations[a]

|  | % of total |  | % of total |
|---|---|---|---|
| United States | 28.9 | Italy | 5.5 |
| Germany | 9.6 | France | 5.4 |
| United Kingdom | 7.7 | Singapore | 3.8 |

## Principal imports

|  | $m cif |  | $m cif |
|---|---|---|---|
| Machinery & transport |  | Chemicals | 164.9 |
| equipment | 304.6 | Cereal & dairy products | 92.5 |
| Textiles | 687.3 |  |  |
| Energy products | 291.2 | Total incl. others | **3,463.0** |

### Main origins of imports[a]

|  | % of total |  | % of total |
|---|---|---|---|
| Japan | 10.5 | Singapore | 6.6 |
| South Korea | 9.4 | India | 6.3 |
| United States | 7.0 | China | 5.8 |

## Balance of payments, reserves and debt, $bn

|  |  |  |  |
|---|---|---|---|
| Visible exports fob | 2.1 | Overall balance | 0.6 |
| Visible imports fob | -3.4 | Change in reserves | 0.6 |
| Trade balance | -1.3 | Level of reserves |  |
| Invisibles inflows | 0.6 | end Dec. | 1.8 |
| Invisibles outflows | -1.0 | No. months import cover | 6.4 |
| Net transfers | 1.8 | Foreign debt | 13.2 |
| Current account balance | 0.2 | – as % of GDP | 55.7 |
| – as % of GDP | 0.7 | Debt service | 0.58 |
| Capital balance | 0.5 | Debt service ratio | 17.1 |

## Family life

|  |  |  |  |
|---|---|---|---|
| No. households | 14.8m | Divorces per 1,000 pop. | ... |
| Av. no. per household | 5.7 | Cost of living, Sept. 1993 |  |
| Marriages per 1,000 pop. | 11.3 | New York = 100 | 62 |

a 1991.

# BELGIUM

| | | | |
|---|---|---|---|
| Area | 30,513 sq km | Currency | Belgian franc (BFr) |
| Capital | Brussels | | |

## People

| | | | |
|---|---|---|---|
| Population | 10.0m | Life expectancy: men | 73 yrs |
| Pop. per sq km | 329 | women | 79 yrs |
| Av. ann. growth | | Adult literacy | 99.0% |
| in pop. 1985–92 | 0.3% | Fertility rate (per woman) | 1.7 |
| Pop. under 15 | 17.9% | | |
| Pop. over 65 | 15.7% | | *per 1,000 pop.* |
| No. of men per 100 women | 96 | Crude birth rate | 12.1 |
| Human Development Index | 95 | Crude death rate | 11.3 |

## The economy

| | | | |
|---|---|---|---|
| GDP | BFr6,752bn | GDP per head | $20,878 |
| GDP | $210bn | GDP per head in purchasing | |
| Av. ann. growth in real | | power parity (USA=100) | 76 |
| GDP 1985–92 | 2.4% | | |

| Origins of GDP[a] | | Components of GDP[a] | |
|---|---|---|---|
| | *% of total* | | *% of total* |
| Agriculture | 2.3 | Private consumption | 63.9 |
| Industry, of which: | 31.4 | Public consumption | 15.4 |
| manufacturing | 22.0 | Investment | 18.1 |
| Services | 62.3 | Exports | 66.5 |
| | | Imports | -63.0 |

## Structure of manufacturing

| | *% of total* | | *% of total* |
|---|---|---|---|
| Agric. & food processing | 17 | Other | 52 |
| Textiles & clothing | 8 | Av. ann. increase in industrial | |
| Machinery & transport | 23 | output 1980–91 | 2.2% |

## Energy

| | *'000 TCE* | | |
|---|---|---|---|
| Total output | 16,603 | % output exported[c] | 169.8 |
| Total consumption | 68,896 | % consumption imported[c] | 131.0 |
| Consumption per head, | | | |
| kg coal equivalent | 6,900 | | |

## Inflation and finance

| | | | |
|---|---|---|---|
| Consumer price | | *av. ann. increase 1987–91* | |
| inflation 1993 | 2.8% | Narrow money (M1) | 4.4% |
| Av. ann. inflation 1988–93 | 2.7% | Broad money | 8.3% |

## Exchange rates

| | *end 1993* | | *end June 1993* |
|---|---|---|---|
| BFr per $ | 36.11 | Effective rates | *1985 = 100* |
| BFr per SDR | 49.60 | – nominal | 115.4 |
| BFr per Ecu | 40.44 | – real | 107.9 |

## Principal exports[a]

| | $bn fob | | $bn fob |
|---|---|---|---|
| Machinery & transport equipment | 33.4 | Textiles & clothing | 8.8 |
| | | Precious stones & jewellery | 7.7 |
| Chemicals | 18.1 | Petroleum & products | 4.0 |
| Metals & products | 13.8 | | |
| Agric. products & foodstuffs | 10.7 | Total incl. others | **123.4** |

### Main export destinations

| | % of total | | % of total |
|---|---|---|---|
| Germany | 22.8 | Italy | 5.9 |
| France | 19.3 | United States | 3.9 |
| Netherlands | 13.7 | Japan | 1.0 |
| United Kingdom | 7.8 | EU | 74.9 |

## Principal imports[a]

| | $bn cif | | $bn cif |
|---|---|---|---|
| Machinery & transport equipment | 32.0 | Metals & products | 9.5 |
| | | Energy & products | 9.3 |
| Chemicals | 14.9 | Textiles & clothing | 7.7 |
| Agric. products & foodstuffs | 10.6 | Precious stones & jewellery | 7.4 |
| | | Total incl. others | **125.2** |

### Main origins of imports

| | % of total | | % of total |
|---|---|---|---|
| Germany | 23.9 | Italy | 4.5 |
| Netherlands | 17.5 | United States | 4.4 |
| France | 16.5 | Japan | 2.2 |
| United Kingdom | 7.7 | EU | 73.5 |

## Balance of payments[a], reserves and aid, $bn

| | | | |
|---|---|---|---|
| Visible exports fob | 116.6 | Capital balance | -6.1 |
| Visible imports fob | -116.4 | Overall balance | 0.6 |
| Trade balance | 0.2 | Change in reserves | 0.6 |
| Invisibles inflows | 126.7 | Level of reserves | |
| Invisibles outflows | -118.9 | end Dec. | 22.1 |
| Net transfers | -2.5 | No. months import cover | 2.3 |
| Current account balance | 5.4 | Aid given | 0.9 |
| – as % of GDP | 2.6 | – as % of GDP | 0.39 |

## Family life

| | | | |
|---|---|---|---|
| No. of households | 3.6m | Divorces per 1,000 pop. | 1.9 |
| Av. no. per household | 2.7 | Cost of living, Sept. 1993 | |
| Marriages per 1,000 pop. | 6.2 | New York = 100 | 104 |

a  Including Luxembourg.
b  1990.
c  Energy trade data are distorted by transitory and oil refining activities.

# BRAZIL

| | | | |
|---|---|---|---|
| Area | 8,511,965 sq km | Currency | Cruzeiro (Cr) |
| Capital | Brasília | | |

## People

| | | | |
|---|---|---|---|
| Population | 153.8m | Life expectancy: men | 64 yrs |
| Pop. per sq km | 19 | women | 69 yrs |
| Av. ann. growth | | Adult literacy | 81.1% |
| in pop. 1985–92 | 1.8% | Fertility rate (per woman) | 2.8 |
| Pop. under 15 | 32.2% | | |
| Pop. over 65 | 5.2% | | *per 1,000 pop.* |
| No. of men per 100 women | 99 | Crude birth rate | 23.3 |
| Human Development Index | 73 | Crude death rate | 7.4 |

## The economy

| | | | |
|---|---|---|---|
| GDP | Cr1,914bn | GDP per head | $2,759 |
| GDP | $424bn | GDP per head in purchasing | |
| Av. ann. growth in real | | power parity (USA=100) | 22 |
| GDP 1985–92 | 2.2% | | |

| Origins of GDP[a] | | Components of GDP[a] | |
|---|---|---|---|
| | *% of total* | | *% of total* |
| Agriculture | 10.8 | Private consumption | 64.7 |
| Industry, of which: | 33.8 | Public consumption | 14.4 |
| manufacturing | 25.0 | Investment | 18.9 |
| Services | 55.4 | Exports | 8.5 |
| | | Imports | -6.5 |

## Structure of manufacturing

| | *% of total* | | *% of total* |
|---|---|---|---|
| Agric. & food processing | 13 | Other | 52 |
| Textiles & clothing | 12 | Av. ann. increase in industrial | |
| Machinery & transport | 23 | output 1980–91 | 1.7% |

## Energy

| | *'000 TCE* | | |
|---|---|---|---|
| Total output | 83,017 | % output exported | 4.9 |
| Total consumption | 121,178 | % consumption imported | 47.1 |
| Consumption per head, | | | |
| kg coal equivalent | 799 | | |

## Inflation and finance

| | | | |
|---|---|---|---|
| Consumer price | | *av. ann. increase 1988–92* | |
| inflation 1993 | 2,110% | Narrow money (M1) | … |
| Av. ann. inflation 1988–93 | 1,179% | Broad money | … |

## Exchange rates

| | *end 1993* | | *end June 1993* |
|---|---|---|---|
| Cr per $ | 326 | Effective rates, | *1985 = 100* |
| Cr per SDR | 448 | – Nominal | … |
| Cr per Ecu | 365 | – Real | … |

## Principal exports

| | $bn fob | | $bn fob |
|---|---|---|---|
| Metallurgical products | 6.1 | Metallic ore | 2.5 |
| Transport equipment & parts | 4.2 | Coffee | 1.4 |
| Soya beans | 2.7 | Total incl. others | **36.1** |

### Main export destinations

| | % of total | | % of total |
|---|---|---|---|
| EU | 29.6 | Africa | 3.2 |
| United States | 19.7 | ALADI | 21.1 |
| Asia | 15.5 | | |
| Middle East | 3.5 | | |

## Principal imports

| | $bn cif | | $bn cif |
|---|---|---|---|
| Raw materials | 7.2 | Oil & oil products | 4.1 |
| Capital goods | 6.3 | Total incl. others | **20.6** |

### Main origins of imports

| | % of total | | % of total |
|---|---|---|---|
| United States | 24.2 | Asia | 8.4 |
| EU | 22.3 | Africa | 2.6 |
| ALADI | 17.5 | | |
| Middle East | 13.8 | | |

## Balance of payments, reserves and debt, $bn

| | | | |
|---|---|---|---|
| Visible exports fob | 36.1 | Overall balance | 17.7 |
| Visible imports fob | -20.6 | Change in reserves | 15.0 |
| Trade balance | 15.5 | Level of reserves | |
| Invisibles inflows | 5.0 | end Dec. | 13.6 |
| Invisibles outflows | -16.3 | No. months import cover | 7.7 |
| Net transfers | 2.1 | Foreign debt | 121.1 |
| Current account balance | 6.3 | – as % of GDP | 31.3 |
| – as % of GDP | 1.5 | Debt service | 9.5 |
| Capital balance | 12.6 | Debt service ratio | 31.3 |

## Family life

| | | | |
|---|---|---|---|
| No. of households | 26.8m | Divorces per 1,000 pop. | 0.5 |
| Av. no. per household | 4.4 | Cost of living, Sept. 1993 | |
| Marriages per 1,000 pop. | 5.6 | New York = 100 | 77 |

a 1991.

# CAMEROON

| | | | |
|---|---|---|---|
| Area | 475,442 sq km | Currency | CFA franc (CFAfr) |
| Capital | Yaoundé | | |

## People

| | | | | |
|---|---|---|---|---|
| Population | 12.2m | Life expectancy: men | | 55 yrs |
| Pop. per sq km | 28 | | women | 58 yrs |
| Av. ann. growth | | Adult literacy | | 54.1% |
| in pop. 1985–92 | 3.0% | Fertility rate (per woman) | | 5.7 |
| Pop. under 15 | 44% | | | |
| Pop. over 65 | 3.6% | | | *per 1,000 pop.* |
| No. of men per 100 women | 99 | Crude birth rate | | 40.7 |
| Human Development Index | 31 | Crude death rate | | 12.2 |

## The economy

| | | | |
|---|---|---|---|
| GDP | CFAfr2,647bn | GDP per head | $817 |
| GDP | $10.0bn | GDP per head in purchasing | |
| Av. ann. growth in real | | power parity (USA=100) | 8 |
| GDP 1985–92 | -3.2% | | |

| Origins of GDP[a] | | Components of GDP[a] | |
|---|---|---|---|
| | *% of total* | | *% of total* |
| Agriculture | 27.2 | Private consumption | 71.0 |
| Industry, of which: | 21.7 | Public consumption | 14.1 |
| manufacturing | 12.1 | Investment | 15.0 |
| Services | 51.1 | Exports | 18.0 |
| | | Imports | -18.1 |

## Structure of manufacturing[b]

| | *% of total* | | *% of total* |
|---|---|---|---|
| Agric. & food processing | 61 | Other | 47 |
| Textiles & clothing | -13 | Av. ann. increase in industrial | |
| Metal products & machinery | 5 | output 1980–91 | 2.2% |

## Energy

| | *'000 TCE* | | |
|---|---|---|---|
| Total output | 11,338 | % output exported | 89.2 |
| Total consumption | 1,202 | % consumption imported | 1.9 |
| Consumption per head, | | | |
| kg coal equivalent | 101 | | |

## Inflation and finance

| | | | |
|---|---|---|---|
| Consumer price | | *av. ann. change 1988–92* | |
| inflation 1992 | 2.0% | Narrow money (M1) | 1.2% |
| Av. ann. inflation 1988–92 | 1.2% | Broad money | 1.9% |

## Exchange rates

| | *end 1993* | | *end June 1993* |
|---|---|---|---|
| CFAfr per $ | 295 | Effective rates | *1985 = 100* |
| CFAfr per SDR | 405 | – nominal | 173.8 |
| CFAfr per Ecu | 330 | – real | 109.5 |

## Principal exports[c]

| | $m fob | | $m fob |
|---|---|---|---|
| Crude oil | 934 | Coffee | 112 |
| Timber | 134 | Aluminium | 86 |
| Cocoa | 113 | Total incl. others | **1,912** |

### Main export destinations

| | % of total | | % of total |
|---|---|---|---|
| France | 26.0 | Italy | 12.0 |
| Spain | 17.0 | Netherlands | 9.0 |

## Principal imports[c]

| | $m fob | | $m fob |
|---|---|---|---|
| Manufactures | 1,181 | Fuel | 21 |
| Primary products | 246 | Total incl. others | **1,585** |

### Main origins of imports

| | % of total | | % of total |
|---|---|---|---|
| France | 39.0 | United States | 5.0 |
| Germany | 8.0 | Belgium/Luxembourg | 5.0 |

## Balance of payments[c], reserves and debt, $bn

| | | | |
|---|---|---|---|
| Visible exports fob | 1.3 | Overall balance | -0.2 |
| Visible imports fob | -0.9 | Change in reserves | 0.02 |
| Trade balance | 0.4 | Level of reserves | |
| Invisibles inflows | 0.2 | end Dec. | 0.03 |
| Invisibles outflows | -1.0 | No. months import cover | 0.4 |
| Net transfers | 0.02 | Foreign debt | 6.6 |
| Current account balance | -0.3 | – as % of GDP | 67.2 |
| – as % of GDP | -3.2 | Debt service | 0.35 |
| Capital balance | -0.2 | Debt service ratio | 16.2 |

## Family life

| | | | |
|---|---|---|---|
| No. of households | 1.4m | Divorces per 1,000 pop. | ... |
| Av. no. per household | 5.2 | Cost of living, Sept. 1993 | |
| Marriages per 1,000 pop. | ... | New York = 100 | 130 |

a  Year ending June 30, 1991.
b  1985.
c  1991.

# CANADA

| | | | |
|---|---|---|---|
| Area | 9,203,210ª sq km | Currency | Canadian dollar (C$) |
| Capital | Ottawa | | |

## People

| | | | |
|---|---|---|---|
| Population | 27.9m | Life expectancy: men | 74 yrs |
| Pop. per sq km | 3 | women | 81 yrs |
| Av. ann. growth | | Adult literacy | 99.0% |
| in pop. 1985–92 | 1.4% | Fertility rate (per woman) | 1.8 |
| Pop. under 15 | 20.7% | | |
| Pop. over 65 | 12.0% | | *per 1,000 pop.* |
| No. of men per 100 women | 97 | Crude birth rate | 14.2 |
| Human Development Index | 98 | Crude death rate | 7.7 |

## The economy

| | | | |
|---|---|---|---|
| GDP | C$684bn | GDP per head | $20,320 |
| GDP | $566bn | GDP per head in purchasing | |
| Av. ann. growth in real | | power parity (USA=100) | 90 |
| GDP 1985–92 | 2.3% | | |

| Origins of GDP | | Components of GDP | |
|---|---|---|---|
| | *% of total* | | *% of total* |
| Agriculture | 2.8 | Private consumption | 60.1 |
| Industry, of which: | 30.3 | Public consumption | 21.0 |
| manufacturing | 21.1 | Investment | 21.2 |
| Services | 66.9 | Exports | 32.0 |
| | | Imports | -34.0 |

## Structure of manufacturing

| | *% of total* | | *% of total* |
|---|---|---|---|
| Agric. & food processing | 14 | Other | 54 |
| Textiles & clothing | 6 | Av. ann. increase in industrial | |
| Machinery & transport | 26 | output 1980–91 | 3.0% |

## Energy

| | *'000 TCE* | | |
|---|---|---|---|
| Total output | 404,267 | % output exported | 42.9 |
| Total consumption | 299,484 | % consumption imported | 18.6 |
| Consumption per head, | | | |
| kg coal equivalent | 11,095 | | |

## Inflation and finance

| | | | |
|---|---|---|---|
| Consumer price | | *av. ann. increase 1988–92* | |
| inflation 1993 | 1.8% | Narrow money (M1) | 4.9% |
| Av. ann. inflation 1988–93 | 3.8% | Broad money | 9.2% |

## Exchange rates

| | *end 1993* | | *end June 1993* |
|---|---|---|---|
| C$ per $ | 1.32 | Effective rates | *1985 = 100* |
| C$ per SDR | 1.82 | – nominal | 94.4 |
| C$ per Ecu | 1.48 | – real | 102.6 |

## Principal exports

| | C$bn fob | | C$bn fob |
|---|---|---|---|
| | | Energy products | 15.7 |
| Motor vehicles & other transport equipment | 38.0 | Agric. products & foodstuffs | 14.9 |
| Machinery & industrial equipment | 31.5 | | |
| Industrial supplies | 29.5 | | |
| Forest products | 21.3 | Total incl. others | **161.3** |

### Main export destinations

| | % of total | | % of total |
|---|---|---|---|
| United States | 77.5 | Germany | 1.5 |
| Japan | 4.6 | South Korea | 0.9 |
| United Kingdom | 1.9 | | |

## Principal imports

| | C$bn cif | | C$bn cif |
|---|---|---|---|
| Machinery & industrial equipment | 46.0 | Consumer goods | 18.9 |
| | | Agric. products & foodstuffs | 9.7 |
| Motor vehicles & other transport equipment | 33.8 | Energy products | 6.4 |
| Industrial supplies | 27.1 | Total incl. others | **151.4** |

### Main origins of imports

| | % of total | | % of total |
|---|---|---|---|
| United States | 63.5 | Germany | 2.3 |
| Japan | 7.1 | South Korea | 1.3 |
| United Kingdom | 2.7 | | |

## Balance of payments, reserves and aid, $bn

| | | | |
|---|---|---|---|
| Visible exports fob | 133.3 | Capital balance | 13.8 |
| Visible imports fob | -125.1 | Overall balance | -5.8 |
| Trade balance | 8.2 | Change in reserves | -5.8 |
| Invisibles inflows | 24.6 | Level of reserves | |
| Invisibles outflows | -56.0 | end Dec. | 11.9 |
| Net transfers | 0.3 | No. months import cover | 1.1 |
| Current account balance | -23.0 | Aid given | 2.52 |
| – as % of GDP | -4.1 | – as % of GDP | 0.46 |

## Family life

| | | | |
|---|---|---|---|
| No. of households | 10.0m | Divorces per 1,000 pop. | 3.1 |
| Av. no. per household | 2.7 | Cost of living, Sept. 1993 | |
| Marriages per 1,000 pop. | 7.3 | New York = 100 | 86 |

a  Land only.

# CHILE

| | | | |
|---|---|---|---|
| Area | 756,945 sq km | Currency | Chilean peso (peso) |
| Capital | Santiago | | |

## People

| | | | | |
|---|---|---|---|---|
| Population | 13.6m | Life expectancy: men | | 69 yrs |
| Pop. per sq km | 19 | | women | 76 yrs |
| Av. ann. growth | | Adult literacy | | 93.4% |
| in pop. 1985–92 | 1.7% | Fertility rate (per woman) | | 2.7 |
| Pop. under 15 | 30.4% | | | |
| Pop. over 65 | 6.4% | | | *per 1,000 pop.* |
| No. of men per 100 women | 98 | Crude birth rate | | 22.5 |
| Human Development Index | 86 | Crude death rate | | 6.4 |

## The economy

| | | | |
|---|---|---|---|
| GDP | 13,416bn pesos | GDP per head | $2,725 |
| GDP | $37bn | GDP per head in purchasing | |
| Av. ann. growth in real | | power parity (USA=100) | 24 |
| GDP 1985–92 | 6.2% | | |

| **Origins of GDP** | | **Components of GDP** | |
|---|---|---|---|
| | *% of total* | | *% of total* |
| Agriculture | 8.6 | Private consumption | 65.5 |
| Industry, of which: | 36.0 | Public consumption | 8.6 |
| manufacturing | 20.8 | Investment | 23.0 |
| Services | 55.4 | Exports | 33.5 |
| | | Imports | -30.6 |

## Structure of manufacturing[a]

| | *% of total* | | *% of total* |
|---|---|---|---|
| Agric. & food processing | 24 | Other | 64 |
| Textiles & clothing | 7 | Av. ann. increase in industrial | |
| Metal products & machinery | 5 | output 1980–91 | 3.6% |

## Energy

| | *'000 TCE* | | |
|---|---|---|---|
| Total output | 7,225 | % output exported | 1.8 |
| Total consumption | 15,825 | % consumption imported | 64.1 |
| Consumption per head, | | | |
| kg coal equivalent | 1,182 | | |

## Inflation and finance

| | | | *av. ann. increase 1988–92* |
|---|---|---|---|
| Consumer price | | | |
| inflation 1993 | 12.6% | Narrow money (M1) | 32.5% |
| Av. ann. inflation 1988–93 | 17.9% | Broad money | 26.6% |

## Exchange rates

| | *end 1993* | | *end June 1993* |
|---|---|---|---|
| | | | *1985 = 100* |
| Peso per $ | 429 | Effective rates | |
| Peso per SDR | 589 | – nominal | 256.5 |
| Peso per Ecu | 480 | – real | 79.2 |

## Principal exports

| | $bn fob | | $bn fob |
|---|---|---|---|
| Industrial products incl. other mining prods. | 4.7 | Agric. products & foodstuffs | 1.2 |
| Copper | 3.9 | Total incl. others | **10.0** |

### Main export destinations

| | % of total | | % of total |
|---|---|---|---|
| Japan | 16.7 | Taiwan | 5.0 |
| United States | 16.1 | South Korea | 4.6 |
| Germany | 5.8 | Brazil | 4.4 |
| United Kingdom | 5.8 | | |

## Principal imports

| | $bn cif | | $bn cif |
|---|---|---|---|
| Industrial supplies | 5.4 | Consumer goods | 1.9 |
| Capital goods | 2.8 | Total incl. others | **10.1** |

### Main origins of imports

| | % of total | | % of total |
|---|---|---|---|
| United States | 20.0 | Germany | 6.5 |
| Brazil | 10.2 | Nigeria | 3.3 |
| Japan | 10.1 | France | 2.9 |
| Argentina | 6.6 | | |

## Balance of payments, reserves and debt, $bn

| | | | |
|---|---|---|---|
| Visible exports fob | 10.0 | Overall balance | 2.5 |
| Visible imports fob | -9.2 | Change in reserves | 1.9 |
| Trade balance | 0.8 | Level of reserves | |
| Invisibles inflows | 3.0 | end Dec. | 9.7 |
| Invisibles outflows | -4.7 | No. months import cover | 12.7 |
| Net transfers | 0.4 | Foreign debt | 19.4 |
| Current account balance | -0.6 | – as % of GDP | 49.3 |
| – as % of GDP | -1.6 | Debt service | 2.71 |
| Capital balance | 2.9 | Debt service ratio | 20.9 |

## Family life

| | | | |
|---|---|---|---|
| No. of households | 3.3m | Divorces per 1,000 pop. | 0.5 |
| Av. no. per household | 4.1 | Cost of living, Sept. 1993 | |
| Marriages per 1,000 pop. | 7.5 | New York = 100 | 65 |

# CHINA

| | | | |
|---|---|---|---|
| Area | 9,561,000 sq km | Currency | Yuan |
| Capital | Beijing | | |

## People

| | | | |
|---|---|---|---|
| Population | 1,166.1m | Life expectancy: men | 69 yrs |
| Pop. per sq km | 129 | women | 73 yrs |
| Av. ann. growth | | Adult literacy | 73.3% |
| in pop. 1985–92 | 1.5% | Fertility rate (per woman) | 2.2 |
| Pop. under 15 | 27.3% | | |
| Pop. over 65 | 6.3% | | *per 1,000 pop.* |
| No. of men per 100 women | 106 | Crude birth rate | 20.8 |
| Human Development Index | 57 | Crude death rate | 6.5 |

## The economy

| | | | |
|---|---|---|---|
| GDP | Yuan2,437bn | GDP per head | $379 |
| GDP | $442bn | GDP per head in purchasing | |
| Av. ann. growth in real | | power parity (USA=100) | 9 |
| GDP 1985–92 | 9.2% | | |

| Origins of GDP[a] | | Components of NMP[b] | |
|---|---|---|---|
| | *% of total* | | *% of total* |
| Agriculture | 32.7 | Private consumption | 52.0 |
| Industry, of which: | 47.8 | Public consumption | 9.0 |
| manufacturing | … | Investment | 36.0 |
| Services | 19.5 | Exports | 20.0 |
| | | Imports | -17.0 |

## Structure of manufacturing

| | *% of total* | | *% of total* |
|---|---|---|---|
| Agric. & food processing | 15 | Other | 46 |
| Textiles & clothing | 15 | Av. ann. increase in industrial | |
| Metal products & machinery | 24 | output 1980–91 | 11.0% |

## Energy

| | *'000 TCE* | | |
|---|---|---|---|
| Total output | 1,014,037 | % output exported | 5.5 |
| Total consumption | 933,020 | % consumption imported | 2.1 |
| Consumption per head, | | | |
| kg coal equivalent | 811 | | |

## Inflation and finance

| | | | |
|---|---|---|---|
| Consumer price | | *av. ann. increase 1988–92* | |
| inflation 1993 | 20.0% | Narrow money (M1) | 20.7% |
| Av. ann. inflation 1988–93 | 11.8% | Broad money | 25.0% |

## Exchange rates

| | *end 1993* | | *end June 1993* |
|---|---|---|---|
| Yuan per $ | 5.80 | Effective rates | *1985 = 100* |
| Yuan per SDR | 7.97 | – nominal | … |
| Yuan per Ecu | 6.50 | – real | … |

## Principal exports

|  | $bn fob |  | $bn fob |
|---|---|---|---|
| Light industry | 19.0 | Fuels | 5.5 |
| Machinery & transport | | Chemicals | 5.1 |
| equipment | 15.6 | | |
| Food | 9.8 | Total incl. others | **85.0** |

### Main export destinations

|  | % of total |  | % of total |
|---|---|---|---|
| Hong Kong | 43.5 | Germany | 2.8 |
| Japan | 11.9 | South Korea | 2.8 |
| United States | 10.0 | Singapore | 2.3 |

## Principal imports

|  | $bn fob |  | $bn fob |
|---|---|---|---|
| Manufactured goods | 44.7 | Fuels | 4.4 |
| Consumer goods | 5.0 | | |
| Food | 4.9 | Total incl. others | **80.6** |

### Main origins of imports

|  | % of total |  | % of total |
|---|---|---|---|
| Hong Kong | 25.1 | Germany | 4.9 |
| Japan | 16.8 | Ex-Soviet Union | 4.8 |
| United States | 10.9 | South Korea | 3.2 |

## Balance of payments, reserves and debt, $bn

| | | | |
|---|---|---|---|
| Visible exports fob | 69.6 | Overall balance | -2.1 |
| Visible imports fob | -64.4 | Change in reserves | 14.6 |
| Trade balance | 5.2 | Level of reserves | |
| Invisibles inflows | 14.8 | end Dec. | 21.2 |
| Invisibles outflows | -14.7 | No. months import cover | 4.0 |
| Net transfers | 1.2 | Foreign debt | 69.3 |
| Current account balance | 6.4 | - as % of GDP | 16.0 |
| - as % of GDP | 1.4 | Debt service | 8.7 |
| Capital balance | -0.3 | Debt service ratio | 9.6 |

## Family life

| | | | |
|---|---|---|---|
| No. of households | 220.1m | Divorces per 1,000 pop. | ... |
| Av. no. per household | 4.4 | Cost of living, Sept. 1993 | |
| Marriages per 1,000 pop. | ... | New York = 100 | 103 |

a 1990.
b 1989.
c 1991.

# COLOMBIA

| | | | |
|---|---|---|---|
| Area | 1,138,914 sq km | Currency | Colombian peso (peso) |
| Capital | Bogota | | |

## People

| | | | | |
|---|---|---|---|---|
| Population | 33.4m | Life expectancy: men | | 66 yrs |
| Pop. per sq km | 31 | | women | 72 yrs |
| Av. ann. growth | | Adult literacy | | 86.7% |
| in pop. 1985–92 | 1.8% | Fertility rate (per woman) | | 2.7 |
| Pop. under 15 | 32.9% | | | |
| Pop. over 65 | 4.5% | | | *per 1,000 pop.* |
| No. of men per 100 women | 98 | Crude birth rate | | 24.0 |
| Human Development Index | 77 | Crude death rate | | 6.0 |

## The economy

| | | | |
|---|---|---|---|
| GDP | 34,168bn pesos | GDP per head | $1,334 |
| GDP | $45bn | GDP per head in purchasing | |
| Av. ann. growth in real | | power parity (USA=100) | 20 |
| GDP 1985–92 | 4.0% | | |

| Origins of GDP | | Components of GDP | |
|---|---|---|---|
| | *% of total* | | *% of total* |
| Agriculture | 15.7 | Private consumption | 67.4 |
| Industry, of which: | 35.0 | Public consumption | 11.7 |
| manufacturing | 19.8 | Investment | 17.6 |
| Services | 49.3 | Exports | 19.3 |
| | | Imports | -16.0 |

## Structure of manufacturing

| | *% of total* | | *% of total* |
|---|---|---|---|
| Agric. & food processing | 30 | Other | 45 |
| Textiles & clothing | 15 | Av. ann. increase in industrial | |
| Machinery & transport | 10 | output 1980–91 | 4.8% |

## Energy

| | *'000 TCE* | | |
|---|---|---|---|
| Total output | 61,663 | % output exported | 53.4 |
| Total consumption | 27,527 | % consumption imported | 6.1 |
| Consumption per head, | | | |
| kg coal equivalent | 838 | | |

## Inflation and finance

| Consumer price | | *av. ann. increase 1991–92* | |
|---|---|---|---|
| inflation 1993 | 22.4% | Narrow money (M1) | 37.8 |
| Av. ann. inflation 1988–93 | 27.1% | Broad money | 32.4 |

## Exchange rates

| | *end 1993* | | *end June 1993* |
|---|---|---|---|
| Peso per $ | 917 | Effective rates | *1985 = 100* |
| Peso per SDR | 1,260 | – nominal | 57.3 |
| Peso per Ecu | 1,207 | – real | 62.9 |

## Principal exports

| | $bn fob | | $bn fob |
|---|---|---|---|
| Petroleum & products | 1.4 | Gold | 0.4 |
| Coffee | 1.3 | Ferro-nickel | 0.1 |
| Coal | 0.5 | Total incl. others | **7.3** |

### Main export destinations

| | % of total | | % of total |
|---|---|---|---|
| United States | 39.2 | Netherlands | 3.9 |
| Germany | 8.5 | Peru | 3.5 |
| Venezuela | 8.5 | | |

## Principal imports

| | $bn fob | | $bn fob |
|---|---|---|---|
| Industrial supplies | 3.3 | Energy & others | 0.3 |
| Capital goods | 2.2 | | |
| Consumer goods | 0.9 | Total incl. others | **6.7** |

### Main origins of imports

| | % of total | | % of total |
|---|---|---|---|
| United States | 38.5 | Germany | 6.3 |
| Japan | 7.4 | Brazil | 4.0 |
| Venezuela | 6.7 | | |

## Balance of payments, reserves and debt, $bn

| | | | |
|---|---|---|---|
| Visible exports fob | 7.3 | Overall balance | 1.2 |
| Visible imports fob | -6.0 | Change in reserves | 1.2 |
| Trade balance | 1.3 | Level of reserves | |
| Invisibles inflows | 2.4 | end Dec. | 7.6 |
| Invisibles outflows | -2.8 | No. months import cover | 15.2 |
| Net transfers | 1.7 | Foreign debt | 17.2 |
| Current account balance | 0.9 | – as % of GDP | 36.7 |
| – as % of GDP | 2.0 | Debt service | 3.8 |
| Capital balance | 0.3 | Debt service ratio | 35.3 |

## Family life

| | | | |
|---|---|---|---|
| No. of households | 5.3m | Divorces per 1,000 pop. | ... |
| Av. no. per household | 5.2 | Cost of living, Sept. 1993 | |
| Marriages per 1,000 pop. | 2.4 | New York = 100 | 63 |

# CÔTE D'IVOIRE

| | | | |
|---|---|---|---|
| Area | 322,463 sq km | Currency | CFA franc (CFAfr) |
| Capital | Abidjan | | |

## People

| | | | |
|---|---|---|---|
| Population | 12.8m | Life expectancy: men | 50 yrs |
| Pop. per sq km | 45 | women | 53 yrs |
| Av. ann. growth | | Adult literacy | 53.8% |
| in pop. 1985–92 | 4.0% | Fertility rate (per woman) | 7.4 |
| Pop. under 15 | 49.0% | | |
| Pop. over 65 | 2.6% | | per 1,000 pop. |
| No. of men per 100 women | 103 | Crude birth rate | 49.9 |
| Human Development Index | 29 | Crude death rate | 14.7 |

## The economy

| | | | |
|---|---|---|---|
| GDP | CFAfr1,853bn | GDP per head | $674 |
| GDP | $7bn | GDP per head in purchasing | |
| Av. ann. growth in real | | power parity (USA=100) | 6 |
| GDP 1985–92 | 0.1% | | |

| Origins of GDP[a] | | Components of GDP[a] | |
|---|---|---|---|
| | % of total | | % of total |
| Agriculture | 37.8 | Private consumption | 67.3 |
| Industry, of which: | 22.5 | Public consumption | 17.5 |
| manufacturing | ... | Investment | 10.4 |
| Services | 39.7 | Exports | 36.7 |
| | | Imports | -31.9 |

## Structure of manufacturing

| | % of total | | % of total |
|---|---|---|---|
| Agric. & food processing | ... | Other | ... |
| Textiles & clothing | ... | Av. ann. increase in industrial | |
| Metal products & machinery | ... | output 1980–91 | -1.6% |

## Energy

| | '000 TCE | | |
|---|---|---|---|
| Total output | 653 | % output exported | 58.3 |
| Total consumption | 2,696 | % consumption imported | 109.4 |
| Consumption per head, | | | |
| kg coal equivalent | 217 | | |

## Inflation and finance

| | | | |
|---|---|---|---|
| Consumer price | | | av. ann. change 1988–92 |
| inflation 1993 | 4.0% | Narrow money (M1) | -3.9% |
| Av. ann. inflation 1988–93 | 2.7% | Broad money | -2.1% |

## Exchange rates

| | end 1993 | | end June 1993 |
|---|---|---|---|
| CFAfr per $ | 295 | Effective rates | 1985 = 100 |
| CFAfr per SDR | 405 | – nominal | 308.0 |
| CFAfr per Ecu | 330 | – real | 134.3 |

## Principal exports

| | $m fob | | $m fob |
|---|---|---|---|
| Cocoa beans & products | 968 | Coffee & products | 210 |
| Petroleum & products | 322 | Raw cotton | 110 |
| Sawn timber | 236 | Total incl. others | **2,880** |

### Main export destinations[a]

| | % of total | | % of total |
|---|---|---|---|
| France | 15.1 | Italy | 7.6 |
| Germany | 9.9 | Netherlands | 7.4 |

## Principal imports

| | $m cif | | $m cif |
|---|---|---|---|
| Crude oil | 438 | Pharmaceuticals | 129 |
| Non-road transport | 208 | Fresh fish | 101 |
| Machinery | 154 | Total incl. others | **1,884** |

### Main origins of imports[a]

| | % of total | | % of total |
|---|---|---|---|
| France | 36.0 | Netherlands | 4.4 |
| Nigeria | 20.2 | United States | 3.9 |

## Balance of payments, reserves and debt, $bn

| | | | |
|---|---|---|---|
| Visible exports fob | 2.9 | Overall balance | -1.2 |
| Visible imports fob | -1.9 | Change in reserves | 0.1 |
| Trade balance | 0.9 | Level of reserves | |
| Invisibles inflows | 0.6 | end Dec. | 0.02 |
| Invisibles outflows | -2.6 | No. months import cover | 0.1 |
| Net transfers | -0.3 | Foreign debt | 18.0 |
| Current account balance | -1.3 | – as % of GDP | 207.1 |
| – as % of GDP | -15.1 | Debt service | 1.1 |
| Capital balance | -0.1 | Debt service ratio | 31.5 |

## Family life

| | | | |
|---|---|---|---|
| No. of households | 1.8m | Divorces per 1,000 pop. | ... |
| Av. no. per household | 6.0 | Cost of living, Sept. 1993 | |
| Marriages per 1,000 pop. | ... | New York = 100 | 134 |

a 1991.

# CZECH REPUBLIC

| | | | |
|---|---|---|---|
| Area | 78,664 sq km | Currency | Koruna (Kc) |
| Capital | Prague | | |

## People

| | | | |
|---|---|---|---|
| Population | 10.4m | Life expectancy: men[b] | 69 yrs |
| Pop. per sq km[a] | 131 | women | 76 yrs |
| Av. ann. growth | | Adult literacy[b] | 99.0% |
| in pop. 1985–92 | 0.1% | Fertility rate (per woman)[b] | 2.0 |
| Pop. under 15[b] | 20.9% | | |
| Pop. over 65[b] | 12.1% | | *per 1,000 pop.* |
| No. of men per 100 women[b] | 95 | Crude birth rate[c] | 13.3 |
| Human Development Index[b] | 89 | Crude death rate | 11.3 |

## The economy

| | | | |
|---|---|---|---|
| GDP | Kcs707bn | GDP per head | $2,438 |
| GDP | $25bn | GDP per head in purchasing | |
| Av. ann. growth in real | | power parity (USA=100) | 34 |
| GDP 1985–92[b] | -1.4% | | |

| Origins of NMP[d] | | Components of NMP[d] | |
|---|---|---|---|
| | *% of total* | | *% of total* |
| Agriculture | 8.9 | Private consumption[c] | 57.0 |
| Industry, of which: | 68.9 | Public consumption | 23.9 |
| manufacturing | ... | Investment | 19.1 |
| Services | 22.2 | Exports | ... |
| | | Imports | ... |

## Structure of manufacturing

| | *% of total* | | *% of total* |
|---|---|---|---|
| Agric. & food processing | 10 | Other | 44 |
| Textiles & clothing | 11 | Av. ann. increase in industrial | |
| Metal products & machinery | 35 | output 1980–91 | 0.3% |

## Energy[b]

| | *'000 TCE* | | |
|---|---|---|---|
| Total output | 60,724 | % output exported | 9.2 |
| Total consumption | 88,927 | % consumption imported | 42.4 |
| Consumption per head, | | | |
| kg coal equivalent | 5,666 | | |

## Inflation and finance[b]

| | | | |
|---|---|---|---|
| Consumer price | | *av. ann. increase 1988–92* | |
| inflation 1993 | 20.8% | Narrow money (M1) | 9.7% |
| Av. ann. inflation 1988–93 | 15.9% | Broad money | 12.1% |

## Exchange rates

| | *end 1993* | | *end June 1993* |
|---|---|---|---|
| Kc per $ | 29.96 | Effective rates | *1985 = 100* |
| Kc per SDR | 41.15 | – nominal | ... |
| Kc per Ecu | 33.56 | – real | ... |

## Principal exports[ce]

| | $bn fob | | $bn fob |
|---|---|---|---|
| Manufactured goods | 2.1 | Chemicals | 0.8 |
| Machinery & industrial | | Food products | 0.6 |
| equipment | 1.4 | Total incl. others | **6.6** |

### Main export destinations[e]

| | % of total | | % of total |
|---|---|---|---|
| Germany | 25.1 | EU | 40.7 |
| Ex-Soviet Union | 19.4 | Other Eastern Europe | 13.4 |

## Principal imports[ce]

| | $bn fob | | $bn fob |
|---|---|---|---|
| Machinery & industrial | | Raw materials | 0.5 |
| equipment | 2.4 | Agric. products & foodstuffs | 0.6 |
| Chemicals & products | 0.8 | Total incl. others | **5.7** |

### Main origins of imports[e]

| | % of total | | % of total |
|---|---|---|---|
| Ex-Soviet Union | 31.8 | EU | 33.0 |
| Germany | 20.3 | Other Eastern Europe | 7.8 |

## Balance of payments[b], reserves[b] and debt[b], $bn

| | | | |
|---|---|---|---|
| Visible exports fob | 11.5 | Overall balance | -0.4 |
| Visible imports fob | -13.3 | Change in reserves | -2.3 |
| Trade balance | -1.8 | Level of reserves | |
| Invisibles inflows | 4.8 | end Dec. | 1.3 |
| Invisibles outflows | -3.1 | No. months import cover | 1.2 |
| Net transfers | 0.1 | Foreign debt | 9.3 |
| Current account balance | -0.03 | – as % of GDP | 28.8 |
| – as % of GDP | -0.1 | Debt service | 2.0 |
| Capital balance | -0.2 | Debt service ratio | ... |

## Family life[b]

| | | | |
|---|---|---|---|
| No. of households | 5.4m | Divorces per 1,000 pop. | 2.4 |
| Av. no. per household | 2.8 | Cost of living, Sept. 1993 | |
| Marriages per 1,000 pop. | 6.7 | New York = 100 | 52 |

Czechoslovakia split into the Czech Republic and Slovakia on January 1, 1993.

*Basic data for Slovakia*

| | | | |
|---|---|---|---|
| Area, sq km | 49,000 | Population, m | 5.3 |
| Capital | Bratislava | GDP, $bn | 10 |
| Currency | Koruna (Sk) | GDP per head | $1,917 |
| $1=Sk33.22, end 1993 | | | |

a  1992.
b  Ex-Czechoslovakia.
c  1991.
d  1990.
e  Western countries.

# DENMARK

| | | | |
|---|---|---|---|
| Area | 43,069 sq km | Currency | Danish krone (DKr) |
| Capital | Copenhagen | | |

## People

| | | | |
|---|---|---|---|
| Population | 5.1m | Life expectancy: men | 73 yrs |
| Pop. per sq km | 121 | women | 79 yrs |
| Av. ann. growth | | Adult literacy | 99.0% |
| in pop. 1985–92 | 0.1 | Fertility rate (per woman) | 1.7 |
| Pop. under 15 | 17.1% | | |
| Pop. over 65 | 15.4% | | *per 1,000 pop.* |
| No. of men per 100 women | 98 | Crude birth rate | 12.5 |
| Human Development Index | 96 | Crude death rate | 11.6 |

## The economy

| | | | |
|---|---|---|---|
| GDP | DKr809bn | GDP per head | $25,927 |
| GDP | $134bn | GDP per head in purchasing | |
| Av. ann. growth in real | | power parity (USA=100) | 78 |
| GDP 1985–92 | 1.8% | | |

| Origins of GDP[a] | | Components of GDP | |
|---|---|---|---|
| | *% of total* | | *% of total* |
| Agriculture | 6.4 | Private consumption | 52.0 |
| Industry, of which: | 28.7 | Public consumption | 25.4 |
| manufacturing[a] | 21.9 | Investment | 14.9 |
| Services | 64.9 | Exports | 37.0 |
| | | Imports | -29.3 |

## Structure of manufacturing

| | *% of total* | | *% of total* |
|---|---|---|---|
| Agric. & food processing | 21 | Other | 51 |
| Textiles & clothing | 4 | Av. ann. increase in industrial | |
| Machinery & transport | 23 | output 1980–91 | 2.9% |

## Energy

| | *'000 TCE* | | |
|---|---|---|---|
| Total output | 15,390 | % output exported | 84.0 |
| Total consumption | 26,170 | % consumption imported | 96.9 |
| Consumption per head, | | | |
| kg coal equivalent | 5,084 | | |

## Inflation and finance

| | | | |
|---|---|---|---|
| Consumer price | | *av. ann. increase 1988–92* | |
| inflation 1993 | 1.3% | Narrow money (M1) | 6.3% |
| Av. ann. inflation 1988–93 | 2.9% | Broad money | 3.3% |

## Exchange rates

| | *end 1993* | | *end June 1993* |
|---|---|---|---|
| DKr per $ | 6.78 | Effective rates | *1985 = 100* |
| DKr per SDR | 9.30 | – nominal | 117.7 |
| DKr per Ecu | 7.59 | – real | 118.9 |

## Principal exports[a]

|  | $bn fob |  | $bn fob |
|---|---|---|---|
| Agric. products & foodstuffs | 9.0 | Furniture | 1.5 |
| Machinery & electrical products | 8.3 | Energy & products | 1.5 |
|  |  | Transport equipment | 1.0 |
| Chemicals | 3.4 | Total incl. others | **35.9** |

### Main export destinations[a]

|  | % of total |  | % of total |
|---|---|---|---|
| Germany | 22.4 | Norway | 5.5 |
| Sweden | 11.5 | EU | 54.0 |
| United Kingdom | 10.3 | Efta | 24.5 |
| France | 5.8 |  |  |

## Principal imports[a]

|  | $bn cif |  | $bn cif |
|---|---|---|---|
| Machinery & electrical products | 6.9 | Textiles & clothing | 2.3 |
|  |  | Energy & products | 2.2 |
| Chemicals | 2.7 | Iron & steel | 1.6 |
| Transport equipment | 2.7 | Total incl. others | **32.3** |

### Main origins of imports[a]

|  | % of total |  | % of total |
|---|---|---|---|
| Germany | 22.1 | Netherlands | 5.7 |
| Sweden | 10.8 | EU | 52.7 |
| United Kingdom | 8.0 | Efta | 22.8 |
| United States | 6.3 |  |  |

## Balance of payments, reserves and aid, $bn

|  |  |  |  |
|---|---|---|---|
| Visible exports fob | 40.6 | Capital balance | -5.0 |
| Visible imports fob | -33.4 | Overall balance | -0.2 |
| Trade balance | 7.2 | Change in reserves | 3.7 |
| Invisibles inflows | 30.2 | Level of reserves end Dec. | 11.6 |
| Invisibles outflows | -32.2 |  |  |
| Net transfers | -0.5 | No. months import cover | 4.2 |
| Current account balance | 4.7 | Aid given | 1.39 |
| – as % of GDP | 3.5 | – as % of GDP | 1.02 |

## Family life

|  |  |  |  |
|---|---|---|---|
| No. of households | 2.3m | Divorces per 1,000 pop. | 3.0 |
| Av. no. per household | 2.2 | Cost of living, Sept. 1993 |  |
| Marriages per 1,000 pop. | 6.0 | New York = 100 | 109 |

a 1991.

# EGYPT

| Area | 1,001,449 sq km | Currency | Egyptian pound (£E) |
|---|---|---|---|
| Capital | Cairo | | |

## People

| | | | |
|---|---|---|---|
| Population | 54.8m | Life expectancy: men | 60 yrs |
| Pop. per sq km | 58 | women | 63 yrs |
| Av. ann. growth | | Adult literacy | 48.4% |
| in pop. 1985–92 | 2.4% | Fertility rate (per woman) | 4.1 |
| Pop. under 15 | 37.9% | | |
| Pop. over 65 | 4.2% | | *per 1,000 pop.* |
| No. of men per 100 women | 103 | Crude birth rate | 31.3 |
| Human Development Index | 39 | Crude death rate | 9.1 |

## The economy

| | | | |
|---|---|---|---|
| GDP | £E117bn | GDP per head | $630 |
| GDP | $35bn | GDP per head in purchasing | |
| Av. ann. growth in real | | power parity (USA=100) | 9 |
| GDP 1985–92 | 3.8% | | |

| **Origins of GDP**[a] | | **Components of GDP**[a] | |
|---|---|---|---|
| | *% of total* | | *% of total* |
| Agriculture | 19.6 | Private consumption | 72.6 |
| Industry, of which: | 28.0 | Public consumption | 10.4 |
| manufacturing | ... | Investment | 19.9 |
| Services | 52.4 | Exports | 29.0 |
| | | Imports | -31.9 |

## Structure of manufacturing

| | *% of total* | | *% of total* |
|---|---|---|---|
| Agric. & food processing | 31 | Other | 44 |
| Textiles & clothing | 16 | Av. ann. increase in industrial | |
| Machinery & transport | 9 | output 1980–91 | 4.2% |

## Energy

| | *'000 TCE* | | |
|---|---|---|---|
| Total output | 79,151 | % output exported | 47.2 |
| Total consumption | 38,246 | % consumption imported | 4.9 |
| Consumption per head, | | | |
| kg coal equivalent | 713 | | |

## Inflation and finance

| | | | |
|---|---|---|---|
| Consumer price | | *av. ann. increase 1988–92* | |
| inflation 1993 | 12.1% | Narrow money (M1) | 11.1% |
| Av. ann. inflation 1988–93 | 16.8% | Broad money | 21.2% |

## Exchange rates

| | *end 1993* | | *end June 1993* |
|---|---|---|---|
| | | | *1985 = 100* |
| £E per $ | 3.37 | Effective rates | |
| £E per SDR | 4.63 | – nominal | ... |
| £E per Ecu | 3.77 | – real | ... |

## Principal exports[b]

|  | $m fob |  | $m fob |
|---|---|---|---|
| Petroleum & products | 1,651 | Other agric. products | 211 |
| Cotton yarn & textiles | 564 | Raw cotton | 35 |
| Industrial goods | 361 | Total incl. others | **3,636** |

**Main export destinations**

|  | % of total |  | % of total |
|---|---|---|---|
| Italy | 20.6 | France | 6.2 |
| United States | 8.2 | Singapore | 5.3 |
| Spain | 6.9 | Greece | 5.2 |

## Principal imports[b]

|  | $m cif |  | $m cif |
|---|---|---|---|
| Machinery & transport equipment | 2,356 | Chemicals & rubber | 1,115 |
|  |  | Wood, paper & textiles | 967 |
| Agric. products & foodstuffs | 1,912 | Raw materials | 956 |
|  |  | Total incl. others | **10,040** |

**Main origins of imports**

|  | % of total |  | % of total |
|---|---|---|---|
| United States | 25.4 | France | 7.0 |
| Germany | 10.1 | Japan | 4.8 |
| Italy | 8.7 | United Kingdom | 3.7 |

## Balance of payments, reserves and debt, $bn

|  |  |  |  |
|---|---|---|---|
| Visible exports fob | 3.4 | Overall balance | 3.4 |
| Visible imports fob | -8.9 | Change in reserves | 5.4 |
| Trade balance | -5.5 | Level of reserves |  |
| Invisibles inflows | 8.9 | end Dec. | 11.4 |
| Invisibles outflows | -7.7 | No. months import cover | 15.4 |
| Net transfers | 7.1 | Foreign debt | 40.4 |
| Current account balance | 2.8 | – as % of GDP | 116.8 |
| – as % of GDP | 8.1 | Debt service | 2.5 |
| Capital balance | -0.2 | Debt service ratio | 15.4 |

## Family life

|  |  |  |  |
|---|---|---|---|
| No. of households | 9.7m | Divorces per 1,000 pop. | 1.6 |
| Av. no. per household | 4.9 | Cost of living, Sept. 1993 |  |
| Marriages per 1,000 pop. | 9.1 | New York = 100 | 90 |

a  1991.
b  Year ending June 30, 1992.

# FINLAND

| Area | 337,032 sq km | Currency | Markka (Fmk) |
|------|---------------|----------|--------------|
| Capital | Helsinki | | |

## People

| | | | |
|---|---|---|---|
| Population | 5.06m | Life expectancy: men | 72 yrs |
| Pop. per sq km | 15 | women | 80 yrs |
| Av. ann. growth | | Adult literacy | 99% |
| in pop. 1985–92 | 0.4% | Fertility rate (per woman) | 1.8 |
| Pop. under 15 | 18.9% | | |
| Pop. over 65 | 14.1% | | *per 1,000 pop.* |
| No. of men per 100 women | 95 | Crude birth rate | 12.8 |
| Human Development Index | 95 | Crude death rate | 10.2 |

## The economy

| | | | |
|---|---|---|---|
| GDP | Fmk520bn | GDP per head | $22,977 |
| GDP | $116bn | GDP per head in purchasing | |
| Av. ann. growth in real | | power parity (USA=100) | 77 |
| GDP 1985–92 | 1.1% | | |

| **Origins of GDP** | | **Components of GDP** | |
|---|---|---|---|
| | *% of total* | | *% of total* |
| Agriculture | 6.3 | Private consumption | 55.6 |
| Industry, of which: | 34.4 | Public consumption | 23.0 |
| manufacturing | 25.3 | Investment | 21.8 |
| Services | 59.3 | Exports | 31.1 |
| | | Imports | -31.5 |

## Structure of manufacturing

| | *% of total* | | *% of total* |
|---|---|---|---|
| Agric. & food processing | 13 | Other | 60 |
| Textiles & clothing | 4 | Av. ann. increase in industrial | |
| Machinery & transport | 23 | output 1980–91 | 3.0% |

## Energy

| | *'000 TCE* | | |
|---|---|---|---|
| Total output | 10,804 | % output exported[a] | 37.1 |
| Total consumption | 34,190 | % consumption imported[a] | 78.7 |
| Consumption per head, | | | |
| kg coal equivalent | 6,845 | | |

## Inflation and finance

| | | | |
|---|---|---|---|
| Consumer price | | *av. ann. increase 1988–92* | |
| inflation 1993 | 2.1% | Narrow money (M1) | 34.8% |
| Av. ann. inflation 1988–93 | 4.4% | Broad money | 7.9% |

## Exchange rates

| | *end 1993* | | *end June 1993* |
|---|---|---|---|
| Fmk per $ | 5.78 | Effective rates | *1985 = 100* |
| Fmk per SDR | 7.95 | – nominal | 77.7 |
| Fmk per Ecu | 6.47 | – real | 73.1 |

## Principal exports

| | $bn fob | | $bn fob |
|---|---|---|---|
| Metals & engineering equipment | 8.0 | Chemicals | 2.7 |
| | | Wood & products | 1.8 |
| Paper & products | 7.3 | Total incl. others | **24.0** |

### Main export destinations

| | % of total | | % of total |
|---|---|---|---|
| Germany | 15.6 | Netherlands | 5.2 |
| Sweden | 12.8 | Denmark | 3.6 |
| United Kingdom | 10.7 | Russia | 2.8 |
| France | 6.7 | EU | 53.2 |
| United States | 5.9 | | |

## Principal imports

| | $bn cif | | $bn cif |
|---|---|---|---|
| Raw materials | 11.1 | Energy & products | 2.2 |
| Consumer goods | 4.6 | | |
| Capital goods | 3.0 | Total incl. others | **22.5** |

### Main origins of imports

| | % of total | | % of total |
|---|---|---|---|
| Germany | 16.9 | Japan | 5.5 |
| Sweden | 11.7 | France | 4.6 |
| United Kingdom | 8.6 | Norway | 4.0 |
| Russia | 7.1 | EU | 47.2 |
| United States | 6.1 | Efta | 19.0 |

## Balance of payments, reserves and aid, $bn

| | | | |
|---|---|---|---|
| Visible exports fob | 23.6 | Capital balance | 3.4 |
| Visible imports fob | -19.7 | Overall balance | -2.2 |
| Trade balance | 3.9 | Change in reserves | -2.4 |
| Invisibles inflows | 6.4 | Level of reserves | |
| Invisibles outflows | -14.5 | end Dec. | 5.6 |
| Net transfers | -0.9 | No. months import cover | 3.4 |
| Current account balance | -5.1 | Aid given | 0.64 |
| – as % of GDP | -4.4 | – as % of GDP | 0.62 |

## Family life

| | | | |
|---|---|---|---|
| No. of households | 2.0m | Divorces per 1,000 pop. | 2.9 |
| Av. no. per household | 2.5 | Cost of living, Sept. 1993 | |
| Marriages per 1,000 pop. | 4.7 | New York = 100 | 93 |

a  Energy trade data are distorted by transitory and oil refinery activities.

# FRANCE

| Area | 552,000sq km | Currency | Franc (FFr) |
|---|---|---|---|
| Capital | Paris | | |

## People

| | | | |
|---|---|---|---|
| Population | 57.3m | Life expectancy: men | 73 yrs |
| Pop. per sq km | 105 | women | 81 yrs |
| Av. ann. growth | | Adult literacy | 99.0% |
| in pop. 1985–92 | 0.6% | Fertility rate (per woman) | 1.8 |
| Pop. under 15 | 19.8% | | |
| Pop. over 65 | 14.9% | | *per 1,000 pop.* |
| No. of men per 100 women | 95 | Crude birth rate | 13.5 |
| Human Development Index | 97 | Crude death rate | 9.8 |

## The economy

| | | | |
|---|---|---|---|
| GDP | FFr6,771bn | GDP per head | $22,300 |
| GDP | $1,279bn | GDP per head in purchasing | |
| Av. ann. growth in real | | power parity (USA=100) | 81 |
| GDP, 1985–92 | 2.5% | | |

| **Origins of GDP** | | **Components of GDP** | |
|---|---|---|---|
| | *% of total* | | *% of total* |
| Agriculture | 3.1 | Private consumption | 60.5 |
| Industry, of which: | 31.0 | Public consumption | 18.6 |
| manufacturing | 21.9 | Investment | 19.7 |
| Services | 65.9 | Exports | 23.1 |
| | | Imports | -21.8 |

## Structure of manufacturing

| | *% of total* | | *% of total* |
|---|---|---|---|
| Agric. & food processing | 13 | Other | 50 |
| Textiles & clothing | 6 | Av. ann. increase in industrial | |
| Metal products & machinery | 31 | output 1980–91 | 0.9% |

## Energy

| | *'000 TCE* | | |
|---|---|---|---|
| Total output | 148,922 | % output exported | 17.8 |
| Total consumption | 311,021 | % consumption imported | 66.1 |
| Consumption per head, | | | |
| kg coal equivalent | 6,845 | | |

## Inflation and finance

| Consumer price | | *av. ann. increase 1988–92* | |
|---|---|---|---|
| inflation 1993 | 2.1% | Narrow money (M1) | 2.3% |
| Av. ann. inflation 1988–93 | 2.9% | Broad money | 2.2% |

## Exchange rates

| | *end 1993* | | *end June 1993* |
|---|---|---|---|
| FFr per $ | 5.90 | Effective rates | *1985 = 100* |
| FFr per SDR | 8.10 | – nominal | 109.7 |
| FFr per Ecu | 6.61 | – real | 98.9 |

## Principal exports

| | $bn fob | | $bn fob |
|---|---|---|---|
| Capital equipment | 64.2 | Chemicals | 33.8 |
| Agric. products | | Motor vehicles & other | |
| & foodstuffs | 37.9 | transport equipment | 32.5 |
| Non-durable consumer | | Steel & other metals | 20.9 |
| goods | 35.5 | Total incl. others | **236.0** |

### Main export destinations

| | % of total | | % of total |
|---|---|---|---|
| Germany | 17.6 | Spain | 7.2 |
| Italy | 10.9 | United States | 6.5 |
| United Kingdom | 9.2 | Netherlands | 4.9 |
| Belgium/Luxembourg | 9.2 | EU | 62.7 |

## Principal imports

| | $bn cif | | $bn cif |
|---|---|---|---|
| Capital equipment | 58.4 | Motor vehicles & other | |
| Non-durable consumer | | transport equipment | 26.4 |
| goods | 40.5 | Steel & other metals | 21.1 |
| Chemicals | 37.0 | Energy products | 20.4 |
| Agric. products | | | |
| & foodstuffs | 27.8 | Total incl. others | **230.9** |

### Main origins of imports

| | % of total | | % of total |
|---|---|---|---|
| Germany | 18.7 | United Kingdom | 7.7 |
| Italy | 10.6 | Spain | 5.4 |
| Belgium/Luxembourg | 8.7 | Netherlands | 5.1 |
| United States | 8.4 | EU | 59.7 |

## Balance of payments, reserves and aid, $bn

| | | | |
|---|---|---|---|
| Visible exports fob | 225.2 | Capital balance | -19.0 |
| Visible imports fob | -223.6 | Overall balance | -13.1 |
| Trade balance | 1.7 | Change in reserves | -5.4 |
| Invisibles inflows | 181.4 | Level of reserves | |
| Invisibles outflows | -170.4 | end Dec. | 53.3 |
| Net transfers | -8.5 | No. months import cover | 2.9 |
| Current account balance | 4.1 | Aid given[a] | 8.3 |
| – as % of GDP | 0.3 | – as % of GDP | 0.63 |

## Family life

| | | | |
|---|---|---|---|
| No. of households | 21.5m | Divorces per 1,000 pop. | 1.9 |
| Av. no. per household | 2.6 | Cost of living, Sept. 1993 | |
| Marriages per 1,000 pop. | 5.0 | New York = 100 | 123 |

a  Including aid to French overseas territories.

# GERMANY

| | | | |
|---|---|---|---|
| Area | 357,039 sq km | Currency | Deutschemark (DM) |
| Capital | Berlin[a] | | |

## People

| | | | |
|---|---|---|---|
| Population | 80.5m | Life expectancy: men | 73 yrs |
| Pop. per sq km | 228 | women | 79 yrs |
| Av. ann. growth | | Adult literacy | 99.0% |
| in pop. 1985–92 | 0.6% | Fertility rate (per woman) | 1.5 |
| Pop. under 15 | 17.1% | | |
| Pop. over 65 | 14.8% | | *per 1,000 pop.* |
| No. of men per 100 women | 95 | Crude birth rate | 11.3 |
| Human Development Index | 96 | Crude death rate | 11.4 |

## The economy

| | | | |
|---|---|---|---|
| GDP | DM2,883bn | GDP per head | $22,917 |
| GDP | $1,846bn | GDP per head in purchasing | |
| Av. ann. growth in real | | power parity (USA=100) | 85 |
| GDP 1985–92[b] | 2.8% | | |

| **Origins of GDP**[b] | | **Components of GDP**[b] | |
|---|---|---|---|
| | *% of total* | | *% of total* |
| Agriculture | 1.2 | Private consumption | 54.0 |
| Industry, of which: | 37.2 | Public consumption | 17.9 |
| manufacturing | 33.4 | Investment | 21.0 |
| Services | 58.1 | Exports | 38.2 |
| | | Imports | -31.1 |

## Structure of manufacturing[b]

| | *% of total* | | *% of total* |
|---|---|---|---|
| Agric. & food processing | 9 | Other | 45 |
| Textiles & clothing | 4 | Av. ann. increase in industrial | |
| Machinery & transport | 42 | output 1980–91 | 0.9 |

## Energy

| | *'000 TCE* | | |
|---|---|---|---|
| Total output | 272,896 | % output exported | 9.8 |
| Total consumption | 509,233 | % consumption imported | 54.5 |
| Consumption per head, | | | |
| kg coal equivalent | 6,375 | | |

## Inflation[b] and finance

| | | *av. ann. increase 1991–92* | |
|---|---|---|---|
| Consumer price | | | |
| inflation 1993 | 4.1% | Narrow money (M1) | 7.8% |
| Av. ann. inflation 1988–93 | 3.1% | Broad money | 7.2% |

## Exchange rates

| | *end 1993* | | *end June 1993* |
|---|---|---|---|
| DM per $ | 1.73 | Effective rates | *1985 = 100* |
| DM per SDR | 2.37 | – nominal | 124.1 |
| DM per Ecu | 1.94 | – real | 136.9 |

## Principal exports

| | $bn fob | | $bn fob |
|---|---|---|---|
| Motor vehicles | 120.8 | Electrical engineering | |
| Mechanical engineering | | products | 80.0 |
| products | 100.9 | Agric. products & foodstuffs | 39.1 |
| Chemicals | 85.3 | Textiles | 24.0 |
| | | Total incl. others | **430.4** |

### Main export destinations

| | % of total | | % of total |
|---|---|---|---|
| France | 13.0 | Belgium/Luxembourg | 7.4 |
| Italy | 9.3 | EU | 54.3 |
| Netherlands | 8.3 | | |
| United Kingdom | 7.7 | | |

## Principal imports

| | $bn cif | | $bn cif |
|---|---|---|---|
| Agric. products & | | Chemicals | 57.6 |
| foodstuffs | 73.7 | Mechanical engineering | |
| Motor vehicles | 69.8 | products | 43.5 |
| Electrical engineering | | Textiles | 33.4 |
| products | 64.8 | Total incl. others | **408.5** |

### Main origins of imports

| | % of total | | % of total |
|---|---|---|---|
| France | 12.0 | United Kingdom | 6.8 |
| Netherlands | 9.6 | EU | 52.0 |
| Italy | 9.2 | | |
| Belgium/Luxembourg | 7.0 | | |

## Balance of payments, reserves and aid, $bn

| | | | |
|---|---|---|---|
| Visible exports fob | 406.9 | Capital balance | 68.1 |
| Visible imports fob | -374.0 | Overall balance | 43.0 |
| Trade balance | 32.9 | Change in reserves | 36.3 |
| Invisibles inflows | 156.0 | Level of reserves | |
| Invisibles outflows | -182.5 | end Dec. | 99.4 |
| Net transfers | -32.0 | No. months import cover | 3.2 |
| Current account balance | -25.6 | Aid given | 7.6 |
| – as % of GDP | -1.4 | – as % of GDP | 0.39 |

## Family life

| | | | |
|---|---|---|---|
| No. of households | 32.7m | Divorces per 1,000 pop. | 1.9 |
| Av. no. per household | 2.3 | Cost of living, Sept. 1993 | |
| Marriages per 1,000 pop. | 6.5 | New York = 100 | 107 |

a  Date of government move from Bonn unknown.
b  Western Germany.

# GREECE

| | | | |
|---|---|---|---|
| Area | 131,944 sq km | Currency | Drachma (Dr) |
| Capital | Athens | | |

## People

| | | | |
|---|---|---|---|
| Population | 10.4m | Life expectancy: men | 75 yrs |
| Pop. per sq km | 78 | women | 80 yrs |
| Av. ann. growth | | Adult literacy | 93.2% |
| in pop. 1985–92 | 0.7% | Fertility rate (per woman) | 1.5 |
| Pop. under 15 | 17.3% | | |
| Pop. over 65 | 15.4% | | *per 1,000 pop.* |
| No. of men per 100 women | 97 | Crude birth rate | 10.4 |
| Human Development Index | 90 | Crude death rate | 9.8 |

## The economy

| | | | |
|---|---|---|---|
| GDP | Dr14,297bn | GDP per head | $7,184 |
| GDP | $75bn | GDP per head in purchasing | |
| Av. ann. growth in real | | power parity (USA=100) | 34 |
| GDP 1985–92 | 1.8% | | |

| Origins of GDP | | Components of GDP | |
|---|---|---|---|
| | *% of total* | | *% of total* |
| Agriculture | 14.9 | Private consumption | 71.8 |
| Industry, of which: | 26.1 | Public consumption | 19.8 |
| manufacturing | 16.7 | Investment | 18.1 |
| Services | 59.0 | Exports | 23.2 |
| | | Imports | -33.1 |

## Structure of manufacturing

| | *% of total* | | *% of total* |
|---|---|---|---|
| Agric. & food processing | 22 | Other | 45 |
| Textiles & clothing | 21 | Av. ann. increase in industrial | |
| Metal products & machinery | 12 | output 1980–91 | 1.2% |

## Energy

| | *'000 TCE* | | |
|---|---|---|---|
| Total output | 11,661 | % output exported | 56.8 |
| Total consumption | 32,176 | % consumption imported | 90.2 |
| Consumption per head, | | | |
| kg coal equivalent | 3,169 | | |

## Inflation and finance

| | | | |
|---|---|---|---|
| Consumer price | | *av. ann. increase 1988–92* | |
| inflation 1993 | 14.4% | Narrow money (M1) | 17.6% |
| Av. ann. inflation 1988–93 | 16.2% | Broad money[b] | 14.9% |

## Exchange rates

| | *end 1993* | | *end June 1993* |
|---|---|---|---|
| Dr per $ | 249 | Effective rates | *1985 = 100* |
| Dr per SDR | 342 | – nominal | 44.1 |
| Dr per Ecu | 279 | – real | 110.8 |

## Principal exports[a]

|  | $bn fob |  | $bn fob |
|---|---|---|---|
| Manufactured products | 3.1 | Raw materials & industrial | |
| Food & beverages | 1.5 | supplies | 0.2 |
| Petroleum products | 0.6 | Tobacco | 0.2 |
| Minerals | 0.3 | Total incl. others | **9.5** |

### Main export destinations

|  | % of total |  | % of total |
|---|---|---|---|
| Germany | 23.0 | United Kingdom | 6.9 |
| Italy | 18.0 | United States | 4.0 |
| France | 7.2 | EU | 64.1 |

## Principal imports[a]

|  | $bn cif |  | $bn cif |
|---|---|---|---|
| Manufactured consumer | | Petroleum | 1.2 |
| goods | 8.0 | Chemicals & products | 1.0 |
| Machinery equipment | 3.5 | Iron & steel | 0.6 |
| Foodstuffs | 2.8 | Total incl. others | **23.1** |

### Main origins of imports

|  | % of total |  | % of total |
|---|---|---|---|
| Germany | 20.2 | Netherlands | 6.8 |
| Italy | 14.2 | Japan | 6.4 |
| France | 7.8 | EU | 62.7 |

## Balance of payments, reserves and debt, $bn

|  |  |  |  |
|---|---|---|---|
| Visible exports fob | 6.0 | Overall balance | -0.4 |
| Visible imports fob | -17.6 | Change in reserves | -0.3 |
| Trade balance | -11.6 | Level of reserves | |
| Invisibles inflows | 9.3 | end Dec. | 5.5 |
| Invisibles outflows | -6.3 | No. months import cover | 3.8 |
| Net transfers | 6.5 | Foreign debt | 30.9 |
| Current account balance | -2.1 | – as % of GDP | 39.3 |
| – as % of GDP | -2.8 | Debt service | 5.7 |
| Capital balance | 2.6 | Debt service ratio | 27.9 |

## Family life

|  |  |  |  |
|---|---|---|---|
| No. of households | 3.0m | Divorces per 1,000 pop. | 0.9 |
| Av. no. per household | 3.1 | Cost of living, Sept. 1993 | |
| Marriages per 1,000 pop. | 5.9 | New York = 100 | 89 |

a  Energy trade figures are distorted by transitory and oil refining activities.

# HONG KONG

| Area | 1,074 sq km | Currency | Hong Kong dollar (HK$) |
|------|-------------|----------|------------------------|
| Capital | Victoria | | |

## People

| | | | |
|---|---|---|---|
| Population | 5.8m | Life expectancy: men | 75 yrs |
| Pop. per sq km | 5,677 | women | 80 yrs |
| Av. ann. growth | | Adult literacy | 90.0% |
| in pop. 1985–92 | 0.9% | Fertility rate (per woman) | 1.4 |
| Pop. under 15 | 19.1% | | |
| Pop. over 65 | 10.1% | | *per 1,000 pop.* |
| No. of men per 100 women | 107 | Crude birth rate | 12.7 |
| Human Development Index | 91 | Crude death rate | 6.1 |

## The economy

| | | | |
|---|---|---|---|
| GDP | HK$690bn | GDP per head | $15,379 |
| GDP | $89bn | GDP per head in purchasing | |
| Av. ann. growth in real | | power parity (USA=100) | 73 |
| GDP 1985–92 | 6.1% | | |

| **Origins of GDP**[a] | | **Components of GDP** | |
|---|---|---|---|
| | *% of total* | | *% of total* |
| Agriculture | 0.3 | Private consumption | 30.4 |
| Industry, of which: | 24.9 | Public consumption | 8.2 |
| manufacturing | 16.7 | Investment | 28.4 |
| Services | 74.8 | Net exports of goods | |
| | | & services | 32.9 |

## Structure of manufacturing

| | *% of total* | | *% of total* |
|---|---|---|---|
| Agric. & food processing | 7 | Other | 35 |
| Textiles & clothing | 38 | Av. ann. increase in industrial | |
| Machinery & transport | 20 | output 1980–89 | 6.5% |

## Energy

| | *'000 TCE* | | |
|---|---|---|---|
| Total output | ... | % output exported | ... |
| Total consumption | 11,047 | % consumption imported | 169.1 |
| Consumption per head, | | | |
| kg coal equivalent | 1,920 | | |

## Inflation and finance

| Consumer price | | *av. ann. increase 1988–92* | |
|---|---|---|---|
| inflation 1993 | 8.5% | Narrow money (M1) | ... |
| Av. ann. inflation 1988–93 | 9.5% | Broad money | ... |

## Exchange rates

| | *end 1993* | | *end June 1993* |
|---|---|---|---|
| HK$ per $ | 7.73 | Effective rates | *1985 = 100* |
| HK$ per SDR | 10.62 | – nominal | ... |
| HK$ per Ecu | 8.66 | – real | ... |

## Principal exports[b]

| | $bn fob | | $bn fob |
|---|---|---|---|
| Clothing | 10.0 | Textiles | 2.3 |
| Machinery | 7.9 | | |
| Watches & clocks | 2.4 | Total incl. others | **30.2** |

### Main export destinations[c]

| | % of total | | % of total |
|---|---|---|---|
| China | 29.6 | Japan | 5.2 |
| United States | 23.0 | Taiwan | 4.0 |
| Germany | 5.3 | | |

## Principal imports

| | $bn cif | | $bn cif |
|---|---|---|---|
| Consumer goods | 50.9 | Agric. products & foodstuffs[*] | 5.8 |
| Raw materials & semi-manufactured products | 42.6 | Fuels | 2.3 |
| Capital goods | 21.7 | Total incl. others | **123.4** |

### Main origins of imports

| | % of total | | % of total |
|---|---|---|---|
| China | 37.1 | South Korea | 4.6 |
| Japan | 17.4 | Singapore | 4.1 |
| Taiwan | 9.1 | | |
| United States | 7.4 | | |

## Balance of payments, reserves and debt, $bn

| | | | |
|---|---|---|---|
| Visible exports fob | 119.5 | Overall balance | ... |
| Visible imports cif | 123.8 | Change in reserves | ... |
| Trade balance | -4.3 | Level of reserves | |
| Invisibles inflows | ... | end Dec. | ... |
| Invisibles outflows | ... | No. months import cover | ... |
| Net transfers | ... | Foreign debt | 11.7 |
| Current account balance | 1.7 | – as % of GDP | 13.0 |
| – as % of GDP | 1.9 | Debt service | 1.5 |
| Capital balance | ... | Debt service ratio | 1.1 |

## Family life

| | | | |
|---|---|---|---|
| No. of households | 1.6m | Divorces per 1,000 pop. | 1.0 |
| Av. no. per household | 3.4 | Cost of living, Sept. 1993 | |
| Marriages per 1,000 pop. | 8.1 | New York = 100 | 108 |

a   1990.
b   Domestic.
c   Including re-exports.

# HUNGARY

| | | | |
|---|---|---|---|
| Area | 93,030 sq km | Currency | Forint (Ft) |
| Capital | Budapest | | |

## People

| | | | |
|---|---|---|---|
| Population | 10.2m | Life expectancy: men | 66 yrs |
| Pop. per sq km | 113 | women | 74 yrs |
| Av. ann. growth | | Adult literacy | 99.0% |
| in pop. 1985–92 | -0.6% | Fertility rate (per woman) | 1.8 |
| Pop. under 15 | 18.5% | | |
| Pop. over 65 | 13.9% | | *per 1,000 pop.* |
| No. of men per 100 women | 93 | Crude birth rate | 12.3 |
| Human Development Index | 89 | Crude death rate | 13.8 |

## The economy

| | | | |
|---|---|---|---|
| GDP | Ft2,370bn | GDP per head | $3,006 |
| GDP | $30bn | GDP per head in purchasing | |
| Av. ann. growth in real | | power parity (USA=100) | 29 |
| GDP 1985–92 | 1.7% | | |

| Origins of GDP[a] | | Components of GDP[a] | |
|---|---|---|---|
| | *% of total* | | *% of total* |
| Agriculture | 7.4 | Private consumption | 62.5 |
| Industry, of which: | 32.9 | Public consumption | 10.7 |
| manufacturing | 27.6 | Investment | 23.0 |
| Services | 59.6 | Exports | 32.9 |
| | | Imports | -29.1 |

## Structure of manufacturing

| | *% of total* | | *% of total* |
|---|---|---|---|
| Agric. & food processing | 10 | Other | 54 |
| Textiles & clothing | 9 | Av. ann. increase in industrial | |
| Machinery & transport | 27 | output 1980–91 | -1.6% |

## Energy

| | *'000 TCE* | | |
|---|---|---|---|
| Total output | 20,180 | % output exported | 5.0 |
| Total consumption | 37,646 | % consumption imported | 51.5 |
| Consumption per head, | | | |
| kg coal equivalent | 3,574 | | |

## Inflation and finance

| | | | |
|---|---|---|---|
| Consumer price | | *av. ann. increase 1988–91* | |
| inflation 1993 | 22.5% | Narrow money (M1) | 15.7% |
| Av. ann. inflation 1988–93 | 23.4% | Broad money | 18.5% |

## Exchange rates

| | *end 1993* | | *end June 1993* |
|---|---|---|---|
| Ft per $ | 101 | Effective rates | *1985 = 100* |
| Ft per SDR | 138 | – nominal | 47.8 |
| Ft per Ecu | 113 | – real | 115.0 |

## Principal exports

|  | $bn fob |  | $bn fob |
|---|---|---|---|
| Raw materials | 3.8 | Capital equipment | 1.3 |
| Consumer goods | 2.8 | Fuels & electricity | 0.3 |
| Food products | 2.5 | Total incl. others | **10.7** |

### Main export destinations

|  | % of total |  | % of total |
|---|---|---|---|
| Germany | 27.7 | Eastern Europe | 22.5 |
| Ex-Soviet Union | 13.1 | Efta | 14.7 |
| EU | 49.8 |  |  |

## Principal imports

|  | $bn cif |  | $bn cif |
|---|---|---|---|
| Raw materials | 4.1 | Fuel & electricity | 1.6 |
| Consumer goods | 2.5 | Food products | 0.6 |
| Capital equipment | 2.3 | Total incl. others | **12.4** |

### Main origins of imports

|  | % of total |  | % of total |
|---|---|---|---|
| Germany | 23.6 | Eastern Europe | 24.6 |
| Ex-Soviet Union | 16.8 | Efta | 20.6 |
| EU | 42.8 |  |  |

## Balance of payments, reserves and debt, $bn

|  |  |  |  |
|---|---|---|---|
| Visible exports fob | 10.1 | Overall balance | 0.8 |
| Visible imports fob | -10.1 | Change in reserves | 0.8 |
| Trade balance | -0.01 | Level of reserves |  |
| Invisibles inflows | 3.8 | end Dec. | 4.5 |
| Invisibles outflows | -4.3 | No. months import cover | 5.3 |
| Net transfers | 0.9 | Foreign debt | 21.9 |
| Current account balance | 0.4 | – as % of GDP | 64.6 |
| – as % of GDP | 1.1 | Debt service | 5.0 |
| Capital balance | 0.4 | Debt service ratio | 35.6 |

## Family life

|  |  |  |  |
|---|---|---|---|
| No. of households | 3.9m | Divorces per 1,000 pop. | 2.4 |
| Av. no. per household | 2.7 | Cost of living, Sept. 1993 |  |
| Marriages per 1,000 pop. | 5.7 | New York = 100 | 59 |

a   1990.

# INDIA

| Area | 3,287,590 sq km | Currency | Indian rupee (Rs) |
|------|-----------------|----------|-------------------|
| Capital | New Delhi | | |

## People

| | | | |
|---|---|---|---|
| Population | 883.5m | Life expectancy: men | 60 yrs |
| Pop. per sq km | 283 | women | 61 yrs |
| Av. ann. growth | | Adult literacy | 48.2% |
| in pop. 1985–92 | 2.1% | Fertility rate (per woman) | 3.9 |
| Pop. under 15 | 34.8% | | |
| Pop. over 65 | 4.9% | | *per 1,000 pop.* |
| No. of men per 100 women | 107 | Crude birth rate | 29.2 |
| Human Development Index | 31 | Crude death rate | 10.0 |

## The economy

| | | | |
|---|---|---|---|
| GDP | Rs7,024bn | GDPª per head | $307 |
| GDP | $271bn | GDP per head in purchasing | |
| Av. ann. growth in real | | power parity (USA=100) | 5 |
| GDP 1985–92 | 5.2% | | |

| Origins of GDPª | | Components of GDPª | |
|-----------------|-----------|--------------------|-----------|
| | *% of total* | | *% of total* |
| Agriculture | 32.7 | Private consumption | 66.6 |
| Industry, of which: | 27.4 | Public consumption | 12.2 |
| manufacturing | ... | Investment | 24.1 |
| Services | 39.9 | Exports | 9.6 |
| | | Imports | -12.5 |

## Structure of manufacturing

| | *% of total* | | *% of total* |
|---|---|---|---|
| Agric. & food processing | 12 | Other | 50 |
| Textiles & clothing | 12 | Av. ann. increase in industrial | |
| Machinery & transport | 26 | output 1980–91 | 6.3% |

## Energy

| | *'000 TCE* | | |
|---|---|---|---|
| Total output | 249,972 | % output exported | 0.3 |
| Total consumption | 273,314 | % consumption imported | 18.3 |
| Consumption per head, | | | |
| kg coal equivalent | 317 | | |

## Inflation and finance

| Consumer price | | *av. ann. increase 1988–92* | |
|---|---|---|---|
| inflation 1993 | 8.0% | Narrow money (M1) | 15.6% |
| Av. ann. inflation 1988–93 | 9.7% | Broad money | 16.8% |

## Exchange rates

| | *end 1993* | | *end June 1993* |
|---|---|---|---|
| Rs per $ | 31.38 | Effective rates | *1985 = 100* |
| Rs per SDR | 43.10 | – nominal | ... |
| Rs per Ecu | 35.15 | – real | ... |

## Principal exports[b]

| | $bn fob | | $bn fob |
|---|---|---|---|
| Textiles | 3.5 | Chemicals | 1.6 |
| Gems & jewellery | 2.7 | Leather goods | 1.3 |
| Engineering products | 2.2 | Total incl. others | **18.1** |

### Main export destination

| | % of total | | % of total |
|---|---|---|---|
| United States | 16.4 | Germany | 7.1 |
| Ex-Soviet Union | 9.2 | United Kingdom | 6.4 |
| Japan | 9.2 | EU | 27.0 |

## Principal imports[b]

| | $bn cif | | $bn cif |
|---|---|---|---|
| Crude oil & products | 5.4 | Chemicals | 2.0 |
| Capital goods | 4.2 | Iron & steel | 1.0 |
| Uncut gems & jewellery | 2.2 | Total incl. others | **19.6** |

### Main origins of imports

| | % of total | | % of total |
|---|---|---|---|
| United States | 10.3 | United Kingdom | 6.2 |
| Germany | 8.0 | EU | 29.2 |
| Japan | 7.1 | | |

## Balance of payments[c], reserves and debt, $bn

| | | | |
|---|---|---|---|
| Visible exports fob | 16.1 | Overall balance | -0.3 |
| Visible imports fob | -22.3 | Change in reserves | 0.1 |
| Trade balance | -6.1 | Level of reserves | |
| Invisibles inflows | 4.6 | end Dec. | 8.7 |
| Invisibles outflows | -8.4 | No. months import cover | ... |
| Net transfers | 3.1 | Foreign debt | 77.0 |
| Current account balance[d] | -5.0 | – as % of GDP | 32.3 |
| – as % of GDP[d] | -1.8 | Debt service | 6.6 |
| Capital balance | 7.3 | Debt service ratio | 25.6 |

## Family life

| | | | |
|---|---|---|---|
| No. of households | 118.6m | Divorces per 1,000 pop. | ... |
| Av. no. per household | 5.5 | Cost of living, Sept. 1993 | |
| Marriages per 1,000 pop. | ... | New York = 100 | 38 |

a   Year ending March 31, 1991.
b   Year ending March 31, 1992.
c   1989.
d   1992 estimates.

# INDONESIA

| | | | |
|---|---|---|---|
| Area | 1,904,569 sq km | Currency | Rupiah (Rp) |
| Capital | Jakarta | | |

## People

| | | | |
|---|---|---|---|
| Population | 184.3m | Life expectancy: men | 61 yrs |
| Pop. per sq km | 106 | women | 65 yrs |
| Av. ann. growth | | Adult literacy | 77.0% |
| in pop. 1985–92 | 1.8% | Fertility rate (per woman) | 3.1 |
| Pop. under 15 | 33.4% | | |
| Pop. over 65 | 4.4% | | *per 1,000 pop.* |
| No. of men per 100 women | 99 | Crude birth rate | 26.6 |
| Human Development Index | 52 | Crude death rate | 8.5 |

## The economy

| | | | |
|---|---|---|---|
| GDP | Rp249,678bn | GDP per head | $667 |
| GDP | $123bn | GDP per head in purchasing | |
| Av. ann. growth in real | | power parity (USA=100) | 10 |
| GDP 1985–92 | 5.8% | | |

| **Origins of GDP** | | **Components of GDP** | |
|---|---|---|---|
| | *% of total* | | *% of total* |
| Agriculture | 19.2 | Private consumption | 53.0 |
| Industry, of which: | 39.6 | Public consumption | 9.6 |
| manufacturing | 21.0 | Investment | 34.6 |
| Services | 41.2 | Exports | 29.3 |
| | | Imports | -26.6 |

## Structure of manufacturing

| | *% of total* | | *% of total* |
|---|---|---|---|
| Agric. & food processing | 24 | Other | 52 |
| Textiles & clothing | 14 | Av. ann. increase in industrial | |
| Machinery & transport | 10 | output 1980–91 | 5.9% |

## Energy

| | *'000 TCE* | | |
|---|---|---|---|
| Total output | 180,506 | % output exported | 68.0 |
| Total consumption | 65,314 | % consumption imported | 25.7 |
| Consumption per head, | | | |
| kg coal equivalent | 348 | | |

## Inflation and finance

| | | | |
|---|---|---|---|
| Consumer price | | *av. ann. increase 1988–92* | |
| inflation 1993 | 9.7% | Narrow money (M1) | 17.8% |
| Av. ann. inflation 1988–93 | 8.1% | Broad money | 28.6% |

## Exchange rates

| | *end 1993* | | *end June 1993* |
|---|---|---|---|
| Rp per $ | 2,110 | Effective rates | 1985 = 100 |
| Rp per SDR | 2,898 | – nominal | ... |
| Rp per Ecu | 2,363 | – real | ... |

## Principal exports

|  | $bn fob |  | $bn fob |
|---|---|---|---|
| Petroleum & products | 6.6 | Rubber & products | 2.5 |
| Textiles & clothing | 6.0 | Shrimp | 0.8 |
| Timber | 4.2 |  |  |
| Natural gas | 4.1 | Total incl. others | **34.0** |

### Main export destinations

|  | % of total |  | % of total |
|---|---|---|---|
| Japan | 31.7 | China | 4.1 |
| United States | 13.0 | Taiwan | 3.8 |
| Singapore | 9.8 | Netherlands | 3.2 |
| South Korea | 6.1 |  |  |

## Principal imports

|  | $bn cif |  | $bn cif |
|---|---|---|---|
| Machinery & transport |  | Fuels | 2.1 |
| equipment | 11.7 | Food, drink & tobacco | 1.4 |
| Chemicals | 3.8 |  |  |
| Raw materials | 2.4 | Total incl. others | **27.3** |

### Main origins of imports

|  | % of total |  | % of total |
|---|---|---|---|
| Japan | 22.0 | Singapore | 6.1 |
| United States | 14.0 | Australia | 5.2 |
| Germany | 7.8 | Taiwan | 4.7 |
| South Korea | 6.9 |  |  |

## Balance of payments, reserves and debt, $bn

|  |  |  |  |
|---|---|---|---|
| Visible exports fob | 32.5 | Overall balance | 2.1 |
| Visible imports fob | -26.5 | Change in reserves | 1.3 |
| Trade balance | 6.0 | Level of reserves |  |
| Invisibles inflows | 3.8 | end Dec. | 11.4 |
| Invisibles outflows | -13.8 | No. months import cover | 5.2 |
| Net transfers | 0.3 | Foreign debt | 84.4 |
| Current account balance | -3.7 | – as % of GDP | 67.4 |
| – as % of GDP | -3.0 | Debt service | 11.7 |
| Capital balance | 5.9 | Debt service ratio | 32.1 |

## Family life

|  |  |  |  |
|---|---|---|---|
| No. of households | 39.7m | Divorces per 1,000 pop. | 0.8 |
| Av. no. per household | 4.5 | Cost of living, Sept. 1993 |  |
| Marriages per 1,000 pop. | 7.4 | New York = 100 | 88 |

# IRAN

| | | | |
|---|---|---|---|
| Area | 1,648,000 sq km | Currency | Rial (IR) |
| Capital | Tehran | | |

## People

| | | | | |
|---|---|---|---|---|
| Population | 59.8m | Life expectancy: men | | 67 yrs |
| Pop. per sq km | 40 | women | | 68 yrs |
| Av. ann. growth | | Adult literacy | | 54.0% |
| in pop. 1985–92 | 3.7% | Fertility rate (per woman) | | 6.0 |
| Pop. under 15 | 45.9% | | | |
| Pop. over 65 | 3.8% | | | *per 1,000 pop.* |
| No. of men per 100 women | 104 | Crude birth rate | | 39.9 |
| Human Development Index | 56 | Crude death rate | | 7.0 |

## The economy

| | | | |
|---|---|---|---|
| GDP | IR8,587bn | GDP per head | $2,189 |
| GDP | $131bn | GDP per head in purchasing | |
| Av. ann. growth in real | | power parity (USA=100) | 15 |
| GDP 1985–92 | 1.7% | | |

| Origins of GDP[a] | | Components of GDP[a] | |
|---|---|---|---|
| | *% of total* | | *% of total* |
| Agriculture | 17.8 | Private consumption | 77.5 |
| Industry, of which: | 35.2 | Public consumption | 12.8 |
| manufacturing | ... | Investment | 20.4 |
| Services | 47.0 | Exports | 19.7 |
| | | Imports | -30.4 |

## Structure of manufacturing[b]

| | *% of total* | | *% of total* |
|---|---|---|---|
| Agric. & food processing | 23 | Other | 46 |
| Textiles & clothing | 19 | Av. ann. increase in industrial | |
| Metal products & machinery | 12 | output 1980–91 | 3.9% |

## Energy

| | *'000 TCE* | | |
|---|---|---|---|
| Total output | 284,345 | % output exported | 65.5 |
| Total consumption | 99,136 | % consumption imported | 12.2 |
| Consumption per head, | | | |
| kg coal equivalent | 1,654 | | |

## Inflation and finance

| Consumer price | | *av. ann. increase 1988–91* | |
|---|---|---|---|
| inflation 1993 | 35.0% | Narrow money (M1) | 17.4% |
| Av. ann. inflation 1988–93 | 22.0% | Broad money | 21.5% |

## Exchange rates

| | *end 1993* | | *end June 1993* |
|---|---|---|---|
| IR per $ | 1,759 | Effective rates | *1985 = 100* |
| IR per SDR | 2,415 | – nominal | ... |
| IR per Ecu | 1,970 | – real | ... |

## Principal exports[c]

|  | $bn fob |  | $bn fob |
|---|---|---|---|
| Crude oil | 14.2 |  |  |
| Others | 1.8 | Total incl. others | **16.0** |

### Main export destinations

|  | % of total |  | % of total |
|---|---|---|---|
| Japan | 15.0 | Belgium/Luxembourg | 6.0 |
| Italy | 9.4 | Germany | 4.2 |
| Netherlands | 8.1 | India | 3.7 |
| France | 6.3 | Spain | 2.0 |

## Principal imports[c]

|  | $bn cif |  | $bn cif |
|---|---|---|---|
| Manufactures | 17.8 |  |  |
| Raw materials | 3.8 | Total incl. others | **21.7** |

### Main origins of imports

|  | % of total |  | % of total |
|---|---|---|---|
| Germany | 24.2 | United Kingdom | 4.8 |
| Japan | 12.6 | United States | 3.6 |
| Italy | 9.7 | France | 3.5 |
| UAE | 5.0 | Turkey | 2.3 |

## Balance of payments[d], reserves and debt, $bn

|  |  |  |  |
|---|---|---|---|
| Visible exports fob | 18.4 | Overall balance | -2.1 |
| Visible imports fob | -25.0 | Change in reserves | -2.1 |
| Trade balance | -6.6 | Level of reserves | |
| Invisibles inflows | 1.7 | end Dec. | ... |
| Invisibles outflows | -5.5 | No. months import cover | ... |
| Net transfers | 2.5 | Foreign debt | 14.2 |
| Current account balance | -7.9 | – as % of GDP | 12.8 |
| – as % of GDP | -6.0 | Debt service | 0.8 |
| Capital balance | 5.5 | Debt service ratio | 3.9 |

## Family life

|  |  |  |  |
|---|---|---|---|
| No. of households | 10.8m | Divorces per 1,000 pop. | 0.7 |
| Av. no. per household | 5.2 | Cost of living, Sept. 1993 | |
| Marriages per 1,000 pop. | 8.3 | New York = 100 | 41 |

a   Iranian year ending March 20, 1991.
b   1989.
c   1991.
d   Iranian year ending March 20, 1992.

# IRAQ

| | | | |
|---|---|---|---|
| Area | 438,317 sq km | Currency | Iraqi dinar (ID) |
| Capital | Baghdad | | |

## People

| | | | | |
|---|---|---|---|---|
| Population | 19.1m | Life expectancy: men | | 65 yrs |
| Pop. per sq km | 48 | | women | 68 yrs |
| Av. ann. growth | | Adult literacy | | 59.7% |
| in pop. 1985–92 | 3.3% | Fertility rate (per woman) | | 5.7 |
| Pop. under 15 | 43.7% | | | |
| Pop. over 65 | 3.0% | | | *per 1,000 pop.* |
| No. of men per 100 women | 104 | Crude birth rate | | 38.8 |
| Human Development Index | 59 | Crude death rate | | 6.8 |

## The economy

| | | | |
|---|---|---|---|
| GDP[a] | ID6.8bn | GDP per head[a] | $12,104 |
| GDP[a] | $22bn | GDP per head in purchasing | |
| Av. ann. growth in real | | power parity (USA=100)[a] | 16 |
| GDP 1987–92 | -14.3% | | |

| Origins of GDP[b] | | Components of GDP[c] | |
|---|---|---|---|
| | *% of total* | | *% of total* |
| Agriculture | 5.1 | Private consumption | 52.7 |
| Industry, of which: | 72.9 | Public consumption | 30.0 |
| manufacturing | 11.6 | Investment | 21.9 |
| Services | 22.0 | Exports | 24.6 |
| | | Imports | -29.1 |

## Structure of manufacturing

| | | | |
|---|---|---|---|
| | *% of total* | | *% of total* |
| Agric. & food processing | ... | Other | ... |
| Textiles & clothing | ... | Av. ann. increase in industrial | |
| Machinery & transport | ... | output 1980–91 | ... |

## Energy

| | | | |
|---|---|---|---|
| | *'000 TCE* | | |
| Total output | 20,685 | % output exported | 19.2 |
| Total consumption | 18,116 | % consumption imported | 0.0 |
| Consumption per head, | | | |
| kg coal equivalent | 970 | | |

## Inflation and finance[a]

| | | | |
|---|---|---|---|
| Consumer price | | | *av. ann. increase 1988–92* |
| inflation 1993 | 175% | Narrow money (M1) | ... |
| Av. ann. inflation 1988–93 | 147.6% | Broad money | ... |

## Exchange rates

| | *end 1993* | | *end June 1993* |
|---|---|---|---|
| | | | *1985 = 100* |
| ID per $ | 0.31 | Effective rates | |
| ID per SDR | 0.43 | – nominal | 66.9 |
| ID per Ecu | 0.35 | – real | ... |

## Principal exports[a][b][e]

| | $bn fob | | $bn fob |
|---|---|---|---|
| Crude oil | 14.5 | Total incl. others | **14.6** |

### Main export destinations[a][d]

| | % of total | | % of total |
|---|---|---|---|
| United States | 28.5 | Netherlands | 7.4 |
| Brazil | 9.9 | Spain | 4.6 |
| Turkey | 9.8 | France | 3.5 |
| Japan | 7.8 | | |

## Principal imports[a]

| | $bn cif | | $bn cif |
|---|---|---|---|
| Civilian goods | 5.0 | | |
| Military goods | 2.7 | Total incl. others | **7.7** |

### Main origins of imports[a][d]

| | % of total | | % of total |
|---|---|---|---|
| Germany | 13.3 | United Kingdom | 8.4 |
| United States | 10.7 | Japan | 4.5 |
| Turkey | 9.2 | Italy | 4.5 |
| France | 8.7 | Brazil | 3.1 |

## Balance of payments[b][e], reserves and debt[c], $bn

| | | | |
|---|---|---|---|
| Visible exports fob | 9.5 | Overall balance | ... |
| Visible imports fob | 5.1 | Change in reserves | ... |
| Trade balance | 4.4 | Level of reserves | |
| Invisibles inflows | ... | end Dec. | ... |
| Invisibles outflows | ... | No. months import cover | ... |
| Net transfers | ... | Foreign debt | 82.9 |
| Current account balance | -0.9 | – as % of GDP | ... |
| – as % of GDP | ... | Debt service | 161 |
| Capital balance | ... | Debt service ratio | ... |

## Family life

| | | | |
|---|---|---|---|
| No. of households | 2.1m | Divorces per 1,000 pop. | 0.1 |
| Av. no. per household | 7.1 | Cost of living, Sept. 1993 | |
| Marriages per 1,000 pop. | 8.5 | New York = 100 | ... |

a  Estimate.
b  1989.
c  1985.
d  1988.
e  Trade, balance of payments and debt data for Iraq are estimates based on limited and frequently inconsistent information.

# IRELAND

| | | | |
|---|---|---|---|
| Area | 70,283 sq km | Currency | Punt (I£) |
| Capital | Dublin | | |

## People

| | | | |
|---|---|---|---|
| Population | 3.5m | Life expectancy: men | 73 yrs |
| Pop. per sq km | 49 | women | 78 yrs |
| Av. ann. growth | | Adult literacy | 99.0% |
| in pop. 1985–92 | -0.1% | Fertility rate (per woman) | 2.1 |
| Pop. under 15 | 24.7% | | |
| Pop. over 65 | 11.6% | | *per 1,000 pop.* |
| No. of men per 100 women | 100 | Crude birth rate | 14.4 |
| Human Development Index | 93 | Crude death rate | 9.2 |

## The economy

| | | | |
|---|---|---|---|
| GDP | I£25bn | GDP per head | $12,104 |
| GDP | $43bn | GDP per head in purchasing | |
| Av. ann. growth in real | | power parity (USA=100) | 49 |
| GDP 1985–92 | 4.8% | | |

| Origins of GDP | | Components of GDP | |
|---|---|---|---|
| | *% of total* | | *% of total* |
| Agriculture | 10.0 | Private consumption | 56.0 |
| Industry, of which: | 38.0 | Public consumption | 16.0 |
| manufacturing | ... | Investment | 19.0 |
| Services | 52.0 | Exports | 62.0 |
| | | Imports | -53.0 |

## Structure of manufacturing

| | *% of total* | | *% of total* |
|---|---|---|---|
| Agric. & food processing | 26 | Other | 38 |
| Textiles & clothing | 4 | Av. ann. increase in industrial | |
| Machinery & transport | 32 | output 1980–89 | -4.3% |

## Energy

| | *'000 TCE* | | |
|---|---|---|---|
| Total output | 4,733 | % output exported | 22.6 |
| Total consumption | 14,473 | % consumption imported | 74.3 |
| Consumption per head, | | | |
| kg coal equivalent | 4,143 | | |

## Inflation and finance

| | | | |
|---|---|---|---|
| Consumer price | | *av. ann. increase 1988–92* | |
| inflation 1993 | 1.4% | Narrow money (M1) | 4.3% |
| Av. ann. inflation 1988–93 | 2.9% | Broad money | 10.7% |

## Exchange rates

| | *end 1993* | | *end June 1993* |
|---|---|---|---|
| I£ per $ | 0.71 | Effective rates | *1985 = 100* |
| I£ per SDR | 0.97 | – nominal | 104.4 |
| I£ per Ecu | 0.80 | – real | ... |

## Principal exports

| | $bn fob | | $bn fob |
|---|---|---|---|
| Machinery & transport equipment | 7.7 | Chemicals | 5.5 |
| | | Other products | 4.3 |
| Agric. products & foodstuffs | 6.3 | Total incl. others | **28.4** |

### Main export destinations

| | % of total | | % of total |
|---|---|---|---|
| United Kingdom | 31.5 | Netherlands | 7.0 |
| Germany | 12.8 | Belgium/Luxembourg | 4.9 |
| France | 9.6 | Japan | 2.9 |
| United States | 8.2 | EU | 74.1 |

## Principal imports

| | $bn cif | | $bn cif |
|---|---|---|---|
| Machinery & transport equipment | 8.0 | Chemicals | 2.9 |
| Manufactured goods | 6.7 | Total incl. others | **22.5** |

### Main origins of imports

| | % of total | | % of total |
|---|---|---|---|
| United Kingdom | 42.4 | France | 4.5 |
| United States | 14.2 | Netherlands | 4.4 |
| Germany | 8.3 | Italy | 2.4 |
| Japan | 5.0 | EU | 66.5 |

## Balance of payments, reserves and aid, $bn

| | | | |
|---|---|---|---|
| Visible exports fob | 27.9 | Capital balance | -6.2 |
| Visible imports fob | -21.1 | Overall balance | -3.5 |
| Trade balance | 6.8 | Change in reserves | -2.3 |
| Invisibles inflows | 6.6 | Level of reserves | |
| Invisibles outflows | -13.7 | end Dec. | 3.5 |
| Net transfers | 3.0 | No. months import cover | 2.0 |
| Current account balance | 2.6 | Aid given | 0.07 |
| – as % of GDP | 6.1 | – as % of GDP | 0.16 |

## Family life

| | | | |
|---|---|---|---|
| No. of households | 0.9m | Divorces per 1,000 pop. | ... |
| Av. no. per household | 3.6 | Cost of living, Sept. 1993 | |
| Marriages per 1,000 pop. | 5.2 | New York = 100 | 94 |

# ISRAEL

| | | | |
|---|---|---|---|
| Area | 20,770 sq km | Currency | New Shekel (NIS) |
| Capital | Jerusalem | | |

## People

| | | | | |
|---|---|---|---|---|
| Population | 5.1m | Life expectancy: men | | 75 yrs |
| Pop. per sq km | 279 | women | | 78 yrs |
| Av. ann. growth | | Adult literacy | | 95.8% |
| in pop. 1985–92 | 2.7% | Fertility rate (per woman) | | 2.9 |
| Pop. under 15 | 28.8% | | | |
| Pop. over 65 | 9.7% | | | *per 1,000 pop.* |
| No. of men per 100 women | 98 | Crude birth rate | | 21.1 |
| Human Development Index | 94 | Crude death rate | | 6.9 |

## The economy

| | | | |
|---|---|---|---|
| GDP | NIS167bn | GDP per head | $13,233 |
| GDP | $68bn | GDP per head in purchasing | |
| Av. ann. growth in real | | power parity (USA=100) | 50 |
| GDP 1985–92 | 4.6% | | |

| **Origins of NDP** | | **Components of GDP** | |
|---|---|---|---|
| | *% of total* | | *% of total* |
| Agriculture | 2.6 | Private consumption | 63.1 |
| Industry, of which: | 32.1 | Public consumption | 28.8 |
| manufacturing | 21.7 | Investment | 23.8 |
| Services | 65.3 | Exports | 33.6 |
| | | Imports | -49.3 |

## Structure of manufacturing

| | *% of total* | | *% of total* |
|---|---|---|---|
| Agric. & food processing | 13 | Other | 47 |
| Textiles & clothing | 9 | Av. ann. increase in industrial | |
| Machinery & transport | 32 | output 1980–90 | ... |

## Energy

| | *'000 TCE* | | |
|---|---|---|---|
| Total output | 50 | % output exported[a] | 3,588.0 |
| Total consumption | 14,606 | % consumption imported[a] | 118.0 |
| Consumption per head, | | | |
| kg coal equivalent | 2,999 | | |

## Inflation and finance

| | | | |
|---|---|---|---|
| Consumer price | | *av. ann. increase 1988–91* | |
| inflation 1993 | 11.1% | Narrow money (M1) | 24.3% |
| Av. ann. inflation 1988–93 | 15.8% | Broad money | 20.1% |

## Exchange rates

| | *end 1993* | | *end June 1993* |
|---|---|---|---|
| NIS per $ | 2.99 | Effective rates | *1985 = 100* |
| NIS per SDR | 4.10 | – nominal | ... |
| NIS per Ecu | 3.35 | – real | ... |

## Principal exports

|  | $bn fob |  | $bn fob |
|---|---|---|---|
| Metal, machinery & electronics | 5.1 | Textiles & clothing | 0.9 |
| | | Agric. products & foodstuffs | 0.6 |
| Diamonds | 3.0 | | |
| Chemicals | 1.9 | Total incl. others | **12.4** |

**Main export destinations**

|  | % of total |  | % of total |
|---|---|---|---|
| United States | 30.9 | Germany | 5.3 |
| United Kingdom | 5.5 | Japan | 5.2 |
| Belgium/Luxembourg | 5.4 | France | 3.9 |

## Principal imports

|  | $bn cif |  | $bn cif |
|---|---|---|---|
| Investment goods | 3.6 | Energy & products | 1.7 |
| Diamonds | 3.4 | Durable consumer products | 1.0 |
| Non-durable consumer products | 2.5 | Total incl. others | **18.6** |

**Main origins of imports**

|  | % of total |  | % of total |
|---|---|---|---|
| United States | 17.7 | United Kingdom | 8.6 |
| Belgium/Luxembourg | 12.2 | Switzerland | 7.4 |
| Germany | 10.4 | Italy | 7.3 |

## Balance of payments, reserves and debt, $bn

| | | | |
|---|---|---|---|
| Visible exports fob | 13.3 | Overall balance | -1.3 |
| Visible imports fob | -18.3 | Change in reserves | -1.4 |
| Trade balance | -5.0 | Level of reserves | |
| Invisibles inflows | 7.5 | end Dec. | 5.1 |
| Invisibles outflows | -9.4 | No. months import cover | 3.3 |
| Net transfers | 6.9 | Foreign debt | 30.0 |
| Current account balance | 0.1 | – as % of GDP | 46.2 |
| – as % of GDP | 0.1 | Debt service | 3.4 |
| Capital balance | -2.8 | Debt service ratio | 16.3 |

## Family life

| | | | |
|---|---|---|---|
| No. of households | 1.1m | Divorces per 1,000 pop. | 1.3 |
| Av. no. per household | 3.5 | Cost of living, Sept. 1993 | |
| Marriages per 1,000 pop. | 7.0 | New York = 100 | 108 |

a Energy trade data are distorted by transitory and oil refining activities.

# ITALY

| Area | 301,225 sq km | Currency | Lira (L) |
|------|------|------|------|
| Capital | Rome | | |

## People

| | | | |
|------|------|------|------|
| Population | 57.8m | Life expectancy: men | 74 yrs |
| Pop. per sq km | 192 | women | 80 yrs |
| Av. ann. growth | | Adult literacy | 97.1% |
| in pop. 1985–92 | 0.2% | Fertility rate (per woman) | 1.3 |
| Pop. under 15 | 15.4% | | |
| Pop. over 65 | 15.6% | | *per 1,000 pop.* |
| No. of men per 100 women | 95 | Crude birth rate | 10.0 |
| Human Development Index | 92 | Crude death rate | 10.0 |

## The economy

| | | | |
|------|------|------|------|
| GDP | L1,462,859bn | GDP per head | $20,513 |
| GDP | $1,187bn | GDP per head in purchasing | |
| Av. ann. growth in real | | power parity (USA=100) | 74 |
| GDP 1985–92 | 2.5% | | |

| Origins of GDP | | Components of GDP | |
|------|------|------|------|
| | *% of total* | | *% of total* |
| Agriculture | 3.1 | Private consumption | 63.1 |
| Industry, of which: | 31.8 | Public consumption | 17.7 |
| manufacturing | 25.9 | Investment | 19.4 |
| Services | 65.2 | Exports | 18.1 |
| | | Imports | -18.3 |

## Structure of manufacturing

| | *% of total* | | *% of total* |
|------|------|------|------|
| Agric. & food processing | 8 | Other | 46 |
| Textiles & clothing | 13 | Av. ann. increase in industrial | |
| Machinery & transport | 33 | output 1980–91 | 2.1% |

## Energy

| | *'000 TCE* | | |
|------|------|------|------|
| Total output | 39,774 | % output exported | 73.3 |
| Total consumption | 230,905 | % consumption imported | 95.4 |
| Consumption per head, | | | |
| kg coal equivalent | 3,998 | | |

## Inflation and finance

| | | | |
|------|------|------|------|
| Consumer price | | *av. ann. increase 1988–92* | |
| inflation 1993 | 4.3% | Narrow money (M1) | 7.9% |
| Av. ann. inflation 1988–93 | 5.6% | Broad money | 8.5% |

## Exchange rates

| | *end 1993* | | *end June 1993* |
|------|------|------|------|
| L per $ | 1,704 | Effective rates | *1985 = 100* |
| L per SDR | 2,341 | – nominal | 81.3 |
| L per Ecu | 1,908 | – real | 89.8 |

## Principal exports[a]

| | $bn fob | | $bn fob |
|---|---|---|---|
| Engineering products | 28.2 | Leather & footwear | 10.1 |
| Textiles & clothing | 20.2 | Metal products | 8.6 |
| Transport equipment | 12.4 | | |
| Chemicals | 12.4 | Total incl. others | **169.0** |

### Main export destinations[a]

| | % of total | | % of total |
|---|---|---|---|
| Germany | 21.0 | Spain | 5.1 |
| France | 15.2 | Switzerland | 4.2 |
| United States | 6.9 | EU | 59.0 |
| United Kingdom | 6.7 | Opec | 4.8 |

## Principal imports[a]

| | $bn cif | | $bn cif |
|---|---|---|---|
| Chemicals | 22.0 | Energy | 16.4 |
| Transport equipment | 17.0 | Electrical equipment | 16.3 |
| Metals | 16.6 | Total incl. others | **181.9** |

### Main origins of imports[a]

| | % of total | | % of total |
|---|---|---|---|
| Germany | 20.9 | Switzerland | 4.4 |
| France | 14.2 | Spain | 3.5 |
| United Kingdom | 5.7 | EU | 57.7 |
| United States | 5.6 | Opec | 7.1 |

## Balance of payments, reserves and aid, $bn

| | | | |
|---|---|---|---|
| Visible exports fob | 177.7 | Capital balance | 5.0 |
| Visible imports fob | -175.2 | Overall balance | -31.7 |
| Trade balance | 2.4 | Change in reserves | -21.0 |
| Invisibles inflows | 90.0 | Level of reserves | |
| Invisibles outflows | -112.1 | end Dec. | 50.8 |
| Net transfers | -5.7 | No. months import cover | 3.5 |
| Current account balance | -25.4 | Aid given | 4.1 |
| – as % of GDP | -2.1 | – as % of GDP | 0.34 |

## Family life

| | | | |
|---|---|---|---|
| No. of households | 19.8m | Divorces per 1,000 pop. | 0.5 |
| Av. no. per household | 2.8 | Cost of living, Sept. 1993 | |
| Marriages per 1,000 pop. | 5.4 | New York = 100 | 90 |

a 1991.

# JAPAN

| Area | 377,708 sq km | Currency | Yen (¥) |
|---|---|---|---|
| Capital | Tokyo | | |

## People

| | | | |
|---|---|---|---|
| Population | 124.3m | Life expectancy: men | 76 yrs |
| Pop. per sq km | 333 | women | 82 yrs |
| Av. ann. growth | | Adult literacy | 99.0% |
| in pop. 1985–92 | 0.4% | Fertility rate (per woman) | 1.7 |
| Pop. under 15 | 16.8% | | |
| Pop. over 65 | 13.9% | | *per 1,000 pop.* |
| No. of men per 100 women | 97 | Crude birth rate | 11.2 |
| Human Development Index | 98 | Crude death rate | 7.5 |

## The economy

| | | | |
|---|---|---|---|
| GDP | ¥444,288bn | GDP per head | $28,217 |
| GDP | $3,508bn | GDP per head in purchasing | |
| Av. ann. growth in real | | power parity (USA=100) | 82 |
| GDP 1985–92 | 4.1% | | |

| Origins of NDP[a] | | Components of GDP | |
|---|---|---|---|
| | *% of total* | | *% of total* |
| Agriculture | 2.3 | Private consumption | 57.1 |
| Industry, of which: | 42.0 | Public consumption | 9.3 |
| manufacturing | 29.0 | Investment | 31.2 |
| Services | 55.7 | Exports | 10.2 |
| | | Imports | -7.8 |

## Structure of manufacturing

| | *% of total* | | *% of total* |
|---|---|---|---|
| Agric. & food processing | 9 | Other | 47 |
| Textiles & clothing | 5 | Av. ann. increase in industrial | |
| Machinery & transport | 39 | output 1980–91 | 4.9% |

## Energy

| | *'000 TCE* | | |
|---|---|---|---|
| Total output | 104,816 | % output exported[b] | 12.6 |
| Total consumption | 589,599 | % consumption imported[b] | 89.5 |
| Consumption per head, | | | |
| kg coal equivalent | 4,754 | | |

## Inflation and finance

| Consumer price | | *av. ann. increase 1988–92* | |
|---|---|---|---|
| inflation 1993 | 1.2% | Narrow money (M1) | 5.7% |
| Av. ann. inflation 1988–93 | 2.0% | Broad money | 6.3% |

## Exchange rates

| | *end 1993* | | *end June 1993* |
|---|---|---|---|
| ¥ per $ | 111.9 | Effective rates | 1985 = 100 |
| ¥ per SDR | 153.6 | – nominal | 172.4 |
| ¥ per Ecu | 125.8 | – real | 161.0 |

## Principal exports

| | $bn fob | | $bn fob |
|---|---|---|---|
| Motor vehicles | 60.5 | Iron & steel products | 13.3 |
| Office machinery | 25.4 | | |
| Chemicals | 19.1 | | |
| Scientific & optical equipment | 13.5 | Total incl. others | **330.9** |

### Main export destinations

| | % of total | | % of total |
|---|---|---|---|
| United States | 28.2 | Germany | 6.0 |
| Taiwan | 6.2 | South Korea | 5.2 |
| Hong Kong | 6.1 | Singapore | 3.8 |

## Principal imports

| | $bn cif | | $bn cif |
|---|---|---|---|
| Energy | 52.7 | Textiles | 15.3 |
| Agric. products & foodstuffs | 37.3 | Wood | 7.6 |
| Chemicals | 17.4 | Total incl. others | **198.5** |

### Main origins of imports

| | % of total | | % of total |
|---|---|---|---|
| United States | 22.4 | Indonesia | 5.3 |
| China | 7.3 | South Korea | 5.0 |
| Australia | 5.3 | Germany | 4.6 |

## Balance of payments, reserves and aid, $bn

| | | | |
|---|---|---|---|
| Visible exports fob | 330.9 | Capital balance | -106.6 |
| Visible imports fob | -198.5 | Overall balance | 0.6 |
| Trade balance | 132.4 | Change in reserves | -0.1 |
| Invisibles inflows | 194.1 | Level of reserves | |
| Invisibles outflows | -204.2 | end Dec. | 72.8 |
| Net transfers | -4.6 | No. months import cover | 4.4 |
| Current account balance | 117.6 | Aid given | 11.15 |
| – as % of GDP | 3.4 | – as % of GDP | 0.30 |

## Family life

| | | | |
|---|---|---|---|
| No. of households | 40.7m | Divorces per 1,000 pop. | 1.3 |
| Av. no. per household | 3.0 | Cost of living, Sept. 1993 | |
| Marriages per 1,000 pop. | 6.0 | New York = 100 | 213 |

a   1991.
b   Energy trade data are distorted by transitory and oil refining activities.

# KENYA

| Area | 580,367 sq km | Currency | Kenya shilling (KSh) |
|---|---|---|---|
| Capital | Nairobi | | |

## People

| | | | |
|---|---|---|---|
| Population | 25.8m | Life expectancy: men | 57 yrs |
| Pop. per sq km | 48 | women | 61 yrs |
| Av. ann. growth | | Adult literacy | 69.0% |
| in pop. 1985–92 | 3.5% | Fertility rate (per woman) | 6.3% |
| Pop. under 15 | 47.4% | | |
| Pop. over 65 | 2.9% | | *per 1,000 pop.* |
| No. of men per 100 women | 100 | Crude birth rate | 43.7 |
| Human Development Index | 37 | Crude death rate | 10.3 |

## The economy

| | | | |
|---|---|---|---|
| GDP | KSh274bn | GDP per head | $327 |
| GDP | $8.5bn | GDP per head in purchasing | 5 |
| Av. ann. growth in real | | power parity (USA=100) | |
| GDP 1985–92 | 4.3% | | |

| **Origins of GDP** | | **Components of GDP** | |
|---|---|---|---|
| | *% of total* | | *% of total* |
| Agriculture | 25.6 | Private consumption | 68.9 |
| Industry, of which: | 39.2 | Public consumption | 15.7 |
| manufacturing | 11.3 | Investment | 16.1 |
| Services | 34.9 | Exports | 25.8 |
| | | Imports | -26.5 |

## Structure of manufacturing

| | *% of total* | | *% of total* |
|---|---|---|---|
| Agric. & food processing | 38 | Other | 42 |
| Textiles & clothing | 10 | Av. ann. increase in industrial | |
| Machinery & transport | 10 | output 1980–91 | 8.6% |

## Energy

| | *'000 TCE* | | |
|---|---|---|---|
| Total output | 706 | % output exported[a] | 130.6 |
| Total consumption | 2,661 | % consumption imported[a] | 118.2 |
| Consumption per head, | | | |
| kg coal equivalent | 109 | | |

## Inflation and finance

| | | | *av. ann. increase 1988–92* |
|---|---|---|---|
| Consumer price | | | |
| inflation 1993 | 45.7% | Narrow money (M1) | 19.7% |
| Av. ann. inflation 1988–93 | 21.9% | Broad money | 19.5% |

## Exchange rates

| | *end 1993* | | *end June 1993* |
|---|---|---|---|
| | | | *1985 = 100* |
| KSh per $ | 68.16 | Effective rates | |
| KSh per SDR | 93.63 | – nominal | ... |
| KSh per Ecu | 76.34 | – real | ... |

## Principal exports

|  | $m fob |  | $m fob |
|---|---|---|---|
| Tea | 295 | Coffee | 128 |
| Petroleum products | 146 | | |
| Horticultural products | 130 | Total incl. others | **1,081** |

### Main export destinations

|  | % of total |  | % of total |
|---|---|---|---|
| United Kingdom | 18.3 | Germany | 6.5 |
| Uganda | 7.1 | Tanzania | 4.6 |

## Principal imports

|  | $m cif |  | $m cif |
|---|---|---|---|
| Petroleum & products | 341 | Motor vehicles & chassis | 90 |
| Industrial machinery | 314 | | |
| Iron & steel | 114 | Total incl. others | **1,834** |

### Main origins of imports

|  | % of total |  | % of total |
|---|---|---|---|
| UAE | 16.3 | Japan | 9.4 |
| United Kingdom | 11.5 | United States | 8.2 |

## Balance of payments, reserves and debt, $bn

|  |  |  |  |
|---|---|---|---|
| Visible exports fob | 1.0 | Overall balance | -0.3 |
| Visible imports fob | -1.6 | Change in reserves | 0.2 |
| Trade balance | -0.6 | Level of reserves | |
| Invisibles inflows | 1.1 | end Dec. | 0.05 |
| Invisibles outflows | -0.9 | No. months import cover | 0.4 |
| Net transfers | 0.3 | Foreign debt | 6.4 |
| Current account balance | -0.1 | – as % of GDP | 75.9 |
| – as % of GDP | -1.2 | Debt service | 0.6 |
| Capital balance | -0.3 | Debt service ratio | 24.5 |

## Family life

|  |  |  |  |
|---|---|---|---|
| No. of households | 3.0m | Divorces per 1,000 pop. | ... |
| Av. no. per household | 5.1 | Cost of living, Sept. 1993 | |
| Marriages per 1,000 pop. | ... | New York = 100 | 45 |

a   Energy trade data are distorted by transitory and oil refining activities.

# MALAYSIA

| | | | |
|---|---|---|---|
| Area | 329,749 sq km | Currency | Malaysian dollar/ringgit |
| Capital | Kuala Lumpur | | (M$) |

## People

| | | | |
|---|---|---|---|
| Population | 18.6m | Life expectancy: men | 69 yrs |
| Pop. per sq km | 61 | women | 73 yrs |
| Av. ann. growth | | Adult literacy | 78.4% |
| in pop. 1985–92 | 2.5% | Fertility rate (per woman) | 3.6 |
| Pop. under 15 | 37.9% | | |
| Pop. over 65 | 3.9% | | *per 1,000 pop.* |
| No. of men per 100 women | 102 | Crude birth rate | 28.6 |
| Human Development Index | 79 | Crude death rate | 5.1 |

## The economy

| | | | |
|---|---|---|---|
| GDP | M$132bn | GDP per head | $2,790 |
| GDP | $52bn | GDP per head in purchasing | |
| Av. ann. growth in real | | power parity (USA=100) | 29 |
| GDP 1985–92 | 6.2% | | |

| **Origins of GDP** | | **Components of GDP** | |
|---|---|---|---|
| | *% of total* | | *% of total* |
| Agriculture | 18.6 | Private consumption | 51.5 |
| Industry, of which: | 40.0 | Public consumption | 13.5 |
| manufacturing | 26.8 | Investment | 33.9 |
| Services | 41.4 | Exports | 78.4 |
| | | Imports | -77.3 |

## Structure of manufacturing

| | *% of total* | | *% of total* |
|---|---|---|---|
| Agric. & food processing | 13 | Other | 50 |
| Textiles & clothing | 6 | Av. ann. increase in industrial | |
| Machinery & transport | 31 | output 1980–91 | 7.7% |

## Energy

| | *'000 TCE* | | |
|---|---|---|---|
| Total output | 66,531 | % output exported | 79.2 |
| Total consumption | 28,133 | % consumption imported | 50.0 |
| Consumption per head, | | | |
| kg coal equivalent | 1,534 | | |

## Inflation and finance

| | | | |
|---|---|---|---|
| Consumer price | | *av. ann. increase 1988–91* | |
| inflation 1993 | 3.6% | Narrow money (M1) | 14.3% |
| Av. ann. inflation 1988–93 | 3.5% | Broad money | 12.3% |

## Exchange rates

| | *end 1993* | | *end June 1993* |
|---|---|---|---|
| M$ per $ | 2.70 | Effective rates | *1985 = 100* |
| M$ per SDR | 3.71 | – nominal | 73.0 |
| M$ per Ecu | 3.04 | – real | 68.8 |

## Principal exports

| | $bn fob | | $bn fob |
|---|---|---|---|
| Electronic components | 16.3 | Palm oil | 2.0 |
| Petroleum & products | 4.4 | Rubber | 0.8 |
| Timber & products | 2.8 | Total incl. others | **40.6** |

### Main export destinations

| | % of total | | % of total |
|---|---|---|---|
| Singapore | 23.8 | Germany | 4.1 |
| United States | 14.8 | United Kingdom | 4.0 |
| Japan | 13.2 | Thailand | 3.7 |

## Principal imports

| | $bn cif | | $bn cif |
|---|---|---|---|
| Manufacturing supplies | 16.4 | Agric. products & foodstuffs | 1.5 |
| Machinery & transport equipment | 7.9 | Durables & consumer goods | 1.3 |
| Metal products | 2.2 | Total incl. others | **39.8** |

### Main origins of imports

| | % of total | | % of total |
|---|---|---|---|
| Japan | 25.9 | Taiwan | 5.6 |
| Singapore | 20.6 | United Kingdom | 3.4 |
| United States | 15.7 | Australia | 2.6 |

## Balance of payments, reserves and debt, $bn

| | | | |
|---|---|---|---|
| Visible exports fob | 39.7 | Overall balance | 6.6 |
| Visible imports fob | -36.9 | Change in reserves | 6.9 |
| Trade balance | 2.8 | Level of reserves | |
| Invisibles inflows | 7.1 | end Dec. | 17.3 |
| Invisibles outflows | -11.8 | No. months import cover | 5.6 |
| Net transfers | 0.1 | Foreign debt | 19.8 |
| Current account balance | -1.7 | as % of GDP | 36.1 |
| – as % of GDP | -3.3 | Debt service | 3.1 |
| Capital balance | 6.3 | Debt service ratio | 6.6 |

## Family life

| | | | |
|---|---|---|---|
| No. households | 2.5m | Divorces per 1,000 pop. | ... |
| Av. no. per household | 5.2 | Cost of living, Sept. 1993 | |
| Marriages per 1,000 pop. | 3.2 | New York = 100 | 77 |

a 1990.

# MEXICO

| Area | 1,958,201 sq km | Currency | Mexican peso (PS) |
|---|---|---|---|
| Capital | Mexico City | | |

## People

| | | | |
|---|---|---|---|
| Population | 85.0m | Life expectancy: men | 67 yrs |
| Pop. per sq km | 48 | women | 74 yrs |
| Av. ann. growth | | Adult literacy | 87.3% |
| in pop. 1985–92 | 1.8% | Fertility rate (per woman) | 3.2 |
| Pop. under 15 | 36.0% | | |
| Pop. over 65 | 4.0% | | *per 1,000 pop.* |
| No. of men per 100 women | 99 | Crude birth rate | 27.9 |
| Human Development Index | 81 | Crude death rate | 5.5 |

## The economy

| | | | |
|---|---|---|---|
| GDP | 913bn New pesos | GDP per head | $3,470 |
| GDP | $295bn | GDP per head in purchasing | 28 |
| Av. ann. growth in real | | power parity (USA=100) | |
| GDP 1985–92 | 1.9% | | |

| Origins of GDP | | Components of GDP | |
|---|---|---|---|
| | *% of total* | | *% of total* |
| Agriculture | 7.3 | Private consumption | 68.1 |
| Industry, of which: | 32.9 | Public consumption | 10.7 |
| manufacturing | 22.7 | Investment | 20.7 |
| Services | 59.8 | Exports | 18.2 |
| | | Imports | -17.8 |

## Structure of manufacturing

| | *% of total* | | *% of total* |
|---|---|---|---|
| Agric. & food processing | 22 | Other | 52 |
| Machinery & transport | 9 | Av. ann. increase in industrial | |
| Textiles & clothing | 23 | output 1980–91 | 1.3% |

## Energy

| | *'000 TCE* | | |
|---|---|---|---|
| Total output | 274,721 | % output exported | 39.2 |
| Total consumption | 164,943 | % consumption imported | 7.2 |
| Consumption per head, | | | |
| kg coal equivalent | 1,911 | | |

## Inflation and finance

| Consumer price | | *av. ann. increase 1988–92* | |
|---|---|---|---|
| inflation 1993 | 9.8% | Narrow money (M1) | 57.5% |
| Av. ann. inflation 1988–93 | 31.0% | Broad money | 41.9% |

## Exchange rates

| | *end 1993* | | *end June 1993* |
|---|---|---|---|
| PS per $ | 3.11 | Effective rates | *1985 = 100* |
| PS per SDR | 4.27 | – nominal | ... |
| PS per Ecu | 3.48 | – real | ... |

## Principal exports

| | $bn fob | | $bn fob |
|---|---|---|---|
| Manufactured products | 35.2 | Agric. products & foodstuffs | 2.1 |
| Petroleum & products | 8.3 | Total incl. others | **46.2** |

### Main export destinations

| | % of total | | % of total |
|---|---|---|---|
| United States | 68.7 | Canada | 2.8 |
| Spain | 4.4 | France | 2.0 |
| Japan | 3.2 | | |

## Principal imports

| | $bn cif | | $bn cif |
|---|---|---|---|
| Industrial supplies | 42.8 | Consumer goods | 7.7 |
| Capital goods | 11.6 | Total incl. others | **62.1** |

### Main origins of imports

| | % of total | | % of total |
|---|---|---|---|
| United States | 65.2 | France | 2.7 |
| Japan | 6.3 | Italy | 2.3 |
| Germany | 5.1 | | |

## Balance of payments, reserves and debt, $bn

| | | | |
|---|---|---|---|
| Visible exports fob | 27.5 | Overall balance | 1.7 |
| Visible imports fob | -48.2 | Change in reserves | 1.9 |
| Trade balance | -20.7 | Level of reserves | |
| Invisibles inflows | 17.0 | end Dec. | 18.9 |
| Invisibles outflows | -21.5 | No. months import cover | 4.7 |
| Net transfers | 2.4 | Foreign debt | 113.4 |
| Current account balance | -22.8 | – as % of GDP | 35.2 |
| – as % of GDP | -7.7 | Debt service | 20.7 |
| Capital balance | 26.4 | Debt service ratio | 44.4 |

## Family life

| | | | |
|---|---|---|---|
| No. of households | 16.2m | Divorces per 1,000 pop. | 0.6 |
| Av. no. per household | 5.0 | Cost of living, Sept. 1993 | |
| Marriages per 1,000 pop. | 7.4 | New York = 100 | 86 |

# MOROCCO

| | | | |
|---|---|---|---|
| Area | 446,550 sq km | Currency | Dirham (Dh) |
| Capital | Rabat | | |

## People

| | | | |
|---|---|---|---|
| Population | 26.2m | Life expectancy: men | 62 yrs |
| Pop. per sq km | 63 | women | 65 yrs |
| Av. ann. growth | | Adult literacy | 49.5% |
| in pop. 1985–92 | 2.5% | Fertility rate (per woman) | 4.4 |
| Pop. under 15 | 38.7% | | |
| Pop. over 65 | 3.9% | | *per 1,000 pop.* |
| No. of men per 100 women | 100 | Crude birth rate | 32.3 |
| Human Development Index | 43 | Crude death rate | 8.3 |

## The economy

| | | | |
|---|---|---|---|
| GDP | Dh231bn | GDP per head | $1,036 |
| GDP | $27bn | GDP per head in purchasing | |
| Av. ann. growth in real | | power parity (USA=100) | 11 |
| GDP 1985–92 | 3.8% | | |

| Origins of GDP | | Components of GDP[a] | |
|---|---|---|---|
| | *% of total* | | *% of total* |
| Agriculture | 14.4 | Private consumption | 65.4 |
| Industry, of which: | 32.6 | Public consumption | 15.8 |
| manufacturing | 18.8 | Investment | 24.6 |
| Services | 53.0 | Exports | 22.8 |
| | | Imports | -28.6 |

## Structure of manufacturing

| | *% of total* | | *% of total* |
|---|---|---|---|
| Agric. & food processing | 31 | Other | 48 |
| Textiles & clothing | 25 | Av. ann. increase in industrial | |
| Machinery & transport | 6 | output 1980–91 | 3.0% |

## Energy

| | *'000 TCE* | | |
|---|---|---|---|
| Total output | 775 | % output exported | 0.3 |
| Total consumption | 9,865 | % consumption imported | 104.6 |
| Consumption per head, | | | |
| kg coal equivalent | 384 | | |

## Inflation and finance

| | | | |
|---|---|---|---|
| Consumer price | | *av. ann. increase 1988–91* | |
| inflation 1993 | 5.0% | Narrow money (M1) | 14.0% |
| Av. ann. inflation 1988–93 | 5.0% | Broad money | 15.4% |

## Exchange rates

| | *end 1993* | | *end June 1993* |
|---|---|---|---|
| Dh per $ | 9.65 | Effective rates | *1985 = 100* |
| Dh per SDR | 13.26 | – nominal | 112.9 |
| Dh per Ecu | 10.81 | – real | 87.3 |

## Principal exports

| | $bn fob | | $bn fob |
|---|---|---|---|
| Agric. products & foodstuffs | 1.1 | Phosphoric acid | 0.4 |
| | | Fertilisers | 0.3 |
| Consumer goods | 1.1 | | |
| Semi-finished goods | 1.0 | Total incl. others | **4.0** |

### Main export destinations

| | % of total | | % of total |
|---|---|---|---|
| France | 32.8 | Italy | 5.6 |
| Spain | 9.0 | Japan | 4.9 |
| India | 6.0 | | |

## Principal imports

| | $bn cif | | $bn cif |
|---|---|---|---|
| Industrial equipment | 2.0 | Agric. products & foodstuffs | 0.9 |
| Semi-manufactured goods | 1.7 | Consumer goods | 0.8 |
| Energy & fuels | 1.1 | Total incl. others | **6.7** |

### Main origins of imports

| | % of total | | % of total |
|---|---|---|---|
| France | 23.8 | Germany | 5.9 |
| Spain | 8.5 | United States | 5.9 |
| Italy | 6.2 | | |

## Balance of payments, reserves and debt, $bn

| | | | |
|---|---|---|---|
| Visible exports fob | 4.0 | Overall balance | 0.9 |
| Visible imports fob | -6.7 | Change in reserves | 0.6 |
| Trade balance | -2.7 | Level of reserves | |
| Invisibles inflows | 2.6 | end Dec. | 3.6 |
| Invisibles outflows | -2.9 | No. months import cover | 6.4 |
| Net transfers | 2.5 | Foreign debt | 21.4 |
| Current account balance | -0.4 | – as % of GDP | 77.8 |
| – as % of GDP | -1.6 | Debt service | 2.1 |
| Capital balance | 1.4 | Debt service ratio | 25.9[a] |

## Family life

| | | | |
|---|---|---|---|
| No. of households | 3.4m | Divorces per 1,000 pop. | … |
| Av. no. per household | 5.9 | Cost of living, Sept. 1993 | |
| Marriages per 1,000 pop. | … | New York = 100 | 77 |

a 1991.

# NETHERLANDS

| | | | |
|---|---|---|---|
| Area[a] | 37,938 sq km | Currency | Guilder (G) |
| Capital | Amsterdam | | |

## People

| | | | |
|---|---|---|---|
| Population | 15.1m | Life expectancy: men | 74 yrs |
| Pop. per sq km | 379 | women | 81 yrs |
| Av. ann. growth | | Adult literacy | 99.0% |
| in pop. 1985–92 | 0.7% | Fertility rate (per woman) | 1.7 |
| Pop. under 15 | 18.7% | | |
| Pop. over 65 | 13.0% | | *per 1,000 pop.* |
| No. of men per 100 women | 98 | Crude birth rate | 13.7 |
| Human Development Index | 97 | Crude death rate | 8.7 |

## The economy

| | | | |
|---|---|---|---|
| GDP | Fl549bn | GDP per head | $20,593 |
| GDP | $312bn | GDP per head in purchasing | |
| Av. ann. growth in real | | power parity (USA=100) | 73 |
| GDP 1985–92 | 2.6% | | |

| Origins of GDP | | Components of GDP | |
|---|---|---|---|
| | *% of total* | | *% of total* |
| Agriculture | 4.0 | Private consumption | 60.1 |
| Industry, of which: | 30.0 | Public consumption | 14.3 |
| manufacturing | 23.9 | Investment | 20.5 |
| Services | 66.0 | Exports | 52.4 |
| | | Imports | -47.3 |

## Structure of manufacturing

| | *% of total* | | *% of total* |
|---|---|---|---|
| Agric. & food processing | 16 | Other | 57 |
| Textiles & clothing | 3 | Av. ann. increase in industrial | |
| Machinery & transport | 25 | output 1980–89 | 1.1% |

## Energy

| | *'000 TCE* | | |
|---|---|---|---|
| Total output | 103,768 | % output exported[b] | 110.4 |
| Total consumption | 109,070 | % consumption imported[b] | 122.0 |
| Consumption per head, | | | |
| kg coal equivalent | 7,248 | | |

## Inflation and finance

| | | | |
|---|---|---|---|
| Consumer price | | *av. ann. increase 1988–92* | |
| inflation 1993 | 2.1% | Narrow money (M1) | 5.4% |
| Av. ann. inflation 1988–93 | 2.3% | Broad money | 6.8% |

## Exchange rates

| | *end 1993* | | *end June 1993* |
|---|---|---|---|
| Fl per $ | 1.94 | Effective rates | *1985 = 100* |
| Fl per SDR | 2.67 | – nominal | 119.0 |
| Fl per Ecu | 2.17 | – real | 109.7 |

## Principal exports

| | $bn fob | | $bn fob |
|---|---|---|---|
| Machinery & transport equipment | 33.3 | Fuels | 12.0 |
| | | Raw materials, oils & fuels | 9.0 |
| Chemicals & plastics | 31.1 | | |
| Agric. products & foodstuffs | 28.7 | Total incl. others | **139.8** |

### Main export destinations

| | % of total | | % of total |
|---|---|---|---|
| Germany | 28.8 | Italy | 6.4 |
| Belgium/Luxembourg | 14.3 | EU | 75.8 |
| France | 10.6 | Asia | 6.2 |
| United Kingdom | 9.2 | | |

## Principal imports

| | $bn cif | | $bn cif |
|---|---|---|---|
| Machinery & transport equipment | 42.4 | Fuels | 11.5 |
| | | Raw materials, oils & fats | 7.1 |
| Chemicals & plastics | 24.7 | | |
| Agric. products & foodstuffs | 16.6 | Total incl. others | **134.3** |

### Main origins of imports

| | % of total | | % of total |
|---|---|---|---|
| Germany | 25.2 | France | 7.9 |
| Belgium/Luxembourg | 14.2 | United States | 7.8 |
| United Kingdom | 8.7 | EU | 64.4 |

## Balance of payments, reserves and aid, $bn

| | | | |
|---|---|---|---|
| Visible exports fob | 128.5 | Capital balance | -0.1 |
| Visible imports fob | -117.8 | Overall balance | 6.4 |
| Trade balance | 10.7 | Change in reserves | 4.1 |
| Invisibles inflows | 63.6 | Level of reserves | |
| Invisibles outflows | -62.8 | end Dec. | 35.6 |
| Net transfers | -4.8 | No. months import cover | 3.6 |
| Current account balance | 6.8 | Aid given | 2.75 |
| – as % of GDP | 2.2 | – as % of GDP | 0.86 |

## Family life

| | | | |
|---|---|---|---|
| No. of households | 5.9m | Divorces per 1,000 pop. | 1.9 |
| Av. no. per household | 2.5 | Cost of living, Sept. 1993 | |
| Marriages per 1,000 pop. | 6.3 | New York = 100 | 103 |

a  Land only.
b  Energy trade data are distorted due to transitory and oil refining activities.

# NEW ZEALAND

| | | | |
|---|---|---|---|
| Area | 269,057 sq km | Currency New Zealand dollar (NZ$) | |
| Capital | Wellington | | |

## People

| | | | |
|---|---|---|---|
| Population | 3.4m | Life expectancy: men | 73 yrs |
| Pop. per sq km | 13 | women | 79 yrs |
| Av. ann. growth | | Adult literacy | 99.0% |
| in pop. 1985–92 | 0.7% | Fertility rate (per woman) | 2.1 |
| Pop. under 15 | 23.0% | | |
| Pop. over 65 | 11.2% | | *per 1,000 pop.* |
| No. of men per 100 women | 98 | Crude birth rate | 17.4 |
| Human Development Index | 95 | Crude death rate | 8.2 |

## The economy

| | | | |
|---|---|---|---|
| GDP | NZ$76bn | GDP per head | $12,060 |
| GDP | $41bn | GDP per head in purchasing | |
| Av. ann. growth in real | | power parity (USA=100) | 63 |
| GDP 1985–92 | 0.2% | | |

| Origins of GDP[a] | | Components of GDP[b] | |
|---|---|---|---|
| | *% of total* | | *% of total* |
| Agriculture | 7.9 | Private consumption | 65.0 |
| Industry, of which: | 28.0 | Public consumption | 17.0 |
| manufacturing | 18.8 | Investment | 25.9 |
| Services | 64.1 | Exports | 37.5 |
| | | Imports | -45.5 |

## Structure of manufacturing

| | *% of total* | | *% of total* |
|---|---|---|---|
| Agric. & food processing | 26 | Other | 47 |
| Textiles & clothing | 9 | Av. ann. increase in industrial | |
| Machinery & transport | 18 | output 1980–91 | 1.3% |

## Energy

| | *'000 TCE* | | |
|---|---|---|---|
| Total output | 15,696 | % output exported | 15.5 |
| Total consumption | 18,157 | % consumption imported | 27.7 |
| Consumption per head, | | | |
| kg coal equivalent | 5,304 | | |

## Inflation and finance

| | | | |
|---|---|---|---|
| Consumer price | | *av. ann. increase 1989–92* | |
| inflation 1993 | 1.3% | Narrow money (M1) | 13.2% |
| Av. ann. inflation 1988–93 | 3.8% | Broad money | 31.6% |

## Exchange rates

| | *end 1993* | | *end June 1993* |
|---|---|---|---|
| NZ$ per $ | 1.79 | Effective rates | *1985 = 100* |
| NZ$ per SDR | 2.46 | – nominal | 82.8 |
| NZ$ per Ecu | 2.00 | – real | 100.6 |

## Principal exports

| | $bn fob | | $bn fob |
|---|---|---|---|
| Meat | 1.6 | Fruit & vegetables | 0.5 |
| Dairy produce | 1.3 | Wool | 0.5 |
| Forest products | 1.0 | | |
| Fish | 0.6 | Total incl. others | **9.8** |

### Main export destinations

| | % of total | | % of total |
|---|---|---|---|
| Australia | 19.7 | United States | 12.3 |
| Japan | 14.9 | EU | 16.2 |

## Principal imports

| | $bn cif | | $bn cif |
|---|---|---|---|
| Machinery & mechanical appliances | 1.3 | Plastic & products | 0.4 |
| Vehicles & aircraft | 1.3 | | |
| Mineral fuels | 0.6 | Total incl. others | **8.1** |

### Main origins of imports

| | % of total | | % of total |
|---|---|---|---|
| Australia | 21.1 | Japan | 14.7 |
| United States | 19.5 | EU | 18.1 |

## Balance of payments, reserves and aid, $bn

| | | | |
|---|---|---|---|
| Visible exports fob | 9.8 | Capital balance | -2.3 |
| Visible imports fob | -8.1 | Overall balance | -1.5 |
| Trade balance | 1.7 | Change in reserves | -1.2 |
| Invisibles inflows | 2.6 | Level of reserves | |
| Invisibles outflows | -5.7 | end Dec. | 3.1 |
| Net transfers | 0.7 | No. months import cover | 4.6 |
| Current account balance | -0.8 | Aid given | 0.10 |
| – as % of GDP | -1.9 | – as % of GDP | 0.26 |

## Family life

| | | | |
|---|---|---|---|
| No. of households | 1.2m | Divorces per 1,000 pop. | 2.7 |
| Av. no. per household | 2.8 | Cost of living, Sept. 1993 | |
| Marriages per 1,000 pop. | 6.8 | New York = 100 | 76 |

a  Year ending March 31, 1991.
b  Year ending March 31, 1993.

# NIGERIA

| Area | 923,768 sq km | Currency | Naira (N) |
|---|---|---|---|
| Capital | Lagos | | |

## People

| | | | |
|---|---|---|---|
| Population | 101.9m | Life expectancy: men | 51 yrs |
| Pop. per sq km | 137 | women | 54 yrs |
| Av. ann. growth | | Adult literacy | 50.7% |
| in pop. 1985–92 | 2.9% | Fertility rate (per woman) | 6.4 |
| Pop. under 15 | 46.9% | | |
| Pop. over 65 | 2.6% | | *per 1,000 pop.* |
| No. of men per 100 women | 98 | Crude birth rate | 45.2 |
| Human Development Index | 25 | Crude death rate | 13.9 |

## The economy

| | | | |
|---|---|---|---|
| GDP | N571bn | GDP per head | $323 |
| GDP | $33bn | GDP per head in purchasing | |
| Av. ann. growth in real | | power parity (USA=100) | 6 |
| GDP 1985–92 | 5.7% | | |

| **Origins of GDP** | | **Components of GDP** | |
|---|---|---|---|
| | *% of total* | | *% of total* |
| Agriculture | 35.4 | Private consumption | 64.7 |
| Industry, of which: | 21.5 | Public consumption | 4.4 |
| manufacturing | 8.6 | Investment | 14.6 |
| Services | 43.1 | Exports | 52.3 |
| | | Imports | -36.0 |

## Structure of manufacturing

| | *% of total* | | *% of total* |
|---|---|---|---|
| Agric. & food processing | ... | Other | ... |
| Textiles & clothing | ... | Av. ann. increase in industrial | |
| Machinery & transport | ... | output 1980–91 | -0.4% |

## Energy

| | *'000 TCE* | | |
|---|---|---|---|
| Total output | 141,399 | % output exported | 81.9 |
| Total consumption | 23,572 | % consumption imported | 11.4 |
| Consumption per head, | | | |
| kg coal equivalent | 210 | | |

## Inflation and finance

| Consumer price | | *av. ann. increase 1988–91* | |
|---|---|---|---|
| inflation 1993 | 80.0% | Narrow money (M1) | 34.4% |
| Av. ann. inflation 1988–93 | 39.4% | Broad money | 28.6% |

## Exchange rates

| | *end 1993* | | *end June 1993* |
|---|---|---|---|
| N per $ | 21.88 | Effective rates | 1985 = 100 |
| N per SDR | 30.06 | – nominal | 3.8 |
| N per Ecu | 24.51 | – real | 12.1 |

## Principal exports

|  | $bn fob |  | $bn fob |
|---|---|---|---|
| Petroleum | 11.6 |  |  |
| Cocoa beans & products | 0.1 | Total incl. others | **12.7** |

**Main export destinations**

|  | % of total |  | % of total |
|---|---|---|---|
| United States | 39.4 | France | 5.4 |
| Germany | 10.8 | Netherlands | 4.3 |
| Spain | 9.6 |  |  |

## Principal imports

|  | $bn cif |  | $bn cif |
|---|---|---|---|
| Machinery & transport equipment | 3.6 | Agric products & foodstuffs | 0.7 |
| Manufactured goods | 2.0 |  |  |
| Chemicals | 1.3 | Total incl. others | **7.5** |

**Main origins of imports**

|  | % of total |  | % of total |
|---|---|---|---|
| United Kingdom | 13.2 | France | 9.4 |
| Germany | 12.3 | Japan | 6.4 |
| United States | 12.0 |  |  |

## Balance of payments, reserves and debt, $bn

| | | | |
|---|---|---|---|
| Visible exports fob | 11.8 | Overall balance | -5.6 |
| Visible imports fob | -7.2 | Change in reserves | -3.5 |
| Trade balance | 4.6 | Level of reserves | |
| Invisibles inflows | 1.2 | end Dec. | 1.0 |
| Invisibles outflows | -4.3 | No. months import cover | 1.7 |
| Net transfers | 0.8 | Foreign debt | 31.0 |
| Current account balance | 2.3 | – as % of GDP | 110.7 |
| – as % of GDP | 6.9 | Debt service | 3.8 |
| Capital balance | -7.8 | Debt service ratio | 30.6 |

## Family life

| | | | |
|---|---|---|---|
| No. households | ... | Divorces per 1,000 pop. | ... |
| Av. no. per household | ... | Cost of living, Sept. 1993 | |
| Marriages per 1,000 pop. | ... | New York = 100 | 61 |

# NORWAY

| Area | 324,219 sq km | Currency | Norwegian krone (Nkr) |
|------|---------------|----------|------------------------|
| Capital | Oslo | | |

## People

| | | | |
|---|---|---|---|
| Population | 4.3m | Life expectancy: men | 74 yrs |
| Pop. per sq km | 13 | women | 81 yrs |
| Av. ann. growth | | Adult literacy | 99.0% |
| in pop. 1985–92 | 0.4% | Fertility rate (per woman) | 2.0 |
| Pop. under 15 | 19.7% | | |
| Pop. over 65 | 15.9% | | *per 1,000 pop.* |
| No. of men per 100 women | 98 | Crude birth rate | 14.7 |
| Human Development Index | 98 | Crude death rate | 10.8 |

## The economy

| | | | |
|---|---|---|---|
| GDP | Nkr684bn | GDP per head | $25,804 |
| GDP | $110bn | GDP per head in purchasing | |
| Av. ann. growth in real | | power parity (USA=100) | 75 |
| GDP 1985–92 | 2.5% | | |

| **Origins of GDP** | | **Components of GDP** | |
|---|---|---|---|
| | *% of total* | | *% of total* |
| Agriculture | 2.8 | Private consumption | 51.8 |
| Industry, of which: | 32.7 | Public consumption | 22.1 |
| manufacturing | 13.5 | Investment | 18.5 |
| Services | 64.5 | Exports | 43.4 |
| | | Imports | -35.8 |

## Structure of manufacturing

| | *% of total* | | *% of total* |
|---|---|---|---|
| Agric. & food processing | 21 | Other | 53 |
| Textiles & clothing | 2 | Av. ann. increase in industrial | |
| Machinery & transport | 24 | output 1980–91 | 5.2% |

## Energy

| | *'000 TCE* | | |
|---|---|---|---|
| Total output | 185,497 | % output exported | 86.2 |
| Total consumption | 29,120 | % consumption imported | 22.2 |
| Consumption per head, | | | |
| kg coal equivalent | 6,818 | | |

## Inflation and finance

| Consumer price | | *av. ann. increase 1988–92* | |
|---|---|---|---|
| inflation 1993 | 2.2% | Narrow money (M1) | 16.2% |
| Av. ann. inflation 1988–93 | 3.9% | Broad money | 6.1% |

## Exchange rates

| | *end 1993* | | *end June 1993* |
|---|---|---|---|
| | | | *1985 = 100* |
| Nkr per $ | 7.52 | Effective rates | |
| Nkr per SDR | 10.33 | – nominal | 87.7 |
| Nkr per Ecu | 8.42 | – real | 95.4 |

## Principal exports

| | $bn fob | | $bn fob |
|---|---|---|---|
| Oil, gas & products | 17.6 | Fish & fish products | 2.3 |
| Non-ferrous metals | 2.4 | Iron & steel | 2.2 |
| Machinery incl. | | Ships & oil platforms | 1.9 |
| electricals | 2.4 | Total incl. others | **35.2** |

### Main export destinations

| | % of total | | % of total |
|---|---|---|---|
| United Kingdom | 24.2 | Netherlands | 7.2 |
| Germany | 13.5 | EU | 67.3 |
| Sweden | 9.4 | Efta | 13.5 |
| France | 7.9 | | |

## Principal imports

| | $bn cif | | $bn cif |
|---|---|---|---|
| Machinery incl. | | Clothing | 1.4 |
| electricals | 6.3 | Iron & steel | 1.2 |
| Transport equipment | | Ships & oil platforms | 0.9 |
| excl.ships | 2.4 | | |
| Food, drink & tobacco | 1.6 | Total incl. others | **27.8** |

### Main origins of imports

| | % of total | | % of total |
|---|---|---|---|
| Sweden | 15.5 | Denmark | 7.5 |
| Germany | 14.7 | EU | 49.1 |
| United Kingdom | 9.4 | Efta | 21.8 |
| United States | 8.4 | | |

## Balance of payments, reserves and aid, $bn

| | | | |
|---|---|---|---|
| Visible exports fob | 35.2 | Capital balance | -0.2 |
| Visible imports fob | -25.9 | Overall balance | -0.5 |
| Trade balance | 9.3 | Change in reserves | -1.3 |
| Invisibles inflows | 17.1 | Level of reserves | |
| Invisibles outflows | -21.6 | end Dec. | 11.9 |
| Net transfers | -1.8 | No. months import cover | 5.5 |
| Current account balance | 2.9 | Aid given | 1.27 |
| – as % of GDP | 2.6 | – as % of GDP | 1.16 |

## Family life

| | | | |
|---|---|---|---|
| No. households | 1.8m | Divorces per 1,000 pop. | 2.4 |
| Av. no. per household | 2.4 | Cost of living, Sept. 1993 | |
| Marriages per 1,000 pop. | 5.2 | New York = 100 | 131 |

# PAKISTAN

| Area | 796,095 sq km | Currency | Pakistan rupee (PRs) |
|---|---|---|---|
| Capital | Islamabad | | |

## People

| | | | |
|---|---|---|---|
| Population | 119.3m | Life expectancy: men | 59 yrs |
| Pop. per sq km | 170 | women | 59 yrs |
| Av. ann. growth | | Adult literacy | 34.8% |
| in pop. 1985–92 | 3.1% | Fertility rate (per woman) | 6.2 |
| Pop. under 15 | 43.6% | | |
| Pop. over 65 | 2.9% | | *per 1,000 pop.* |
| No. of men per 100 women | 108 | Crude birth rate | 40.6 |
| Human Development Index | 31 | Crude death rate | 10.5 |

## The economy

| | | | |
|---|---|---|---|
| GDP | PRs1,229bn | GDP per head | $415 |
| GDP | $49bn | GDP per head in purchasing | |
| Av. ann. growth in real | | power parity (USA=100) | 9 |
| GDP 1985–92 | 5.6% | | |

| Origins of GDP[a] | *% of total* | Components of GDP[b] | *% of total* |
|---|---|---|---|
| Agriculture | 26.2 | Private consumption | 70.2 |
| Industry, of which: | 28.8 | Public consumption | 12.8 |
| manufacturing | 17.4 | Investment | 20.0 |
| Services | 45.0 | Exports | 17.3 |
| | | Imports | -20.4 |

## Structure of manufacturing

| | *% of total* | | *% of total* |
|---|---|---|---|
| Agric. & food processing | 29 | Other | 45 |
| Textiles & clothing | 19 | Av. ann. increase in industrial | |
| Machinery & transport | 7 | output 1980–91 | 7.5% |

## Energy

| | *'000 TCE* | | |
|---|---|---|---|
| Total output | 24,128 | % output exported | 2.0 |
| Total consumption | 35,202 | % consumption imported | 37.1 |
| Consumption per head, | | | |
| kg coal equivalent | 290 | | |

## Inflation and finance

| Consumer price | | *av. ann. increase 1988–92* | |
|---|---|---|---|
| inflation 1993 | 9.4% | Narrow money (M1) | 16.5% |
| Av. ann. inflation 1988–93 | 9.4% | Broad money | 14.7% |

## Exchange rates

| | *end 1993* | | *end June 1993* |
|---|---|---|---|
| PRs per $ | 30.12 | Effective rates | 1985 = 100 |
| PRs per SDR | 41.37 | – nominal | ... |
| PRs per Ecu | 33.73 | – real | ... |

## Principal exports[a]

|  | $bn fob |  | $bn fob |
|---|---|---|---|
| Cotton yarn | 1.2 | Raw cotton | 0.4 |
| Clothing | 0.8 | Rice | 0.4 |
| Cotton fabrics | 0.7 | Total incl. others | **6.2** |

### Main export destinations[a]

|  | % of total |  | % of total |
|---|---|---|---|
| United States | 10.8 | United Kingdom | 7.3 |
| Germany | 8.9 | Hong Kong | 6.3 |
| Japan | 8.3 | South Korea | 3.9 |

## Principal imports[a]

|  | $bn cif |  | $bn cif |
|---|---|---|---|
| Petroleum & products | 1.7 | Transport equipment | 0.4 |
| Non-electrical machinery | 1.4 |  |  |
| Chemicals | 0.7 | Total incl. others | **7.6** |

### Main origins of imports[a]

|  | % of total |  | % of total |
|---|---|---|---|
| Japan | 13.0 | Saudi Arabia | 6.3 |
| United States | 11.8 | United Kingdom | 4.9 |
| Germany | 7.3 | UAE | 3.0 |

## Balance of payments[b], reserves and debt, $bn

| | | | |
|---|---|---|---|
| Visible exports fob | 6.4 | Overall balance | -1.1 |
| Visible imports fob | -8.6 | Change in reserves[d] | 0.0 |
| Trade balance | -2.2 | Level of reserves | |
| Invisibles inflows | 1.6 | end Dec. | 1.5 |
| Invisibles outflows | -3.6 | No. months import cover | 2.1 |
| Net transfers | 2.3 | Foreign debt | 24.1 |
| Current account balance[c] | -3.1 | – as % of GDP | 48.0 |
| – as % of GDP[c] | -6.2 | Debt service | 2.3 |
| Capital balance | 0.9 | Debt service ratio | 23.3 |

## Family life

| | | | |
|---|---|---|---|
| No. households | 12.6m | Divorces per 1,000 pop. | ... |
| Av. no. per household | 6.7 | Cost of living, Sept. 1993 | |
| Marriages per 1,000 pop. | ... | New York = 100 | 56 |

a Fiscal year ending June 30, 1991.
b 1991.
c 1992 estimates.
d Less than $0.01bn.

# PERU

| | | | |
|---|---|---|---|
| Area | 1,285,216 sq km | Currency | Nuevo Sol (New Sol) |
| Capital | Lima | | |

## People

| | | | | |
|---|---|---|---|---|
| Population | 22.3m | Life expectancy: men | | 63 yrs |
| Pop. per sq km | 19 | women | | 66 yrs |
| Av. ann. growth | | Adult literacy[a] | | 85.1% |
| in pop. 1985–92 | 2.1% | Fertility rate (per woman) | | 3.6 |
| Pop. under 15 | 35.5% | | | |
| Pop. over 65 | 4.1% | | *per 1,000 pop.* | |
| No. of men per 100 women | 101 | Crude birth rate | | 29.0 |
| Human Development Index | 64 | Crude death rate | | 7.6 |

## The economy

| | | | |
|---|---|---|---|
| GDP | New Soles 26.2bn | GDP per head | $951 |
| GDP | $21bn | GDP per head in purchasing | |
| Av. ann. growth in real | | power parity (USA=100) | 12 |
| GDP 1985–92 | -0.9% | | |

| Origins of GDP[b] | | Components of GDP[b] | |
|---|---|---|---|
| | *% of total* | | *% of total* |
| Agriculture | 13.6 | Private consumption | 81.8 |
| Industry, of which: | 39.4 | Public consumption | 5.2 |
| manufacturing | 22.3 | Investment | 15.9 |
| Services | 47.0 | Exports | 8.5 |
| | | Imports | -11.5 |

## Structure of manufacturing

| | *% of total* | | *% of total* |
|---|---|---|---|
| Agric. & food processing | 23 | Other | 53 |
| Textiles & clothing | 14 | Av. ann. increase in industrial | |
| Machinery & transport | 10 | output 1980–91 | -1.1% |

## Energy

| | *'000 TCE* | | |
|---|---|---|---|
| Total output | 10,914 | % output exported | 26.6 |
| Total consumption | 9,793 | % consumption imported | 26.7 |
| Consumption per head, | | | |
| kg coal equivalent | 445 | | |

## Inflation and finance

| | | | |
|---|---|---|---|
| Consumer price | | *av. ann. increase 1988–92* | |
| inflation 1993 | 48.6% | Narrow money (M1) | 686% |
| Av. ann. inflation 1988–93 | 702.4% | Broad money | 799% |

## Exchange rates

| | *end 1993* | | *end June 1993* |
|---|---|---|---|
| New Soles per $ | 2.16 | Effective rates | 1985 = 100 |
| New Soles per SDR | 2.97 | – nominal | ... |
| New Soles per Ecu | 2.42 | – real | ... |

## Principal exports

|  | $bn fob |  | $bn fob |
|---|---|---|---|
| Non-traditional products | 1.0 | Zinc | 0.3 |
| Copper | 0.8 | Petroleum & products | 0.2 |
| Fishmeal | 0.4 | Total incl. others | **3.5** |

### Main export destinations

|  | % of total |  | % of total |
|---|---|---|---|
| United States | 21.4 | Italy | 6.0 |
| Japan | 9.9 | Brazil | 4.7 |

## Principal imports

|  | $bn fob |  | $bn fob |
|---|---|---|---|
| Industrial supplies | 1.8 | Consumer goods | 0.8 |
| Capital goods | 1.1 | Total incl. others | **4.1** |

### Main origins of imports

|  | % of total |  | % of total |
|---|---|---|---|
| United States | 27.2 | Argentina | 5.2 |
| Colombia | 8.1 | Germany | 4.6 |

## Balance of payments, reserves and debt, $bn

| | | | |
|---|---|---|---|
| Visible exports fob | 3.5 | Overall balance | -0.1 |
| Visible imports fob | -4.1 | Change in reserves | 0.9 |
| Trade balance | -0.6 | Level of reserves | |
| Invisibles inflows | 1.0 | end Dec. | 3.4 |
| Invisibles outflows | -2.8 | No. months import cover | 10.0 |
| Net transfers | 0.3 | Foreign debt | 20.3 |
| Current account balance | -2.1 | – as % of GDP | 95.4 |
| – as % of GDP | -9.8 | Debt service | 1.0 |
| Capital balance | -0.1 | Debt service ratio | 23.0 |

## Family life

| | | | |
|---|---|---|---|
| No. of households | 4.2m | Divorces per 1,000 pop. | ... |
| Av. no. per household | 5.1 | Cost of living, Sept. 1993 | |
| Marriages per 1,000 pop. | 6.0 | New York = 100 | 64 |

a  Excluding Indian jungle population.
b  1991.

# PHILIPPINES

| | | | |
|---|---|---|---|
| Area | 300,000 sq km | Currency | Philippine peso (P) |
| Capital | Manila | | |

## People

| | | | |
|---|---|---|---|
| Population | 64.2m | Life expectancy: men | 63 yrs |
| Pop. per sq km | 231 | women | 67 yrs |
| Av. ann. growth | | Adult literacy | 89.7% |
| in pop. 1985–92 | 2.3% | Fertility rate (per woman) | 3.9 |
| Pop. under 15 | 38.4% | | |
| Pop. over 65 | 3.3% | | *per 1,000 pop.* |
| No. of men per 100 women | 103 | Crude birth rate | 30.3 |
| Human Development Index | 60 | Crude death rate | 6.8 |

## The economy

| | | | |
|---|---|---|---|
| GDP | P1,250bn | GDP per head | $771 |
| GDP | $49bn | GDP per head in purchasing | |
| Av. ann. growth in real | | power parity (USA=100) | 11 |
| GDP 1985–92 | 2.2% | | |

| Origins of GDP[a] | | Components of GDP | |
|---|---|---|---|
| | *% of total* | | *% of total* |
| Agriculture | 22.8 | Private consumption | 75.8 |
| Industry, of which: | 35.0 | Public consumption | 9.7 |
| manufacturing | 25.5 | Investment | 20.9 |
| Services | 42.2 | Exports | 29.4 |
| | | Imports | -33.4 |

## Structure of manufacturing

| | *% of total* | | *% of total* |
|---|---|---|---|
| Agric. & food processing | 36 | Other | 46 |
| Textiles & clothing | 10 | Av. ann. increase in industrial | |
| Machinery & transport | 8 | output 1980–91 | -0.5% |

## Energy

| | *'000 TCE* | | |
|---|---|---|---|
| Total output | 8,781 | % output exported | 4.0 |
| Total consumption | 25,818 | % consumption imported | 75.5 |
| Consumption per head, | | | |
| kg coal equivalent | 405 | | |

## Inflation and finance

| | | | |
|---|---|---|---|
| Consumer price | | *av. ann. increase 1988–92* | |
| inflation 1993 | 7.6% | Narrow money (M1) | 16.9% |
| Av. ann. inflation 1988–93 | 11.7% | Broad money | 21.5% |

## Exchange rates

| | *end 1993* | | *end June 1993* |
|---|---|---|---|
| | | | *1985 = 100* |
| P per $ | 27.70 | Effective rates | |
| P per SDR | 38.05 | – nominal | 49.9 |
| P per Ecu | 31.02 | – real | 77.1 |

## Principal exports

| | $bn fob | | $bn fob |
|---|---|---|---|
| Electrical & electronic equipment | 2.7 | Copper | 0.4 |
| Clothing | 2.1 | Fish & products | 0.3 |
| Coconut products | 0.6 | Total incl. others | **9.8** |

### Main export destinations

| | % of total | | % of total |
|---|---|---|---|
| United States | 39.0 | United Kingdom | 4.8 |
| Japan | 17.7 | Hong Kong | 4.7 |
| Germany | 5.3 | | |

## Principal imports

| | $bn cif | | $bn cif |
|---|---|---|---|
| Raw materials & intermediaries | 6.7 | Crude oil | 1.6 |
| Capital goods | 4.0 | Total incl. others | **14.5** |

### Main origins of imports

| | % of total | | % of total |
|---|---|---|---|
| Japan | 21.2 | Saudi Arabia | 6.0 |
| United States | 18.0 | Hong Kong | 5.0 |
| Taiwan | 6.6 | South Korea | 4.8 |

## Balance of payments, reserves and debt, $bn

| | | | |
|---|---|---|---|
| Visible exports fob | 9.8 | Overall balance | 1.7 |
| Visible imports fob | -14.5 | Change in reserves | 1.6 |
| Trade balance | -4.7 | Level of reserves | |
| Invisibles inflows | 7.5 | end Dec. | 5.3 |
| Invisibles outflows | -4.5 | No. months import cover | 4.4 |
| Net transfers | 0.8 | Foreign debt | 32.6 |
| Current account balance | -0.9 | – as % of GDP | 60.7 |
| – as % of GDP | -1.9 | Debt service | 4.9 |
| Capital balance | 3.1 | Debt service ratio | 27.7 |

## Family life

| | | | |
|---|---|---|---|
| No. of households | 11.4m | Divorces per 1,000 pop. | ... |
| Av. no. per household | 5.3 | Cost of living, Sept. 1993 | |
| Marriages per 1,000 pop. | 5.0 | New York = 100 | 58 |

a  1991.

# POLAND

| Area | 312,677 sq km | Currency | Zloty (Zl) |
|---|---|---|---|
| Capital | Warsaw | | |

## People

| | | | |
|---|---|---|---|
| Population | 38.4m | Life expectancy: men | 67 yrs |
| Pop. per sq km | 124 | women | 76 yrs |
| Av. ann. growth | | Adult literacy | 98.0% |
| in pop. 1985–92 | 0.4% | Fertility rate (per woman) | 2.1 |
| Pop. under 15 | 23.5% | | |
| Pop. over 65 | 10.9% | | *per 1,000 pop.* |
| No. of men per 100 women | 95 | Crude birth rate | 14.3 |
| Human Development Index | 83 | Crude death rate | 10.1 |

## The economy

| | | | |
|---|---|---|---|
| GDP | Zl1,021,950bn | GDP per head | $1,962 |
| GDP | $75bn | GDP per head in purchasing | |
| Av. ann. growth in real | | power parity (USA=100) | 20 |
| GDP 1985–92 | -0.5% | | |

| Origins of GDP | | Components of GDP | |
|---|---|---|---|
| | *% of total* | | *% of total* |
| Agriculture | 7.3 | Private consumption | 57.1 |
| Industry, of which: | 50.8 | Public consumption | 20.8 |
| manufacturing | ... | Accumulation | 22.1 |
| Services | 41.9 | Exports | ... |
| | | Imports | ... |

## Structure of manufacturing

| | *% of total* | | *% of total* |
|---|---|---|---|
| Agric. & food processing | 21 | Other | 44 |
| Textiles & clothing | 9 | Av. ann. increase in industrial | |
| Machinery & transport | 26 | output 1980–90 | ... |

## Energy

| | *'000 TCE* | | |
|---|---|---|---|
| Total output | 132,130 | % output exported | 16.2 |
| Total consumption | 121,317 | % consumption imported | 23.5 |
| Consumption per head, | | | |
| kg coal equivalent | 3,167 | | |

## Inflation and finance

| Consumer price | | *av. ann. increase 1988–92* | |
|---|---|---|---|
| inflation 1993 | 35.3% | Narrow money (M1) | 111.7% |
| Av. ann. inflation 1988–93 | 124.2% | Broad money | 124.9% |

## Exchange rates

| | *end 1993* | | *end June 1993* |
|---|---|---|---|
| Zl per $ | 21,344 | Effective rates | *1985 = 100* |
| Zl per SDR | 29,317 | – nominal | 0.9 |
| Zl per Ecu | 23,905 | – real | 83.3 |

## Principal exports

|  | $bn fob |  | $bn fob |
|---|---|---|---|
| Machinery | 3.2 | Copper | 0.8 |
| Chemicals | 1.6 | Steel | 0.7 |
| Food & agric. products | 1.3 | Total incl. others | **13.2** |

### Main export destinations

|  | % of total |  | % of total |
|---|---|---|---|
| Germany | 31.4 | United Kingdom | 4.4 |
| Netherlands | 6.0 | Ex-Czechoslovakia | 3.8 |
| Italy | 5.6 | Austria | 3.2 |
| Ex-Soviet Union | 5.5 |  |  |

## Principal imports

|  | $bn fob |  | $bn fob |
|---|---|---|---|
| Machinery | 5.3 | Food & agric. products | 1.4 |
| Chemicals | 2.8 | Light industry | 0.7 |
| Oil | 2.7 | Metals | 0.7 |
|  |  | Total incl. others | **14.1** |

### Main origins of imports

|  | % of total |  | % of total |
|---|---|---|---|
| Germany | 23.9 | Netherlands | 4.8 |
| Ex-Soviet Union | 8.5 | Austria | 4.5 |
| Italy | 6.9 | France | 4.4 |
| United Kingdom | 6.6 |  |  |

## Balance of payments, reserves and debt, $bn

|  |  |  |  |
|---|---|---|---|
| Visible exports fob | 13.9 | Overall balance | -4.3 |
| Visible imports fob | -14.1 | Change in reserves | 0.5 |
| Trade balance | -0.2 | Level of reserves |  |
| Invisibles inflows | 5.5 | end Dec. | 4.3 |
| Invisibles outflows | -8.9 | No. months import cover | 3.7 |
| Net transfers | 0.5 | Foreign debt | 48.5 |
| Current account balance | -3.1 | – as % of GDP | 54.4 |
| – as % of GDP | -4.1 | Debt service | 1.5 |
| Capital balance | -1.0 | Debt service ratio | 9.5 |

## Family life

|  |  |  |  |
|---|---|---|---|
| No. of households | 12.0m | Divorces per 1,000 pop. | 0.9 |
| Av. no. per household | 3.1 | Cost of living, Sept. 1993 |  |
| Marriages per 1,000 pop. | 6.1 | New York = 100 | 60 |

# PORTUGAL

| Area | 92,082 sq km | Currency | Escudo (Esc) |
|---|---|---|---|
| Capital | Lisbon | | |

## People

| | | | |
|---|---|---|---|
| Population | 9.8m | Life expectancy: men | 71 yrs |
| Pop. per sq km | 107 | women | 78 yrs |
| Av. ann. growth | | Adult literacy | 85.0% |
| in pop. 1985–92 | -0.7% | Fertility rate (per woman) | 1.5 |
| Pop. under 15 | 18.5% | | |
| Pop. over 65 | 14.2% | | *per 1,000 pop.* |
| No. of men per 100 women | 93 | Crude birth rate | 11.6 |
| Human Development Index | 85 | Crude death rate | 10.2 |

## The economy

| | | | |
|---|---|---|---|
| GDP | Esc9,855bn | GDP per head | $7,451 |
| GDP | $73bn | GDP per head in purchasing | |
| Av. ann. growth in real | | power parity (USA=100) | 41 |
| GDP 1985–92 | 3.7% | | |

| Origins of GDP | | Components of GDP | |
|---|---|---|---|
| | *% of total* | | *% of total* |
| Agriculture | 4.7 | Private consumption | 65.6 |
| Industry, of which: | 36.1 | Public consumption | 18.6 |
| manufacturing | 28.6 | Investment | 28.2 |
| Services | 59.2 | Exports | 24.8 |
| | | Imports | -37.3 |

## Structure of manufacturing

| | *% of total* | | *% of total* |
|---|---|---|---|
| Agric. & food processing | 18 | Other | 49 |
| Textiles & clothing | 20 | Av. ann. increase in industrial | |
| Machinery & transport | 14 | output 1980–90 | ... |

## Energy

| | *'000 TCE* | | |
|---|---|---|---|
| Total output | 1,292 | % output exported[a] | 238.8 |
| Total consumption | 19,332 | % consumption imported[a] | 123.1 |
| Consumption per head, | | | |
| kg coal equivalent | 1,960 | | |

## Inflation and finance

| | | | |
|---|---|---|---|
| Consumer price | | *av. ann. increase 1989–92* | |
| inflation 1993 | 6.5% | Narrow money (M1) | 17.3% |
| Av. ann. inflation 1988–93 | 10.4% | Broad money | 15.0% |

## Exchange rates

| | *end 1993* | | *end June 1993* |
|---|---|---|---|
| | | | *1985 = 100* |
| Esc per $ | 176.8 | Effective rates | |
| Esc per SDR | 242.9 | – nominal | 75.0 |
| Esc per Ecu | 198.0 | – real | 123.9 |

## Principal exports

| | $bn fob | | $bn fob |
|---|---|---|---|
| Textiles & clothing | 7.0 | Food products | 1.4 |
| Machinery & transport | | Chemicals & plastics | 1.0 |
| equipment | 3.9 | | |
| Forestry products | 1.9 | Total incl. others | **18.2** |

**Main export destinations**

| | % of total | | % of total |
|---|---|---|---|
| Germany | 19.2 | Netherlands | 5.4 |
| Spain | 14.7 | United States | 3.5 |
| France | 14.2 | EU | 74.9 |
| United Kingdom | 11.2 | Efta | 8.8 |

## Principal imports

| | $bn cif | | $bn cif |
|---|---|---|---|
| Machinery & transport | | Textiles & clothing | 3.3 |
| equipment | 11.5 | Energy & fuels | 2.4 |
| Food products | 3.8 | | |
| Chemicals & plastics | 3.4 | Total incl. others | **30.0** |

**Main origins of imports**

| | % of total | | % of total |
|---|---|---|---|
| Spain | 16.6 | United Kingdom | 7.2 |
| Germany | 15.0 | Netherlands | 6.9 |
| France | 12.8 | EU | 73.7 |
| Italy | 10.2 | Opec | 6.0 |

## Balance of payments, reserves and debt, $bn

| | | | |
|---|---|---|---|
| Visible exports fob | 18.2 | Overall balance | -0.2 |
| Visible imports fob | -27.7 | Change in reserves | -1.4 |
| Trade balance | -9.5 | Level of reserves | |
| Invisibles inflows | 7.7 | end Dec. | 24.3 |
| Invisibles outflows | -6.2 | No. months import cover | 10.5 |
| Net transfers | 7.8 | Foreign debt | 32.0 |
| Current account balance | -0.2 | – as % of GDP | 40.1 |
| – as % of GDP | -0.3 | Debt service | 5.6 |
| Capital balance | -1.0 | Debt service ratio | 22.4 |

## Family life

| | | | |
|---|---|---|---|
| No. of households | 3.4m | Divorces per 1,000 pop. | 1.0 |
| Av. no. per household | 2.9 | Cost of living, Sept. 1993 | |
| Marriages per 1,000 pop. | 6.8 | New York = 100 | 81 |

a Energy trade data are distorted by transitory and oil refining activities.

# RUSSIA[a]

| Area | 17,075,400 sq km | Currency | Rouble (Rb) |
|---|---|---|---|
| Capital | Moscow | | |

## People

| | | | |
|---|---|---|---|
| Population | 148.9m | Life expectancy | 70 yrs |
| Pop. per sq km | 9 | Adult literacy[b] | 99.0% |
| Av. ann. growth | | Fertility rate (per woman) | 2.2 |
| in pop. 1985–92 | 0.5% | | |
| Pop. under 15[b] | 23.0% | | |
| Pop. over 65[b] | 10% | | *per 1,000 pop.* |
| No. of men per 100 women[b] | 88 | Crude birth rate | 14.8 |
| Human Development Index | 86 | Crude death rate | 11.0 |

## The economy

| | | | |
|---|---|---|---|
| GDP | Rb88,774bn | GDP per head | $2,671 |
| GDP | $398bn | GDP per head in purchasing | |
| Av. ann. growth in real | | power parity (USA=100) | 37[c] |
| GDP 1987–92 | -4.1% | | |

| Origins of NMP | | Components of GDP[f] | |
|---|---|---|---|
| | *% of total* | | *% of total* |
| Agriculture | 13.4 | Private consumption | 44.4 |
| Industry, of which: | 59.5 | Public consumption | 16.7 |
| manufacturing | ... | Investment | 42.9 |
| Services | 26.8 | Foreign trade balance | 0.3 |

## Structure of manufacturing

| | *% of total* | | *% of total* |
|---|---|---|---|
| Agric. & food processing | ... | Other | ... |
| Textiles & clothing | ... | Av. ann. increase in industrial | |
| Machinery & transport | ... | output 1980–88 | 3.9% |

## Energy[c]

| | '000 TCE | | |
|---|---|---|---|
| Total output | 2,217,666 | % output exported | 12.9 |
| Total consumption | 1,867,297 | % consumption imported | 0.2 |
| Consumption per head, | | | |
| kg coal equivalent | 6,415 | | |

## Inflation and finance

| | | | |
|---|---|---|---|
| Consumer price | | | *av. ann. increase 1988–92* |
| inflation 1993 | 940% | Narrow money (M1) | ... |
| Av. ann. inflation 1988–93 | 162.3% | Broad money | ... |

## Exchange rates

| | *end 1993* | | *end June 1993* |
|---|---|---|---|
| Rb[d] per $ | 1,244 | Effective rates | 1985 = 100 |
| Rb[d] per SDR | 1,710 | – nominal | ... |
| Rb[d] per Ecu | 1,394 | – real | ... |

## Principal exports[f]

| | Rb bn | | Rb bn |
|---|---|---|---|
| Fuels & raw materials | 18.5 | Consumer goods | 1.1 |
| Machinery & equipment | 3.0 | Food | 0.7 |
| Chemicals & rubber | 1.9 | Total incl. others | **29.5** |

### Main export destinations[e]

| | % of total | | % of total |
|---|---|---|---|
| Western countries | 59.5 | Eastern Europe | 20.0 |
| of which: Germany | 14.7 | Others | 20.5 |

## Principal imports[f]

| | Rb bn | | Rb bn |
|---|---|---|---|
| Machinery & equipment | 8.6 | Chemicals & rubber | 2.2 |
| Food products | 6.3 | Semi-processed materials | 1.3 |
| Consumer goods | 4.3 | | |
| Fuels & raw materials | 2.3 | Total incl. others | **25.8** |

### Main origins of imports[be]

| | % of total | | % of total |
|---|---|---|---|
| Western countries | 64.3 | Eastern Europe | 15.2 |
| of which: Germany | 19.2 | Others | 20.5 |

## Balance of payments[bc], reserves and debt, $bn

| | | | |
|---|---|---|---|
| Visible exports fob | 109.8 | Overall balance | ... |
| Visible imports fob | -106.4 | Change in reserves | ... |
| Trade balance | 3.4 | Level of reserves | |
| Invisibles inflows | ... | end Dec. | |
| Invisibles outflows | ... | No. months import cover | ... |
| Net transfers | ... | Foreign debt[g] | 78.7 |
| Current account balance | -2.7 | – as % of GDP | ... |
| – as % of GDP | -0.7 | Debt service | 1.6 |
| Capital balance | ... | Debt service ratio | ... |

## Family life

| | | | |
|---|---|---|---|
| No. of households | 40.5m | Divorces per 1,000 pop. | 3.9 |
| Av. no. per household | 2.9 | Cost of living, Sept.1993 | |
| Marriages per 1,000 pop. | 9.4 | New York = 100 | 104 |

a For selected data on Ukraine and other ex-Soviet republics, see page 192.
b 1990.
c Ex-Soviet Union.
d Moscow Interbank Currency Exchange rate.
e Outside ex-Soviet Union only.
f 1991.
g Ex-Soviet Union convertible currency debt.

# SAUDI ARABIA

| | | | |
|---|---|---|---|
| Area | 2,149,640 sq km | Currency | Riyal (SR) |
| Capital | Riyadh | | |

## People

| | | | |
|---|---|---|---|
| Population | 15.9m | Life expectancy: men | 68 yrs |
| Pop. per sq km | 8 | women | 71 yrs |
| Av. ann. growth | | Adult literacy | 62.4% |
| in pop. 1985–92 | 3.5% | Fertility rate (per woman) | 6.4 |
| Pop. under 15 | 42.0% | | |
| Pop. over 65 | 2.7% | | *per 1,000 pop.* |
| No. of men per 100 women | 124 | Crude birth rate | 35.8 |
| Human Development Index | 69 | Crude death rate | 4.9 |

## The economy

| | | | |
|---|---|---|---|
| GDP | SR472bn | GDP per head | $7,942 |
| GDP | $126bn | GDP per head in purchasing | |
| Av. ann. growth in real | | power parity (USA=100) | 51 |
| GDP 1985–92 | 3.7% | | |

| Origins of GDP[a] | | Components of GDP[a] | |
|---|---|---|---|
| | *% of total* | | *% of total* |
| Agriculture | 7.3 | Private consumption | 46.7 |
| Industry, of which: | 45.5 | Public consumption | 31.1 |
| manufacturing | 8.1 | Investment | 21.6 |
| Services | 44.2 | Exports | 38.0 |
| | | Imports | -37.4 |

## Structure of manufacturing

| | *% of total* | | *% of total* |
|---|---|---|---|
| Agric. & food processing | 7 | Other | 88 |
| Textiles & clothing | 1 | Av. ann. increase in industrial | |
| Machinery & transport | 4 | output 1980–91 | -2.9% |

## Energy

| | *'000 TCE* | | |
|---|---|---|---|
| Total output | 660,709 | % output exported | 78.8 |
| Total consumption | 106,502 | % consumption imported | 0.5 |
| Consumption per head, | | | |
| kg coal equivalent | 6,922 | | |

## Inflation and finance

| | | | |
|---|---|---|---|
| Consumer price | | *av. ann. increase 1988–91* | |
| inflation 1993 | 1.8% | Narrow money (M1) | 7.3% |
| Av. ann. inflation 1988–93 | 1.8% | Broad money | 6.5% |

## Exchange rates

| | *end 1993* | | *end June 1993* |
|---|---|---|---|
| SR per $ | 3.75 | Effective rates | *1985 = 100* |
| SR per SDR | 5.14 | – nominal | 66.0 |
| SR per Ecu | 4.20 | – real | 53.7 |

## Principal exports[a]

| | $bn fob | | $bn fob |
|---|---|---|---|
| Crude oil & refined | | Petrochemicals | 2.4 |
| petroleum | 43.7 | Total incl. others | **48.2** |

### Main export destinations

| | % of total | | % of total |
|---|---|---|---|
| United States | 20.2 | France | 5.0 |
| Japan | 18.4 | Singapore | 4.7 |
| South Korea | 5.3 | Netherlands | 4.2 |

## Principal imports[a]

| | $bn cif | | $bn cif |
|---|---|---|---|
| Transport equipment | 7.0 | Agric. products & foodstuffs | 3.6 |
| Consumer goods | 5.2 | Building materials | 3.3 |
| Machinery & equipment | 4.6 | Total incl. others | **29.0** |

### Main origins of imports

| | % of total | | % of total |
|---|---|---|---|
| United States | 20.9 | Germany | 8.1 |
| Japan | 14.2 | Italy | 5.9 |
| United Kingdom | 10.6 | France | 5.3 |

## Balance of payments, reserves and debt, $bn

| | | | |
|---|---|---|---|
| Visible exports fob | 42.8 | Overall balance | -5.7 |
| Visible imports fob | -29.8 | Change in reserves | -5.7 |
| Trade balance | 13.0 | Level of reserves | |
| Invisibles inflows | 11.6 | end Dec. | 6.2 |
| Invisibles outflows | -29.8 | No. months import cover | 2.5 |
| Net transfers | -14.2 | Foreign debt | 19.0 |
| Current account balance | -19.4 | – as % of GDP | 17.1 |
| – as % of GDP | -15.4 | Debt service | 1.7 |
| Capital balance[a] | 27.8 | Debt service ratio | 3.2 |

## Family life

| | | | |
|---|---|---|---|
| No. of households | ... | Divorces per 1,000 pop. | ... |
| Av. no. per household | ... | Cost of living, Sept. 1993 | |
| Marriages per 1,000 pop. | ... | New York = 100 | 75 |

a  1991.

# SINGAPORE

| | | | |
|---|---|---|---|
| Area | 626 sq km | Currency | Singapore dollar (S$) |
| Capital | Singapore | | |

## People

| | | | |
|---|---|---|---|
| Population | 2.9m | Life expectancy: men | 72 yrs |
| Pop. per sq km | 4,617 | women | 77 yrs |
| Av. ann. growth | | Adult literacy | 88.0% |
| in pop. 1985–92 | 1.8% | Fertility rate (per woman) | 1.8 |
| Pop. under 15 | 22.7% | | |
| Pop. over 65 | 6.4% | | per 1,000 pop. |
| No. of men per 100 women | 103 | Crude birth rate | 15.9 |
| Human Development Index | 85 | Crude death rate | 5.5 |

## The economy

| | | | |
|---|---|---|---|
| GDP | S$72bn | GDP per head | $15,748 |
| GDP | $44bn | GDP per head in purchasing | |
| Av. ann. growth in real | | power parity (USA=100) | 74 |
| GDP 1985–92 | 6.3% | | |

| Origins of GDP | | Components of GDP | |
|---|---|---|---|
| | % of total | | % of total |
| Agriculture | 0.3 | Private consumption | 43.1 |
| Industry, of which: | 37.6 | Public consumption | 9.7 |
| manufacturing | 27.9 | Investment | 40.7 |
| Services | 62.1 | Exports less imports | 6.1 |

## Structure of manufacturing

| | % of total | | % of total |
|---|---|---|---|
| Agric. & food processing | 4 | Other | 39 |
| Textiles & clothing | 3 | Av. ann. increase in industrial | |
| Machinery & transport | 53 | output 1980–91 | 5.8% |

## Energy

| | '000 TCE | | |
|---|---|---|---|
| Total output | ... | % output exported | ... |
| Total consumption | 15,945 | % consumption imported[a] | 559.5 |
| Consumption per head, | | | |
| kg coal equivalent | 5,821 | | |

## Inflation and finance

| | | | |
|---|---|---|---|
| Consumer price | | av. ann. increase 1988–92 | |
| inflation 1992 | -0.1% | Narrow money (M1) | 10.9% |
| Av. ann. inflation 1988–92 | -0.6% | Broad money | 15.3% |

## Exchange rates

| | end 1993 | | end June 1993 |
|---|---|---|---|
| S$ per $ | 1.61 | Effective rates | 1985 = 100 |
| S$ per SDR | 2.21 | – nominal | 101.8 |
| S$ per Ecu | 1.80 | – real | ... |

## Principal exports

|  | $bn fob |  | $bn fob |
|---|---|---|---|
| Machinery & equipment | 34.9 | Agric. products & foodstuffs | 1.8 |
| Minerals & fuels | 8.3 | Crude materials | 1.4 |
| Manufactured products | 4.4 | | |
| Chemicals | 4.1 | Total incl. others | **63.4** |

### Main export destinations

|  | % of total |  | % of total |
|---|---|---|---|
| United States | 21.1 | Thailand | 6.2 |
| Malaysia | 12.5 | Germany | 4.2 |
| Hong Kong | 7.8 | Netherlands | 3.1 |
| Japan | 7.6 | | |

## Principal imports

|  | $bn cif |  | $bn cif |
|---|---|---|---|
| Machinery & equipment | 34.6 | Agric. products & foodstuffs | 3.0 |
| Mineral fuels | 9.2 | Crude minerals | 1.1 |
| Manufactured products | 9.2 | | |
| Chemicals | 5.4 | Total incl. others | **72.1** |

### Main origins of imports

|  | % of total |  | % of total |
|---|---|---|---|
| Japan | 21.1 | Taiwan | 4.0 |
| United States | 16.5 | Germany | 3.2 |
| Malaysia | 14.7 | China | 3.1 |
| Saudi Arabia | 5.1 | | |

## Balance of payments, reserves and debt, $bn

| | | | |
|---|---|---|---|
| Visible exports fob | 61.6 | Overall balance | 6.1 |
| Visible imports fob | -66.5 | Change in reserves | 5.8 |
| Trade balance | -4.9 | Level of reserves | |
| Invisibles inflows | 26.2 | end Dec. | 39.9 |
| Invisibles outflows | -17.7 | No. months import cover | 7.2 |
| Net transfers | -0.6 | Foreign debt | 4.7 |
| Current account balance | 2.9 | – as % of GDP | 10.3 |
| – as % of GDP | 6.6 | Debt service | 0.7 |
| Capital balance | 4.2 | Debt service ratio | 0.8 |

## Family life

| | | | |
|---|---|---|---|
| No. of households | 0.6m | Divorces per 1,000 pop. | 1.6 |
| Av. no. per household | 4.6 | Cost of living, Sept. 1993 | |
| Marriages per 1,000 pop. | 9.0 | New York = 100 | 101 |

a Energy trade data are distorted by transitory and oil refining activities.

# SOUTH AFRICA

| Area | 1,221,031 sq km | Currency | Rand (R) |
|---|---|---|---|
| Capital | Pretoria | | |

## People

| | | | |
|---|---|---|---|
| Population | 39.8m | Life expectancy: men | 60 yrs |
| Pop. per sq km | 35 | women | 66 yrs |
| Av. ann. growth | | Adult literacy | 70.0% |
| in pop. 1985–92 | 2.4% | Fertility rate (per woman) | 4.1 |
| Pop. under 15 | 37.5% | | |
| Pop. over 65 | 4.0% | | *per 1,000 pop.* |
| No. of men per 100 women | 99 | Crude birth rate | 31.3 |
| Human Development Index | 67 | Crude death rate | 8.6 |

## The economy

| | | | |
|---|---|---|---|
| GDP | R302bn | GDP per head | $2,666 |
| GDP | $106bn | GDP per head in purchasing | |
| Av. ann. growth in real | | power parity (USA=100) | 23 |
| GDP 1985–92 | 0.5% | | |

| **Origins of GDP** | | **Components of GDP** | |
|---|---|---|---|
| | *% of total* | | *% of total* |
| Agriculture | 3.9 | Private consumption | 62.2 |
| Industry, of which: | 37.5 | Public consumption | 21.3 |
| manufacturing | 24.9 | Investment | 13.3 |
| Services | 58.6 | Exports | 23.2 |
| | | Imports | -20.0 |

## Structure of manufacturing

| | *% of total* | | *% of total* |
|---|---|---|---|
| Agric. & food processing | 14 | Other | 61 |
| Textiles & clothing | 8 | Av. ann. increase in industrial | |
| Machinery & transport | 18 | output 1980–91 | 0.0% |

## Energy

| | *'000 TCE* | | |
|---|---|---|---|
| Total output | 135,275 | % output exported | 32.1 |
| Total consumption | 107,436 | % consumption imported | 21.0 |
| Consumption per head, | | | |
| kg coal equivalent | 2,431 | | |

## Inflation and finance

| | | | |
|---|---|---|---|
| Consumer price | | *av. ann. increase 1988–90* | |
| inflation 1993 | 9.7% | Narrow money (M1) | 15.9% |
| Av. ann. inflation 1988–93 | 13.5% | Broad money | 27.1% |

## Exchange rates

| | *end 1993* | | *end June 1993* |
|---|---|---|---|
| R per $ | 3.40 | Effective rates | *1985 = 100* |
| R per SDR | 4.67 | – nominal | 46.9 |
| R per Ecu | 3.81 | – real | 107.0 |

## Principal exports[a]

| | $bn fob | | $bn fob |
|---|---|---|---|
| Gold | 7.1 | Platinum[b] | 1.0 |
| Base metals | 3.2 | Agric. products & foodstuffs | 0.7 |
| Mineral products | 2.5 | Total incl. others | **23.7** |

### Main export destinations[c]

| | % of total | | % of total |
|---|---|---|---|
| Italy | 12.6 | United Kingdom | 8.7 |
| Japan | 9.0 | Germany | 8.4 |
| United States | 7.9 | | |

## Principal imports[a]

| | $bn cif | | $bn cif |
|---|---|---|---|
| Machinery & equipment | 4.7 | Oil[b] | 1.5 |
| Transport equipment | 2.2 | Base metals | 0.8 |
| Chemicals | 1.8 | Total incl. others | **17.5** |

### Main origins of imports[c]

| | % of total | | % of total |
|---|---|---|---|
| Germany | 19.0 | Japan | 9.3 |
| United Kingdom | 12.4 | Italy | 4.9 |
| United States | 11.1 | | |

## Balance of payments, reserves and debt, $bn

| | | | |
|---|---|---|---|
| Visible exports fob | 23.6 | Overall balance | 0.1 |
| Visible imports fob | -18.2 | Change in reserves | 0.5 |
| Trade balance | 5.4 | Level of reserves | |
| Invisibles inflows | 4.7 | end Dec. | 3.0 |
| Invisibles outflows | -8.8 | No. months import cover | 2.0 |
| Net transfers | 0.1 | Foreign debt | 17.3 |
| Current account balance | 1.4 | – as % of GDP | 15.1 |
| – as % of GDP | 1.3 | Debt service | 2.6 |
| Capital balance | -0.1 | Debt service ratio | 9.5 |

## Family life

| | | | |
|---|---|---|---|
| No. of households | ... | Divorces per 1,000 pop. | 0.4 |
| Av. no. per household | ... | Cost of living, Sept. 1993 | |
| Marriages per 1,000 pop. | ... | New York = 100 | 74 |

a  1991.
b  Estimate; no official figures published.
c  1990.

# SOUTH KOREA

| | | | |
|---|---|---|---|
| Area | 98,486 sq km | Currency | Won (W) |
| Capital | Seoul | | |

## People

| | | | |
|---|---|---|---|
| Population | 43.6m | Life expectancy: men | 68 yrs |
| Pop. per sq km | 456 | women | 74 yrs |
| Av. ann. growth | | Adult literacy | 96.3% |
| in pop. 1985–92 | 1.0% | Fertility rate (per woman) | 1.8 |
| Pop. under 15 | 23.4% | | |
| Pop. over 65 | 5.4% | | per 1,000 pop. |
| No. of men per 100 women | 102 | Crude birth rate | 16.3 |
| Human Development Index | 87 | Crude death rate | 6.1 |

## The economy

| | | | |
|---|---|---|---|
| GDP | W231,072bn | GDP per head | $6,787 |
| GDP | $296bn | GDP per head in purchasing | |
| Av. ann. growth in real | | power parity (USA=100) | 31 |
| GDP 1985–92 | 8.9% | | |

| Origins of GDP | | Components of GDP | |
|---|---|---|---|
| | % of total | | % of total |
| Agriculture | 7.6 | Private consumption | 53.4 |
| Industry, of which: | 45.0 | Public consumption | 11.3 |
| manufacturing | 27.3 | Investment | 35.8 |
| Services | 47.4 | Exports | 29.9 |
| | | Imports | -31.0 |

## Structure of manufacturing

| | % of total | | % of total |
|---|---|---|---|
| Agric. & food processing | 11 | Other | 44 |
| Textiles & clothing | 13 | Av. ann. increase in industrial | |
| Machinery & transport | 32 | output 1980–91 | 12.1% |

## Energy

| | '000 TCE | | |
|---|---|---|---|
| Total output | 31,218 | % output exported | 42.3 |
| Total consumption | 130,357 | % consumption imported | 96.4 |
| Consumption per head, | | | |
| kg coal equivalent | 2,977 | | |

## Inflation and finance

| | | | |
|---|---|---|---|
| Consumer price | | av. ann. increase 1988–92 | |
| inflation 1993 | 4.8% | Narrow money (M1) | 19.5% |
| Av. ann. inflation 1988–93 | 7.0% | Broad money | 19.0% |

## Exchange rates

| | end 1993 | | end June 1993 |
|---|---|---|---|
| W per $ | 808 | Effective rates | 1985 = 100 |
| W per SDR | 1,110 | – nominal | ... |
| W per Ecu | 905 | – real | ... |

## Principal exports

|  | $bn fob |  | $bn fob |
|---|---|---|---|
| Machinery & transport equipment | 32.5 | Textiles | 5.7 |
|  |  | Footwear | 3.2 |
| Clothing | 6.8 | Total incl. others | **76.6** |

### Main export destinations

|  | % of total |  | % of total |
|---|---|---|---|
| United States | 23.6 | Singapore | 4.2 |
| Japan | 15.1 | Germany | 3.8 |
| Hong Kong | 7.7 |  |  |

## Principal imports

|  | $bn cif |  | $bn cif |
|---|---|---|---|
| Machinery & transport equipment | 29.0 | Chemicals | 7.7 |
|  |  | Food & live animals | 4.1 |
| Mineral fuels & lubricants | 14.6 |  |  |
| Raw materials | 8.3 | Total incl. others | **81.8** |

### Main origins of imports

|  | % of total |  | % of total |
|---|---|---|---|
| Japan | 23.8 | Saudi Arabia | 4.6 |
| United States | 22.4 | Australia | 3.8 |
| Germany | 4.6 |  |  |

## Balance of payments, reserves and debt, $bn

|  |  |  |  |
|---|---|---|---|
| Visible exports fob | 75.2 | Overall balance | 3.7 |
| Visible imports fob | -77.3 | Change in reserves | 3.4 |
| Trade balance | -2.1 | Level of reserves |  |
| Invisibles inflows | 16.0 | end Dec. | 20.3 |
| Invisibles outflows | -18.6 | No. months import cover | 3.2 |
| Net transfers | 0.2 | Foreign debt | 43.0 |
| Current account balance | -4.5 | – as % of GDP | 14.6 |
| – as % of GDP | -1.5 | Debt service | 6.8 |
| Capital balance | 7.2 | Debt service ratio | 7.4 |

## Family life

|  |  |  |  |
|---|---|---|---|
| No. of households | 11.4m | Divorces per 1,000 pop. | 0.8 |
| Av. no. per household | 3.8 | Cost of living, Sept. 1993 |  |
| Marriages per 1,000 pop. | 7.3 | New York = 100 | 108 |

# SPAIN

| | | | |
|---|---|---|---|
| Area | 504,782 sq km | Currency | Peseta (Pta) |
| Capital | Madrid | | |

## People

| | | | |
|---|---|---|---|
| Population | 39.1m | Life expectancy: men | 75 yrs |
| Pop. per sq km | 78 | women | 81 yrs |
| Av. ann. growth | | Adult literacy | 95.4% |
| in pop. 1985–92 | 0.2% | Fertility rate (per woman) | 1.4 |
| Pop. under 15 | 17.1% | | |
| Pop. over 65 | 14.7% | | *per 1,000 pop.* |
| No. of men per 100 women | 97 | Crude birth rate | 10.8 |
| Human Development Index | 92 | Crude death rate | 9.2 |

## The economy

| | | | |
|---|---|---|---|
| GDP | Pta56,104bn | GDP per head | $14,022 |
| GDP | $548bn | GDP per head in purchasing | |
| Av. ann. growth in real | | power parity (USA=100) | 55 |
| GDP 1985–92 | 3.5% | | |

| Origins of GDP | | Components of GDP | |
|---|---|---|---|
| | *% of total* | | *% of total* |
| Agriculture | 3.8 | Private consumption | 63.4 |
| Industry, of which: | 34.5 | Public consumption | 16.2 |
| manufacturing | 25.4 | Investment | 23.4 |
| Services | 61.7 | Exports | 17.5 |
| | | Imports | -20.5 |

## Structure of manufacturing

| | *% of total* | | *% of total* |
|---|---|---|---|
| Agric. & food processing | 18 | Other | 48 |
| Textiles & clothing | 8 | Av. ann. increase in industrial | |
| Machinery & transport | 25 | output 1980–88 | 2.3% |

## Energy

| | *'000 TCE* | | |
|---|---|---|---|
| Total output | 44,800 | % output exported[a] | 37.4 |
| Total consumption | 119,610 | % consumption imported[a] | 86.9 |
| Consumption per head, | | | |
| kg coal equivalent | 3,065 | | |

## Inflation and finance

| Consumer price | | *av. ann. increase 1988–92* | |
|---|---|---|---|
| inflation 1993 | 4.6% | Narrow money (M1) | 6.9% |
| Av. ann. inflation 1988–93 | 5.8% | Broad money | 9.2% |

## Exchange rates

| | *end 1993* | | *end June 199?* |
|---|---|---|---|
| Pta per $ | 142.2 | Effective rates | 1985 = 100 |
| Pta per SDR | 195.3 | – nominal | 93.7 |
| Pta per Ecu | 159.3 | – real | 122.1 |

## Principal exports

| | $bn fob | | $bn fob |
|---|---|---|---|
| Raw materials & | | Agric. products & | |
| intermediate products | 27.0 | foodstuffs | 8.2 |
| Non-food consumer goods | 18.6 | Energy products | 1.6 |
| Capital goods | 9.0 | Total incl. others | **63.9** |

### Main export destinations

| | % of total | | % of total |
|---|---|---|---|
| France | 19.0 | United States | 4.7 |
| Germany | 15.0 | EU | 68.2 |
| Italy | 9.3 | Latin America | 5.7 |
| United Kingdom | 8.4 | Opec | 3.5 |

## Principal imports

| | $bn cif | | $bn cif |
|---|---|---|---|
| Raw materials & intermediate | | Energy products | 9.9 |
| products (excl. fuels) | 44.2 | Agric. products & foodstuffs | 7.6 |
| Non-foods consumer goods | 20.2 | | |
| Capital goods | 17.8 | Total incl. others | **99.7** |

### Main origins of imports

| | % of total | | % of total |
|---|---|---|---|
| France | 16.8 | United States | 6.8 |
| Germany | 15.6 | EU | 60.8 |
| Italy | 9.0 | Opec | 5.8 |
| United Kingdom | 7.6 | Latin America | 4.1 |

## Balance of payments, reserves and aid, $bn

| | | | |
|---|---|---|---|
| Visible exports fob | 63.9 | Capital balance | 6.4 |
| Visible imports fob | -95.0 | Overall balance | -17.5 |
| Trade balance | -31.0 | Change in reserves | -20.3 |
| Invisibles inflows | 45.7 | Level of reserves | |
| Invisibles outflows | -39.0 | end Dec. | 49.7 |
| Net transfers | 5.8 | No. months import cover | 6.3 |
| Current account balance | -18.5 | Aid given | 1.52 |
| – as % of GDP | -3.4 | – as % of GDP | 0.26 |

## Family life

| | | | |
|---|---|---|---|
| No. of households | 10.6m | Divorces per 1,000 pop. | 0.6 |
| Av. no. per household | 3.5 | Cost of living, Sept. 1993 | |
| Marriages per 1,000 pop. | 5.5 | New York = 100 | 93 |

a  Energy trade data are distorted by transitory and oil refining activities.

# SWEDEN

| | | | |
|---|---|---|---|
| Area | 449,964 sq km | Currency | Swedish krona (Skr) |
| Capital | Stockholm | | |

## People

| | | | |
|---|---|---|---|
| Population | 8.7m | Life expectancy: men | 75 yrs |
| Pop. per sq km | 19 | women | 81 yrs |
| Av. ann. growth | | Adult literacy | 99.0% |
| in pop. 1985–92 | 0.6% | Fertility rate (per woman) | 2.1 |
| Pop. under 15 | 18.8% | | |
| Pop. over 65 | 17.4% | | *per 1,000 pop.* |
| No. of men per 100 women | 98 | Crude birth rate | 14.0 |
| Human Development Index | 98 | Crude death rate | 11.5 |

## The economy

| | | | |
|---|---|---|---|
| GDP | Skr1,357bn | GDP per head | $26,784 |
| GDP | $233bn | GDP per head in purchasing | |
| Av. ann. growth in real | | power parity (USA=100) | 79 |
| GDP 1985–92 | 1.2% | | |

| Origins of GDP | | Components of GDP | |
|---|---|---|---|
| | *% of total* | | *% of total* |
| Agriculture | 3.0 | Private consumption | 53.8 |
| Industry, of which: | 28.4 | Public consumption | 27.9 |
| manufacturing | 22.8 | Investment | 16.6 |
| Services | 68.6 | Exports | 27.9 |
| | | Imports | -26.2 |

## Structure of manufacturing

| | *% of total* | | *% of total* |
|---|---|---|---|
| Agric. & food processing | 10 | Other | 56 |
| Textiles & clothing | 2 | Av. ann. increase in industrial | |
| Machinery & transport | 32 | output 1980–91 | 2.8% |

## Energy

| | *'000 TCE* | | |
|---|---|---|---|
| Total output | 36,501 | % output exported | 37.1 |
| Total consumption | 59,344 | % consumption imported | 65.3 |
| Consumption per head, | | | |
| kg coal equivalent | 6,892 | | |

## Inflation and finance

| | | | |
|---|---|---|---|
| Consumer price | | *av. ann. increase 1988–92* | |
| inflation 1993 | 4.7% | Narrow money (M1) | ... |
| Av. ann. inflation 1988–93 | 6.5% | Broad money | 5.4% |

## Exchange rates

| | *end 1993* | | *end June 1993* |
|---|---|---|---|
| Skr per $ | 8.30 | Effective rates | *1985 = 100* |
| Skr per SDR | 11.41 | – nominal | 78.8 |
| Skr per Ecu | 9.30 | – real | 87.6 |

## Principal exports

|  | $bn fob |  | $bn fob |
|---|---|---|---|
| Machinery incl. electricals | 15.6 | Transport equipment | 8.4 |
|  |  | Chemicals | 5.1 |
| Wood products, pulp & paper | 9.7 | Iron & steel | 3.2 |
|  |  | Total incl. others | **56.0** |

### Main export destinations

|  | % of total |  | % of total |
|---|---|---|---|
| Germany | 15.0 | Denmark | 7.2 |
| United Kingdom | 9.7 | EU | 55.8 |
| Norway | 8.4 | Efta | 17.4 |
| United States | 8.3 |  |  |

## Principal imports

|  | $bn cif |  | $bn cif |
|---|---|---|---|
| Machinery incl. electricals | 13.0 | Mineral fuels | 4.3 |
|  |  | Agric. products & foodstuffs | 3.6 |
| Chemicals | 5.3 |  |  |
| Transport equipment | 5.0 | Total incl. others | **49.8** |

### Main origins of imports

|  | % of total |  | % of total |
|---|---|---|---|
| Germany | 18.5 | Norway | 6.9 |
| United States | 8.8 | Finland | 6.2 |
| United Kingdom | 8.6 | EU | 55.6 |
| Denmark | 7.8 | Efta | 16.4 |

## Balance of payments, reserves and aid, $bn

|  |  |  |  |
|---|---|---|---|
| Visible exports fob | 55.4 | Capital balance | 7.4 |
| Visible imports fob | -48.5 | Overall balance | 7.1 |
| Trade balance | 6.9 | Change in reserves | 4.3 |
| Invisibles inflows | 25.3 | Level of reserves |  |
| Invisibles outflows | -34.7 | end Dec. | 22.9 |
| Net transfers | -2.5 | No. months import cover | 5.7 |
| Current account balance | -4.9 | Aid given | 2.46 |
| – as % of GDP | -2.1 | – as % of GDP | 1.03 |

## Family life

|  |  |  |  |
|---|---|---|---|
| No. of households | 3.8m | Divorces per 1,000 pop. | 2.2 |
| Av. no. per household | 2.2 | Cost of living, Sept. 1993 |  |
| Marriages per 1,000 pop. | 4.7 | New York = 100 | 103 |

# SWITZERLAND

| Area | 41,293 sq km | Currency | Swiss franc (SFr) |
|------|--------------|----------|-------------------|
| Capital | Berne | | |

## People

| | | | |
|---|---|---|---|
| Population | 6.7m | Life expectancy: men | 75 yrs |
| Pop. per sq km | 168 | women | 81 yrs |
| Av. ann. growth | | Adult literacy | 99.0% |
| in pop. 1985–92 | 0.9% | Fertility rate (per woman) | 1.7 |
| Pop. under 15 | 17.1% | | |
| Pop. over 65 | 15.1% | | per 1,000 pop. |
| No. of men per 100 women | 96 | Crude birth rate | 12.7 |
| Human Development Index | 98 | Crude death rate | 9.9 |

## The economy

| | | | |
|---|---|---|---|
| GDP | SFr350bn | GDP per head | $36,231 |
| GDP | $249bn | GDP per head in purchasing | |
| Av. ann. growth in real | | power parity (USA=100) | 97 |
| GDP 1985–92 | 2.3% | | |

| Origins of GDP[a] | | Components of GDP | |
|---|---|---|---|
| | % of total | | % of total |
| Agriculture | 3.5 | Private consumption | 61.2 |
| Industry, of which: | 34.5 | Public consumption | 14.5 |
| manufacturing | 25.0 | Investment | 27.6 |
| Services | 62.0 | Exports | 42.5 |
| | | Imports | -45.2 |

## Structure of manufacturing

| | % of total | | % of total |
|---|---|---|---|
| Agric. & food processing | ... | Other | ... |
| Textiles & clothing | ... | Av. ann. increase in industrial | |
| Machinery & transport | ... | output 1980–89[b] | 1.8% |

## Energy

| | '000 TCE | | |
|---|---|---|---|
| Total output | 12,635 | % output exported | 28.6 |
| Total consumption | 31,924 | % consumption imported | 77.6 |
| Consumption per head, | | | |
| kg coal equivalent | 4,701 | | |

## Inflation and finance

| Consumer price | | av. ann. increase 1988–92 | |
|---|---|---|---|
| inflation 1993 | 3.3% | Narrow money (M1) | 0.1% |
| Av. ann. inflation 1988–93 | 3.9% | Broad money | 3.5% |

## Exchange rates

| | end 1993 | | end June1993 |
|---|---|---|---|
| SFr per $ | 1.48 | Effective rates | 1985 = 100 |
| SFr per SDR | 2.03 | – nominal | 111.2 |
| SFr per Ecu | 1.66 | – real | ... |

## Principal exports

|  | $bn fob |  | $bn fob |
|---|---|---|---|
| Machinery | 18.1 | Metals & metal manufactures | 5.5 |
| Chemicals | 15.2 | Textiles & clothing | 3.3 |
| Precision instruments, watches & jewellery | 13.6 | Total incl. others | **65.8** |

### Main export destinations

|  | % of total |  | % of total |
|---|---|---|---|
| Germany | 23.4 | United Kingdom | 6.6 |
| France | 9.5 | Japan | 3.7 |
| Italy | 8.8 | EU | 58.9 |
| United States | 8.5 | Efta | 6.3 |

## Principal imports

|  | $bn cif |  | $bn cif |
|---|---|---|---|
| Machinery | 13.0 | Textiles & clothing | 6.3 |
| Chemicals | 8.2 | Agric. products | 5.7 |
| Precision instruments, watches & jewellery | 7.4 | Energy & fuels | 2.8 |
| Motor vehicles | 7.1 | Total incl. others | **66.0** |

### Main origins of imports

|  | % of total |  | % of total |
|---|---|---|---|
| Germany | 33.4 | United Kingdom | 5.8 |
| France | 10.8 | EU | 72.2 |
| Italy | 10.0 | Efta | 6.9 |
| United States | 6.4 |  |  |

## Balance of payments, reserves and aid, $bn

|  |  |  |  |
|---|---|---|---|
| Visible exports fob | 78.6 | Capital balance | -8.7 |
| Visible imports fob | -78.9 | Overall balance | 4.4 |
| Trade balance | -0.3 | Change in reserves | 4.3 |
| Invisibles inflows | 46.9 | Level of reserves |  |
| Invisibles outflows | -30.2 | end Dec. | 41.4 |
| Net transfers | -2.9 | No. months import cover | 6.3 |
| Current account balance | 13.4 | Aid given | 1.14 |
| – as % of GDP | 5.4 | – as % of GDP | 0.46 |

## Family life

|  |  |  |  |
|---|---|---|---|
| No. of households | 2.5m | Divorces per 1,000 pop. | 2.0 |
| Av. no. per household | 2.5 | Cost of living, Sept. 1993 |  |
| Marriages per 1,000 pop. | 6.9 | New York = 100 | 132 |

a  1985 (Switzerland no longer publishes figures on GDP by origin).
b  Based on index of manufacturing output.

# TAIWAN

| | | | |
|---|---|---|---|
| Area | 36,000 sq km | Currency | Taiwan dollar (T$) |
| Capital | Taipei | | |

## People

| | | | |
|---|---|---|---|
| Population | 20.8m | Life expectancy: men | ... |
| Pop. per sq km[a] | 576 | women | ... |
| Av. ann. growth | | Adult literacy | ... |
| in pop. 1985–92[a] | 1.1% | Fertility rate (per woman) | 1.8 |
| Pop. under 15[a] | 25.8 | | |
| Pop. over 65[a] | 6.8 | | *per 1,000 pop.* |
| No. of men per 100 women[a] | 107 | Crude birth rate | 15.0 |
| Human Development Index | ... | Crude death rate | 5.3 |

## The economy

| | | | |
|---|---|---|---|
| GDP | T$5,159bn | GDP per head | $9,981 |
| GDP | $207bn | GDP per head in purchasing | |
| Av. ann. growth in real | | power parity (USA=100) | ... |
| GDP 1985–92 | 6.5% | | |

### Origins of GDP

| | % of total |
|---|---|
| Agriculture | 3.5 |
| Industry, of which: | 41.4 |
| manufacturing | 32.9 |
| Services | 55.1 |

### Components of GDP

| | % of total |
|---|---|
| Private consumption | 55.8 |
| Public consumption | 17.5 |
| Investment | 24.3 |
| Exports | 44.2 |
| Imports | -41.8 |

## Structure of manufacturing

| | % of total | | % of total |
|---|---|---|---|
| Agric. & food processing | ... | Other | ... |
| Textiles & clothing | ... | Av. ann. increase in industrial | |
| Machinery & transport | ... | output 1980–92 | 5.9% |

## Energy

| | '000 TCE | | |
|---|---|---|---|
| Total output | ... | % output exported | 3.3 |
| Total consumption | ... | % consumption imported | 76.7 |
| Consumption per head, | | | |
| kg coal equivalent | ... | | |

## Inflation and finance

| | | *av. ann. increase 1988–92* | |
|---|---|---|---|
| Consumer price | | | |
| inflation 1993 | 2.9% | Narrow money (M1) | 9.2% |
| Av. ann. inflation 1988–93 | 3.5% | Broad money | 16.3% |

## Exchange rates

| | end 1993 | | end June 1993 |
|---|---|---|---|
| T$ per $ | 26.63 | Effective rates | 1985 = 100 |
| T$ per SDR | 36.58 | – nominal | ... |
| T$ per Ecu | 29.83 | – real | ... |

## Principal exports

| | $bn fob | | $bn fob |
|---|---|---|---|
| Machinery & electrical | | Footwear | 4.3 |
| equipment | 29.7 | Vehicles & ships | 4.3 |
| Textiles & clothing | 11.8 | Toys & sporting goods | 3.3 |
| Plastic & rubber articles | 5.5 | Total incl. others | **81.5** |

### Main export destinations

| | % of total | | % of total |
|---|---|---|---|
| United States | 28.9 | Singapore | 3.1 |
| Hong Kong | 18.9 | Netherlands | 2.7 |
| Japan | 10.9 | United Kingdom | 2.7 |
| Germany | 4.4 | Thailand | 2.2 |

## Principal imports

| | $bn cif | | $bn cif |
|---|---|---|---|
| Machinery & electrical | | Transport equipment | 6.0 |
| equipment | 22.4 | Crude petroleum | 3.1 |
| Metals | 8.4 | Agric. products & foodstuffs | 1.5 |
| Chemicals | 7.1 | Total incl. others | **72.0** |

### Main origins of imports

| | % of total | | % of total |
|---|---|---|---|
| Japan | 28.9 | Australia | 2.9 |
| United States | 21.9 | Hong Kong | 2.5 |
| Germany | 5.4 | Malaysia | 2.5 |
| South Korea | 3.2 | Singapore | 2.4 |

## Balance of payments, reserves and debt, $bn

| | | | |
|---|---|---|---|
| Visible exports fob | 80.7 | Overall balance | -0.6 |
| Visible imports fob | -68.1 | Change in reserves | -0.6 |
| Trade balance | 12.6 | Level of reserves | |
| Invisibles inflows | 18.0 | end Dec.[b] | 88.3 |
| Invisibles outflows | -22.5 | No. months import cover | 15.6 |
| Net transfers | -0.2 | Foreign debt | 20.9 |
| Current account balance | 7.9 | – as % of GDP | 10.1 |
| – as % of GDP | 4.0 | Debt service | 2.3 |
| Capital balance | -4.9 | Debt service ratio | 2.3 |

## Family life

| | | | |
|---|---|---|---|
| No. of households | ... | Divorces per 1,000 pop. | ... |
| Av. no. per household | ... | Cost of living, Sept. 1993 | |
| Marriages per 1,000 pop. | ... | New York = 100 | 103 |

a  1992.
b  Excluding gold.

# THAILAND

| | | | |
|---|---|---|---|
| Area | 513,115 sq km | Currency | Baht (Bt) |
| Capital | Bangkok | | |

## People

| | | | | |
|---|---|---|---|---|
| Population | 58.0m | Life expectancy: men | 67 yrs |
| Pop. per sq km | 114 | women | 72 yrs |
| Av. ann. growth | | Adult literacy | 93.0% |
| in pop. 1985–92 | 1.7% | Fertility rate (per woman) | 2.2 |
| Pop. under 15 | 29.2% | | |
| Pop. over 65 | 4.5% | | *per 1,000 pop.* |
| No. of men per 100 women | 98 | Crude birth rate | 20.5 |
| Human Development Index | 72 | Crude death rate | 5.8 |

## The economy

| | | | |
|---|---|---|---|
| GDP | Bt2,718bn | GDP per head | $1,837 |
| GDP | $107bn | GDP per head in purchasing | |
| Av. ann. growth in real | | power parity (USA=100) | 19 |
| GDP 1985–92 | 8.6% | | |

| Origins of GDP[a] | | Components of GDP[a] | |
|---|---|---|---|
| | *% of total* | | *% of total* |
| Agriculture[b] | 14.4 | Private consumption | 56.5 |
| Industry, of which: | 37.0 | Public consumption | 9.4 |
| manufacturing | 28.1 | Investment | 42.5 |
| Services | 48.6 | Exports | 35.3 |
| | | Imports | -42.3 |

## Structure of manufacturing

| | *% of total* | | *% of total* |
|---|---|---|---|
| Agric. & food processing | 29 | Other | 34 |
| Textiles & clothing | 25 | Av. ann. increase in industrial | |
| Machinery & transport | 12 | output 1980–91 | 9.6% |

## Energy

| | *'000 TCE* | | |
|---|---|---|---|
| Total output | 17,837 | % output exported | 7.2 |
| Total consumption | 43,716 | % consumption imported | 65.9 |
| Consumption per head, | | | |
| kg coal equivalent | 789 | | |

## Inflation and finance

| | | | |
|---|---|---|---|
| Consumer price | | *av. ann. increase 1988–92* | |
| inflation 1993 | 3.6% | Narrow money (M1) | 13.5% |
| Av. ann. inflation 1988–93 | 4.8% | Broad money | 21.2% |

## Exchange rates

| | *end 1993* | | *end June 1993* |
|---|---|---|---|
| Bt per $ | 25.54 | Effective rates | 1985 = 100 |
| Bt per SDR | 35.08 | – nominal | ... |
| Bt per Ecu | 34.61 | – real | ... |

## Principal exports

|  | $bn fob |  | $bn fob |
|---|---|---|---|
| Textiles & clothing | 4.4 | Canned food | 1.7 |
| Electrical appliances | 2.4 | Precious stones | 1.4 |
| Computers & parts | 2.2 | Total incl. others | **32.5** |

### Main export destinations

|  | % of total |  | % of total |
|---|---|---|---|
| United States | 22 | Hong Kong | 5 |
| Japan | 17 | Germany | 4 |
| Singapore | 9 |  |  |

## Principal imports

|  | $bn cif |  | $bn cif |
|---|---|---|---|
| Non-electrical machinery | 5.8 | Iron & steel | 3.2 |
| Electrical machinery | 3.6 | Chemicals | 3.1 |
| Energy & fuel | 3.3 | Total incl. others | **40.5** |

### Main origins of imports

|  | % of total |  | % of total |
|---|---|---|---|
| Japan | 29 | Taiwan | 6 |
| United States | 12 | Germany | 5 |
| Singapore | 7 |  |  |

## Balance of payments, reserves and debt, $bn

| | | | |
|---|---|---|---|
| Visible exports fob | 32.1 | Overall balance | 2.9 |
| Visible imports fob | -36.3 | Change in reserves | 2.7 |
| Trade balance | -4.2 | Level of reserves | |
| Invisibles inflows | 10.2 | end Dec. | 21.2 |
| Invisibles outflows | -13.0 | No. months import cover | 7.0 |
| Net transfers | 0.3 | Foreign debt | 39.4 |
| Current account balance | -6.7 | – as % of GDP | 36.3 |
| – as % of GDP | -6.3 | Debt service | 6.0 |
| Capital balance | 9.6 | Debt service ratio | 13.1 |

## Family life

| | | | |
|---|---|---|---|
| No. of households | 12.2m | Divorces per 1,000 pop. | 0.7 |
| Av. no. per household | 4.5 | Cost of living, Sept. 1993 | |
| Marriages per 1,000 pop. | 8.2 | New York = 100 | 77 |

a  1991.
b  Includes mining.

# TURKEY

| | | | |
|---|---|---|---|
| Area | 779,452 sq km | Currency | Turkish Lira (L) |
| Capital | Ankara | | |

## People

| | | | |
|---|---|---|---|
| Population | 58.5m | Life expectancy: men | 65 yrs |
| Pop. per sq km | 80 | women | 70 yrs |
| Av. ann. growth | | Adult literacy | 80.7% |
| in pop. 1985–92 | 2.2% | Fertility rate (per woman) | 3.5 |
| Pop. under 15 | 33.7% | | |
| Pop. over 65 | 4.8% | | *per 1,000 pop.* |
| No. of men per 100 women | 104 | Crude birth rate | 28.1 |
| Human Development Index | 72 | Crude death rate | 7.1 |

## The economy

| | | | |
|---|---|---|---|
| GDP | L783,454bn | GDP per head | $1,954 |
| GDP | $114bn | GDP per head in purchasing | |
| Av. ann. growth in real | | power parity (USA=100) | 22 |
| GDP 1985–92 | 5.0% | | |

| Origins of GDP[a] | | Components of GDP[b] | |
|---|---|---|---|
| | *% of total* | | *% of total* |
| Agriculture | 16.3 | Private consumption | 60.0 |
| Industry, of which: | 33.2 | Public consumption | 19.4 |
| manufacturing | 27.1 | Investment | 23.9 |
| Services | 50.5 | Exports | 19.7 |
| | | Imports | -23.1 |

## Structure of manufacturing

| | *% of total* | | *% of total* |
|---|---|---|---|
| Agric. & food processing | 16 | Other | 54 |
| Textiles & clothing | 14 | Av. ann. increase in industrial | |
| Machinery & transport | 17 | output 1980–91 | 6.0% |

## Energy

| | *'000 TCE* | | |
|---|---|---|---|
| Total output | 26,315 | % output exported | 14.9 |
| Total consumption | 59,213 | % consumption imported | 64.9 |
| Consumption per head, | | | |
| kg coal equivalent | 1,036 | | |

## Inflation and finance

| | | | |
|---|---|---|---|
| Consumer price | | *av. ann. increase 1988–92* | |
| inflation 1993 | 66% | Narrow money (M1) | 55.4% |
| Av. ann. inflation 1988–93 | 66.5% | Broad money | 69.4% |

## Exchange rates

| | *end 1993* | | *end June 1993* |
|---|---|---|---|
| L per $ | 14,473 | Effective rates | *1985 = 100* |
| L per SDR | 19,879 | – nominal | ... |
| L per Ecu | 16,210 | – real | ... |

## Principal exports

| | $bn fob | | $bn fob |
|---|---|---|---|
| Clothing | 3.7 | Leather | 0.5 |
| Iron & steel | 1.5 | | |
| Synthetic fibres | 0.5 | Total incl. others | **14.9** |

**Main export destinations**[a]

| | % of total | | % of total |
|---|---|---|---|
| Germany | 24.9 | France | 5.5 |
| Italy | 6.4 | United Kingdom | 5.4 |
| United States | 5.9 | EU | 51.7 |

## Principal imports

| | $bn cif | | $bn cif |
|---|---|---|---|
| Machinery | 5.9 | Chemicals | 1.0 |
| Crude oil | 2.6 | Plastics | 0.7 |
| Metals | 2.1 | Total incl. others | **23.1** |

**Main origins of imports**[a]

| | % of total | | % of total |
|---|---|---|---|
| Germany | 16.4 | France | 5.9 |
| United States | 11.4 | Ex-Soviet Union | 5.4 |
| Italy | 8.4 | EU | 43.9 |
| Saudi Arabia | 7.3 | | |

## Balance of payments, reserves and debt, $bn

| | | | |
|---|---|---|---|
| Visible exports fob | 14.9 | Overall balance | 1.5 |
| Visible imports fob | -23.1 | Change in reserves | 1.0 |
| Trade balance | -8.2 | Level of reserves | |
| Invisibles inflows | 10.5 | end Dec. | 7.7 |
| Invisibles outflows | -7.3 | No. months import cover | 4.0 |
| Net transfers | 4.1 | Foreign debt | 54.8 |
| Current account balance | -0.9 | – as % of GDP | 50.6 |
| – as % of GDP | -0.8 | Debt service | 9.1 |
| Capital balance | 3.6 | Debt service ratio | 31.9 |

## Family life

| | | | |
|---|---|---|---|
| No. of households | 9.7m | Divorces per 1,000 pop. | 0.5 |
| Av. no. per household | 5.2 | Cost of living, Sept. 1993 | |
| Marriages per 1,000 pop. | 7.9 | New York = 100 | 65 |

a  1991.
b  1990.

# UKRAINE

| Area | 603,700 sq km | Currency | Karbovanets |
|------|--------------|----------|-------------|
| Capital | Kiev | | |

## People

| | | | |
|---|---|---|---|
| Population | 52.1m | Life expectancy[c] | 71 yrs |
| Pop. per sq km[a] | 86 | | |
| Av. ann. growth | | | *per 1,000 pop.* |
| in pop. 1985–92 | 0.3% | Crude birth rate | 14.2 |
| No. of men per 100 women[b] | 86 | Crude death rate[c] | 12.0 |

## The economy

| | | | |
|---|---|---|---|
| GDP | $87bn | GDP per head | $1,670 |
| Av. ann. growth in real | | GDP per head in purchasing | |
| GDP 1985–92 | 11.5% | power parity (USA=100) | 25 |

| Origins of NMP | | Components of NMP | |
|---|---|---|---|
| | *% of total* | | *% of total* |
| Agriculture | 23.0 | Private consumption | 58.5 |
| Industry | 51.0 | Public consumption | 12.9 |
| Construction | 15.0 | Net investment | 23.8 |
| Other | 11.0 | Net exports | 4.7 |

## Inflation and exchange rates[a]

| | | | |
|---|---|---|---|
| Consumer price | | | *end 1993* |
| inflation 1992 | 1,450% | Karbovanets per $ | 30,948 |
| Av. ann. inflation 1989–92 | 137.0% | Karbovanets per Ecu | 34,528 |

## Principal exports[b]

| | Rb bn | | Rb bn |
|---|---|---|---|
| Machinery & metalworking | 17.9 | Chemicals & products | 3.9 |
| Ferrous metallurgy | 7.6 | Light industry | 2.3 |
| Food industry | 6.7 | Total incl. others | **45.7** |

### Main export destinations[bd]

| | *% of total* | | *% of total* |
|---|---|---|---|
| Other EU | 14.6 | Ex-Czechoslovakia | 8.6 |
| Germany | 11.5 | Other Eastern Europe | 20.8 |
| Bulgaria | 9.3 | | |

## Principal imports[b]

| | Rb bn | | Rb bn |
|---|---|---|---|
| Machinery & metalworking | 18.7 | Food industry | 4.0 |
| Light industry | 9.7 | Oil & gas | 3.9 |
| Chemicals & products | 5.7 | Total incl. others | **53.8** |

### Main origins of imports[bd]

| | *% of total* | | *% of total* |
|---|---|---|---|
| Germany | 17.7 | Other EU | 6.8 |
| Poland | 13.5 | Other Eastern Europe | 22.6 |
| Ex-Czechoslovakia | 9.9 | | |

# EX-SOVIET REPUBLICS

| | Area '000 sq km | Population '000 | Population per sq km[a] | Capital | Currency |
|---|---|---|---|---|---|
| **Armenia** | 29.8 | 3,499 | 117 | Yerevan | Dram |
| **Azerbaijan** | 86.6 | 7,145 | 83 | Baku | Manat |
| **Belorussia** | 207.6 | 10,346 | 50 | Minsk | Rubel |
| **Estonia** | 45.1 | 1,554 | 34 | Tallinn | Kroon |
| **Georgia** | 69.7 | 5,493 | 79 | Tbilisi | Coupon |
| **Kazakhstan** | 2,717.3 | 16,954 | 6 | Alma-Ata | Tenge |
| **Kirgizstan** | 198.5 | 4,472 | 23 | Bishkek | Som |
| **Latvia** | 64.6 | 2,617 | 41 | Riga | Lats |
| **Lithuania** | 65.2 | 3,754 | 58 | Vilnius | Litas |
| **Moldova** | 33.7 | 4,359 | 129 | Kishinev | Leu |
| **Tajikistan** | 143.1 | 5,634 | 39 | Dushanbe | Rouble |
| **Turkmenistan** | 488.1 | 3,852 | 8 | Ashkhabad | Manat |
| **Uzbekistan** | 447.4 | 21,285 | 48 | Tashkent | Som |

## People

| | Av. ann. pop. growth 1985–92 | Pop. under 15[b] % | Life expect.[c] yrs | Birth rate[e] | Death rate[e] | Human Dev. Index |
|---|---|---|---|---|---|---|
| **Armenia** | 1.2 | 30 | 71 | 23 | 6 | 83 |
| **Azerbaijan** | 1.0 | 33 | 70 | 27 | 7 | 77 |
| **Belorussia** | 0.5 | 23 | 72 | 16 | 10 | 86 |
| **Estonia** | 0.2 | 24 | 70 | 16 | 12 | 87 |
| **Georgia** | 0.5 | 25 | 72 | 18 | 9 | 83 |
| **Kazakhstan** | 1.0 | 32 | 69 | 24 | 8 | 80 |
| **Kirgizstan** | 1.7 | 38 | 68 | 31 | 7 | 69 |
| **Latvia** | 0.0 | 24 | 70 | 15 | 12 | 87 |
| **Lithuania** | 0.7 | 24 | 72 | 16 | 10 | 88 |
| **Moldova** | 0.6 | 28 | 68 | 21 | 10 | 76 |
| **Tajikistan** | 3.0 | 43 | 70 | 40 | 7 | 66 |
| **Turkmenistan** | 2.5 | 41 | 65 | 36 | 8 | 75 |
| **Uzbekistan** | 2.4 | 41 | 69 | 36 | 7 | 70 |

## The economy

| | GDP: $bn | Per head $ | PPP USA = 100 | Agric. as % of GDP | Exports $m | Imports $m | Foreign debt $m |
|---|---|---|---|---|---|---|---|
| **Armenia** | 2.7 | 780 | 22 | 20.0 | 40 | 95 | 10 |
| **Azerbaijan** | 6.3 | 870 | 19 | 31.0 | 738 | 329 | 0 |
| **Belorussia** | 30.1 | 2,910 | 27 | 21.3 | 1,061 | 751 | 181.2 |
| **Estonia** | 4.3 | 2,750 | 30 | 17.1 | 242 | 230 | 51.2 |
| **Georgia** | 4.7 | 850 | 31 | 26.8 | 30 | 480 | 84.8 |
| **Kazakhstan** | 28.6 | 1,680 | 22 | 28.5 | 1,546 | 1,608 | 24.9 |
| **Kirgizstan** | 3.7 | 810 | 15 | 28.4 | 33 | 25 | 0 |
| **Latvia** | 5.1 | 1,930 | 30 | 24.0 | 429 | 423 | 60.6 |
| **Lithuania** | 4.9 | 1,310 | 23 | 21.2 | 560 | 340 | 37.7 |
| **Moldova** | 5.5 | 1,700 | 18 | 33.5 | 185 | 205 | 37.5 |
| **Tajikistan** | 2.7 | 480 | 12 | 33.2 | 424 | 706 | 9.7 |
| **Turkmenistan** | 4.9 | 1,270 | 20 | 33.2 | 1,083 | 545 | 0 |
| **Uzbekistan** | 18.4 | 860 | 15 | 33.1 | 869 | 929 | 15.5 |

a  1992.
b  1990.
c  1985-90.
d  Outside ex-Soviet Union; trade with other union republics accounted for 84% of Ukraine's exports and 72% of Ukraine's imports in 1990.
e  Latest.

# UNITED KINGDOM

| Area | 244,046 sq km | Currency | Pound (£) |
|---|---|---|---|
| Capital | London | | |

## People

| | | | |
|---|---|---|---|
| Population | 57.7m | Life expectancy: men | 74 yrs |
| Pop. per sq km | 238 | women | 79 yrs |
| Av. ann. growth | | Adult literacy | 99.0% |
| in pop. 1985–92 | 0.3% | Fertility rate (per woman) | 1.9 |
| Pop. under 15 | 19.7% | | |
| Pop. over 65 | 15.6% | | *per 1,000 pop.* |
| No. of men per 100 women | 96 | Crude birth rate | 13.9 |
| Human Development Index | 96 | Crude death rate | 11.5 |

## The economy

| | | | |
|---|---|---|---|
| GDP | £580bn | GDP per head | $17,760 |
| GDP | $1,024bn | GDP per head in purchasing | |
| Av. ann. growth in real | | power parity (USA=100) | 74 |
| GDP 1985–92 | 2.2% | | |

| **Origins of GDP**[a] | | **Components of GDP** | |
|---|---|---|---|
| | *% of total* | | *% of total* |
| Agriculture | 1.7 | Private consumption | 65.0 |
| Industry, of which: | 31.7 | Public consumption | 21.8 |
| manufacturing | 19.9 | Investment | 15.1 |
| Services | 66.6 | Exports | 23.3 |
| | | Imports | -25.0 |

## Structure of manufacturing

| | *% of total* | | *% of total* |
|---|---|---|---|
| Agric. & food processing | 13 | Other | 49 |
| Textiles & clothing | 5 | Av. ann. increase in industrial | |
| Machinery & transport | 32 | output 1980–91 | 1.3% |

## Energy

| | *'000 TCE* | | |
|---|---|---|---|
| Total output | 299,244 | % output exported | 34.9 |
| Total consumption | 309,253 | % consumption imported | 40.5 |
| Consumption per head, | | | |
| kg coal equivalent | 5,353 | | |

## Inflation and finance

| Consumer price | | *av. ann. increase 1988–92* | |
|---|---|---|---|
| inflation 1993 | 1.6% | Narrow money (M1) | 9.1% |
| Av. ann. inflation 1988–93 | 5.5% | Broad money | 10.9% |

## Exchange rates

| | *end 1993* | | *end June 1993* |
|---|---|---|---|
| £ per $ | 0.68 | Effective rates | *1985 = 100* |
| £ per SDR | 0.93 | – nominal | 80.2 |
| £ per Ecu | 0.76 | – real | 89.4 |

## Principal exports

| | *$bn fob* | | *$bn fob* |
|---|---|---|---|
| Finished manufactured products | 100.7 | Fuels | 12.0 |
| | | Basic materials | 3.3 |
| Semi-manufactured products | 52.7 | | |
| Agric. products & foodstuffs | 15.1 | Total incl. others | **187.4** |

### Main export destinations

| | *% of total* | | *% of total* |
|---|---|---|---|
| Germany | 13.9 | Italy | 5.7 |
| United States | 11.3 | Belgium/Luxembourg | 5.3 |
| France | 10.6 | EU | 56.0 |
| Netherlands | 7.8 | | |

## Principal imports

| | *$bn cif* | | *$bn cif* |
|---|---|---|---|
| Finished manufactured products | 116.9 | Fuels | 12.3 |
| | | Basic materials | 8.2 |
| Semi-manufactured products | 56.8 | | |
| Agric. products & foodstuffs | 23.6 | Total incl. others | **222.4** |

### Main origins of imports

| | *% of total* | | *% of total* |
|---|---|---|---|
| Germany | 15.1 | Japan | 5.9 |
| United States | 10.9 | Italy | 5.4 |
| France | 9.7 | EU | 52.1 |
| Netherlands | 7.9 | | |

## Balance of payments, reserves and aid, $bn

| | | | |
|---|---|---|---|
| Visible exports fob | 187.4 | Capital balance | 17.3 |
| Visible imports fob | -212.1 | Overall balance | -2.1 |
| Trade balance | -24.6 | Change in reserves | -5.3 |
| Invisibles inflows | 175.7 | Level of reserves | |
| Invisibles outflows | -162.8 | end Dec. | 41.3 |
| Net transfers | -9.0 | No. months import cover | 2.3 |
| Current account balance | -20.7 | Aid given | 3.2 |
| – as % of GDP | -2.0 | – as % of GDP | 0.31 |

## Family life

| | | | |
|---|---|---|---|
| No. of households | 20.0m | Divorces per 1,000 pop. | 2.9 |
| Av. no. per household | 2.8 | Cost of living, Sept. 1993 | |
| Marriages per 1,000 pop. | 6.8 | New York = 100 | 104 |

a 1991.

# UNITED STATES

| Area | 9,372,614 sq km | Currency | US dollar ($) |
|---|---|---|---|
| Capital | Washington DC | | |

## People

| | | | |
|---|---|---|---|
| Population | 255.4m | Life expectancy: men | 73 yrs |
| Pop. per sq km | 27 | women | 79 yrs |
| Av. ann. growth | | Adult literacy | 99.0% |
| in pop. 1985–92 | 0.9% | Fertility rate (per woman) | 2.1 |
| Pop. under 15 | 21.9% | | |
| Pop. over 65 | 12.6% | | *per 1,000 pop.* |
| No. of men per 100 women | 95 | Crude birth rate | 15.9 |
| Human Development Index | 98 | Crude death rate | 8.9 |

## The economy

| | | | |
|---|---|---|---|
| GDP | $5,905bn | GDP per head | $23,119 |
| | | GDP per head in purchasing | |
| Av. ann. growth in real | | power parity (USA=100) | 100 |
| GDP 1985–92 | 2.3% | | |

| Origins of GDP | | Components of GDP | |
|---|---|---|---|
| | *% of total* | | *% of total* |
| Agriculture | 2.3 | Private consumption | 68.6 |
| Industry, of which: | 24.4 | Public consumption | 18.8 |
| manufacturing | 18.3 | Investment | 13.0 |
| Services | 73.3 | Exports | 10.6 |
| | | Imports | -11.1 |

## Structure of manufacturing

| | *% of total* | | *% of total* |
|---|---|---|---|
| Agric. & food processing | 12 | Other | 52 |
| Textiles & clothing | 5 | Av. ann. increase in industrial | |
| Machinery & transport | 31 | output 1980–91 | 2.9% |

## Energy

| | *'000 TCE* | | |
|---|---|---|---|
| Total output | 2,317,467 | % output exported | 6.2 |
| Total consumption | 2,757,794 | % consumption imported | 22.0 |
| Consumption per head, | | | |
| kg coal equivalent | 10,921 | | |

## Inflation and finance

| Consumer price | | *av. ann. increase 1988–92* | |
|---|---|---|---|
| inflation 1993 | 3.0% | Narrow money (M1) | 6.3% |
| Av. ann. inflation 1988–93 | 4.1% | Broad money | 4.4% |

## Exchange rates

| | *end 1993* | | *end June 1993* |
|---|---|---|---|
| $ per SDR | 1.37 | Effective rates | *1985 = 100* |
| $ per Ecu | 1.12 | – nominal | 64.2 |
| | | – real | 61.0 |

## Principal exports

|  | $bn fob |  | $bn fob |
|---|---|---|---|
| Machinery & transport equipment | 224.0 | Agric. products & foodstuffs | 40.6 |
| Other manufactures | 180.2 | Total incl. others | **448.2** |

**Main export destinations**

|  | % of total |  | % of total |
|---|---|---|---|
| Canada | 20.2 | Germany | 4.7 |
| Japan | 10.7 | South Korea | 3.3 |
| Mexico | 9.0 | EU | 22.9 |
| United Kingdom | 5.0 |  |  |

## Principal imports

|  | $bn fob |  | $bn fob |
|---|---|---|---|
| Other manufactures | 273.3 | Agric. products & foodstuffs | 28.0 |
| Machinery & transport equipment | 231.4 | Total incl. others | **532.7** |

**Main origins of imports**

|  | % of total |  | % of total |
|---|---|---|---|
| Canada | 18.5 | Taiwan | 4.6 |
| Japan | 18.2 | United Kingdom | 3.7 |
| Mexico | 6.6 | EU | 17.7 |
| Germany | 5.4 |  |  |

## Balance of payments, reserves and aid, $bn

| Visible exports fob | 440.1 | Capital balance | 36.6 |
|---|---|---|---|
| Visible imports fob | -536.3 | Overall balance | -42.0 |
| Trade balance | -96.1 | Change in reserves | -6.4 |
| Invisibles inflows | 290.4 | Level of reserves |  |
| Invisibles outflows | -227.6 | end Dec. | 71.3 |
| Net transfers | -32.9 | No. months import cover | 1.6 |
| Current account balance | -66.3 | Aid given | 11.7 |
| – as % of GDP | -1.1 | – as % of GDP | 0.20 |

## Family life

| No. of households | 95.6m | Divorces per 1,000 pop. | 4.7 |
|---|---|---|---|
| Av. no. per household | 2.6 | Cost of living, Sept. 1993 |  |
| Marriages per 1,000 pop. | 9.4 | New York = 100 | 100 |

# VENEZUELA

| | | | |
|---|---|---|---|
| Area | 912,050 sq km | Currency | Bolivar (Bs) |
| Capital | Caracas | | |

## People

| | | | | |
|---|---|---|---|---|
| Population | 20.3m | Life expectancy: | men | 67 yrs |
| Pop. per sq km | 24 | | women | 74 yrs |
| Av. ann. growth | | Adult literacy | | 88.1% |
| in pop. 1985–92 | 2.5% | Fertility rate (per woman) | | 3.1 |
| Pop. under 15 | 34.7% | | | |
| Pop. over 65 | 4.1% | | | *per 1,000 pop.* |
| No. of men per 100 women | 101 | Crude birth rate | | 26.1 |
| Human Development Index | 82 | Crude death rate | | 5.3 |

## The economy

| | | | |
|---|---|---|---|
| GDP | Bs4,034bn | GDP per head | $2,900 |
| GDP | $59bn | GDP per head in purchasing | |
| Av. ann. growth in real | | power parity (USA=100) | 29 |
| GDP 1985–92 | 3.8% | | |

| Origins of GDP[a] | | Components of GDP | |
|---|---|---|---|
| | *% of total* | | *% of total* |
| Agriculture | 5.5 | Private consumption | 69.9 |
| Industry, of which: | 45.2 | Public consumption | 8.9 |
| manufacturing | 14.8 | Investment | 23.2 |
| Services | 49.3 | Exports | 26.2 |
| | | Imports | -28.2 |

## Structure of manufacturing

| | *% of total* | | *% of total* |
|---|---|---|---|
| Agric. & food processing | 17 | Other | 73 |
| Textiles & clothing | 5 | Av. ann. increase in industrial | |
| Machinery & transport | 5 | output 1980–91 | 2.1% |

## Energy

| | *'000 TCE* | | |
|---|---|---|---|
| Total output | 226,297 | % output exported | 67.0 |
| Total consumption | 68,935 | % consumption imported | 0.5 |
| Consumption per head, | | | |
| kg coal equivalent | 3,490 | | |

## Inflation and finance

| | | *av. ann. increase 1988–92* | |
|---|---|---|---|
| Consumer price | | | |
| inflation 1993 | 38.1% | Narrow money (M1) | 25.1% |
| Av. ann. inflation 1988–93 | 42.0% | Broad money | 35.9% |

## Exchange rates

| | *end 1993* | | *end June 1993* |
|---|---|---|---|
| Bs per $ | 106 | Effective rates | *1985 = 100* |
| Bs per SDR | 145 | – nominal | 12.9 |
| Bs per Ecu | 118 | – real | 57.9 |

## Principal exports

|  | *$bn fob* |  | *$bn fob* |
|---|---|---|---|
| Petroleum & products | 11.2 | Chemicals | 0.3 |
| Metals | 1.2 | Total incl. others | **14.0** |

### Main export destinations

|  | *% of total* |  | *% of total* |
|---|---|---|---|
| United States | 50.8 | Japan | 3.0 |
| Netherlands | 7.8 | Brazil | 2.2 |
| Germany | 4.4 |  |  |

## Principal imports

|  | *$bn cif* |  | *$bn cif* |
|---|---|---|---|
| Machinery | 3.8 | Metals | 1.0 |
| Transport equipment | 2.6 |  |  |
| Chemicals | 1.4 | Total incl. others | **12.3** |

### Main origins of imports

|  | *% of total* |  | *% of total* |
|---|---|---|---|
| United States | 47.7 | Italy | 4.7 |
| Germany | 6.1 | Brazil | 4.1 |
| Japan | 6.0 |  |  |

## Balance of payments, reserves and debt, $bn

|  |  |  |  |
|---|---|---|---|
| Visible exports fob | 14.0 | Overall balance | -1.6 |
| Visible imports fob | -12.3 | Change in reserves | -1.0 |
| Trade balance | 1.7 | Level of reserves |  |
| Invisibles inflows | 3.0 | end Dec. | 13.0 |
| Invisibles outflows | -7.7 | No. months import cover | 12.7 |
| Net transfers | -0.4 | Foreign debt | 37.2 |
| Current account balance | -3.4 | – as % of GDP | 62.5 |
| – as % of GDP | -5.7 | Debt service | 3.3 |
| Capital balance | 2.1 | Debt service ratio | 19.5 |

## Family life

|  |  |  |  |
|---|---|---|---|
| No. households | 3.5m | Divorces per 1,000 pop. | 1.2 |
| Av. no. per household | 5.1 | Cost of living, Sept. 1993 |  |
| Marriages per 1,000 pop. | 5.9 | New York = 100 | 52 |

a 1991.

# ZAIRE

| | | | |
|---|---|---|---|
| Area | 2,344,409 sq km | Currency | Zaire (Z) |
| Capital | Kinshasa | | |

## People

| | | | |
|---|---|---|---|
| Population | 39.8m | Life expectancy: men | 50 yrs |
| Pop. per sq km | 19 | women | 53 yrs |
| Av. ann. growth | | Adult literacy | 71.8% |
| in pop. 1985–92 | 3.3% | Fertility rate (per woman) | 6.7 |
| Pop. under 15 | 48.1% | | |
| Pop. over 65 | 2.8% | | *per 1,000 pop.* |
| No. of men per 100 women | 98 | Crude birth rate | 47.5 |
| Human Development Index | 26 | Crude death rate | 14.6 |

## The economy

| | | | |
|---|---|---|---|
| GDP | Z5,487bn | GDP per head | $214 |
| GDP | $8.5bn | GDP per head in purchasing | |
| Av. ann. growth in real | | power parity (USA=100) | 2 |
| GDP 1985–92 | -0.4% | | |

| Origins of GDP[a] | | Components of GDP[a] | |
|---|---|---|---|
| | *% of total* | | *% of total* |
| Agriculture | 31.3 | Private consumption | 79.6 |
| Industry, of which: | 25.4 | Public consumption | 8.9 |
| manufacturing | 1.3 | Investment | 14.8 |
| Services | 43.3 | Exports | 26.9 |
| | | Imports | -29.6 |

## Structure of manufacturing[b]

| | *% of total* | | *% of total* |
|---|---|---|---|
| Agric. & food processing | 40 | Other | 36 |
| Textiles & clothing | 16 | Av. ann. increase in industrial | |
| Machinery & transport | 8 | output 1980–90 | 2.3% |

## Energy

| | *'000 TCE* | | |
|---|---|---|---|
| Total output | 2,826 | % output exported | 58.6 |
| Total consumption | 2,495 | % consumption imported | 63.2 |
| Consumption per head, | | | |
| kg coal equivalent | 65 | | |

## Inflation and finance

| Consumer price | | *av. ann. increase 1988–92* | |
|---|---|---|---|
| inflation 1992 | 4,129.2% | Narrow money (M1) | 545% |
| Av. ann. inflation 1988–92 | 478.1% | Broad money | 545% |

## Exchange rates

| | *end 1993* | | *end June 1993* |
|---|---|---|---|
| Z per $ | 6.04 | Effective rates | 1985 = 100 |
| Z per SDR | 8.30 | – nominal | ... |
| Z per Ecu | 6.76 | – real | ... |

## Principal exports[c]

| | $m fob | | $m fob |
|---|---|---|---|
| Copper | 1,001 | | |
| Diamonds | 240 | | |
| Crude petroleum | 227 | Total incl. others | **1,539** |

### Main export destinations

| | % of total | | % of total |
|---|---|---|---|
| United States | 42.6 | United Kingdom | 15.7 |
| Belgium/Luxembourg | 27.3 | Switzerland | 6.0 |

## Principal imports[c]

| | $m fob | | $m fob |
|---|---|---|---|
| Imports for Gécamines[d] | 362 | Transport equipment | 95 |
| Petroleum products | 169 | | |
| Agric. products & foodstuffs | 147 | Total incl. others | **1,395** |

### Main origins of imports

| | % of total | | % of total |
|---|---|---|---|
| United States | 33.0 | Germany | 10.3 |
| Belgium/Luxembourg | 23.3 | France | 9.5 |

## Balance of payments[c], reserves and debt, $bn

| | | | |
|---|---|---|---|
| Visible exports fob | 2.1 | Overall balance | -0.8 |
| Visible imports fob | -1.5 | Change in reserves | 0.1 |
| Trade balance | 0.6 | Level of reserves | |
| Invisibles inflows | 0.2 | end Dec. | 0.2 |
| Invisibles outflows | -1.6 | No. months import cover | 1.1 |
| Net transfers | 0.1 | Foreign debt | 10.9 |
| Current account balance | -0.6 | – as % of GDP | ... |
| – as % of GDP | -7.9 | Debt service | 0.8 |
| Capital balance | -0.1 | Debt service ratio | ... |

## Family life

| | | | |
|---|---|---|---|
| No. of households | 5.7m | Divorces per 1,000 pop. | ... |
| Av. no. per household | 5.4 | Cost of living, Sept. 1993 | |
| Marriages per 1,000 pop. | ... | New York = 100 | ... |

a  1987.
b  1986.
c  1990.
d  Gécamines is the giant government-owned mining company, producing all Zairean cobalt, zinc, coal and copper.

# ZIMBABWE

| Area | 390,580 sq km | Currency | Zimbabwe dollar (Z$) |
|---|---|---|---|
| Capital | Harare | | |

## People

| | | | |
|---|---|---|---|
| Population | 10.4m | Life expectancy: men | 54 yrs |
| Pop. per sq km | 30 | women | 57 yrs |
| Av. ann. growth | | Adult literacy | 66.9% |
| in pop. 1985–92 | 3.0% | Fertility rate (per woman) | 5.3 |
| Pop. under 15 | 44.6% | | |
| Pop. over 65 | 2.8% | | *per 1,000 pop.* |
| No. of men per 100 women | 99 | Crude birth rate | 40.6 |
| Human Development Index | 40 | Crude death rate | 11.0 |

## The economy

| | | | |
|---|---|---|---|
| GDP | Z$30.1bn | GDP per head | $570 |
| GDP | $5.9bn | GDP per head in purchasing | |
| Av. ann. growth in real | | power parity (USA=100) | 7 |
| GDP 1985–92 | 2.4% | | |

| Origins of GDP | | Components of GDP[a] | |
|---|---|---|---|
| | *% of total* | | *% of total* |
| Agriculture | 10.0 | Private consumption | 52.4 |
| Industry, of which: | 31.5 | Public consumption | 24.6 |
| manufacturing | 24.3 | Investment | 19.8 |
| Services | 58.5 | Exports | 31.4 |
| | | Imports | -28.3 |

## Structure of manufacturing

| | *% of total* | | *% of total* |
|---|---|---|---|
| Agric. & food processing | 30 | Other | 44 |
| Textiles & clothing | 17 | Av. ann. increase in industrial | |
| Machinery & transport | 8 | output 1980–91 | 2.1% |

## Energy

| | *'000 TCE* | | |
|---|---|---|---|
| Total output | 6,033 | % output exported | 3.2 |
| Total consumption | 6,923 | % consumption imported | 17.0 |
| Consumption per head, | | | |
| kg coal equivalent | 674 | | |

## Inflation and finance

| Consumer price | | *av. ann. increase 1988–92* | |
|---|---|---|---|
| inflation 1993 | 28.0% | Narrow money (M1) | 20.5% |
| Av. ann. inflation 1988–93 | 21.3% | Broad money | 14.6% |

## Exchange rates

| | *end 1993* | | *end June 1993* |
|---|---|---|---|
| Z$ per $ | 6.93 | Effective rates | *1985 = 100* |
| Z$ per SDR | 9.52 | – nominal | ... |
| Z$ per Ecu | 7.77 | – real | ... |

## Principal exports[b]

|  | $m fob |  | $m fob |
|---|---|---|---|
| Tobacco | 433 | Nickel | 93 |
| Gold | 226 | Cotton | 63 |
| Ferro-alloys | 122 | Total incl. others | **1,613** |

### Main export destinations[bc]

|  | % of total |  | % of total |
|---|---|---|---|
| Germany | 11.2 | Japan | 7.2 |
| South Africa | 9.1 | United States | 6.8 |
| United Kingdom | 9.0 |  |  |

## Principal imports

|  | $m fob |  | $m fob |
|---|---|---|---|
| Machinery & transport equipment | 885 | Chemicals | 278 |
| Manufactured products | 366 |  |  |
| Petroleum products & electricity | 352 | Total incl. others | **2,167** |

### Main origins of imports[b]

|  | % of total |  | % of total |
|---|---|---|---|
| South Africa | 27.8 | United States | 8.1 |
| United Kingdom | 10.2 | Germany | 5.6 |

## Balance of payments[b], reserves and debt, $bn

|  |  |  |  |
|---|---|---|---|
| Visible exports fob | 1.7 | Overall balance | -0.1 |
| Visible imports fob | -1.6 | Change in reserves | -0.3 |
| Trade balance | 0.1 | Level of reserves |  |
| Invisibles inflows | 0.3 | end Dec. | 0.3 |
| Invisibles outflows | -0.9 | No. months import cover | 2.3 |
| Net transfers | 0.1 | Foreign debt | 4.0 |
| Current account balance | -0.5 | – as % of GDP | 74.1 |
| – as % of GDP | -8.3 | Debt service | 0.6 |
| Capital balance | 0.4 | Debt service ratio | 31.9 |

## Family life

|  |  |  |  |
|---|---|---|---|
| No. of households | 0.1m | Divorces per 1,000 pop. | ... |
| Av. no. per household | 4.2 | Cost of living, Sept. 1993 |  |
| Marriages per 1,000 pop. | ... | New York = 100 | 45 |

a   1989.
b   1991.
c   Excluding gold.

# Glossary

**ALADI** Latin American Integration Association replaced the Latin American Free Trade Association in 1980. Its members are Argentina, Bolivia, Brazil, Chile, Colombia, Ecuador, Mexico, Paraguay, Peru, Uruguay and Venezuela.

**Balance of payments** The record of a country's transactions with the rest of the world. The **current account** of the balance of payments consists of: visible trade (goods); "invisible" trade (services and income); private transfer payments (eg, remittances from those working abroad); official transfers (eg, payments to international organisations, famine relief). Visible imports and exports are normally compiled on rather different definitions to those used in the trade statistics (shown in principal imports and exports) and therefore the statistics do not match. The **capital account** consists of long- and short-term transactions relating to a country's assets and liabilities (eg, loans and borrowings). Adding the current to the capital account gives the **overall balance**. This is compensated by net monetary movements and changes in reserves. In practice methods of statistical recording are neither complete nor accurate and an errors and omissions item, sometimes quite large, will appear. In the country pages of this book this item is included in the overall balance. **Changes in reserves** are shown without the practice of reversing the sign often followed in balance of payments presentations.

**CFA** Communauté Financière Africaine. Its members, most of the francophone African nations, share a common currency, the CFA franc, which is maintained at a fixed rate of 1FFr = 100 CFAfr by the French treasury.

**Cif/fob** Measures of the value of merchandise trade. Imports include the cost of "carriage, insurance and freight" (cif) from the exporting country to the importing. The value of exports des not include these elements and is recorded 'free on board" (fob). Balance of payments statistics are generally adjusted so that both exports and imports are shown fob; the cif elements are included in invisibles.

**Crude birth rate** The number of live births in a year per 1,000 population. The crude rate will automatically rise relatively high if a large proportion of the population is of childbearing age.

**Crude death rate** The number of deaths in a year per 1,000 population. Also affected by the population's age structure.

**Debt, foreign** Financial obligations owed by a country to the rest of the world and repayable in foreign currency. **Debt service** consists of interest payments on outstanding debt plus any principal repayments due. **The debt service ratio** is debt service expressed as a percentage of the country's earnings from exports of goods and services.

**EU** European Union. Members are: Belgium, Denmark, France, Germany, Greece, Ireland, Italy, Luxembourg, Netherlands, Portugal, Spain and the United Kingdom.

**Ecu** European currency unit. An accounting measure used within the EU and composed of a weighted basket of the currencies of all EU members.

**Effective exchange rate** This measures a currency's depreciation (figures below 100) or appreciation (figures over 100) from a base date against a trade weighted basket of the currencies of the country's main trading partners.

**Efta** European Free Trade Association. An organisation of West European states that are not members of the European